Cleared to land!

DEDICATION

For the youngsters — Tina, Robert, Mark, Dickon, Andria, Matt, Jenny and Sarah — may they always have happy landings!

Cleared to land!

The FAA Story
by Frank Burnham

AERO PUBLISHERS, INC.
329 West Aviation Road, Fallbrook, CA 92028

Library of Congress Cataloging in Publication Data

Burnham, Frank A
　Cleared to land!

　1. United States. Federal Aviation Administra-
tion. I. Title.
HE9803.A4B84　　353.008'77'7　　75-38050
ISBN 0-8168-4500-X

Printed and Published in the United States by Aero Publishers, Inc.

PREFACE

Checking the shelves of the local library one finds any number of books directed in whole or in part to the subject of America's burgeoning aviation industry and its regulatory body - the Federal Aviation Administration.

Many of these volumes are exposes chronicling the shortcomings of the FAA or are slashing critiques of that agency and its policies by self-styled experts (many of whom offer credentials supporting their expert status that are at best somewhat questionable).

Each year the nation's newspapers and popular magazines carry hundreds of column inches of text usually critical of regulatory policies, procedures and philosophies as practiced by the FAA and several of the nation's foremost aviation publications carry on a continuing editorial attack against the agency. Rarely, if ever, is anything good said about the FAA. And, when an FAA employee makes an error (in the case of controllers, human errors can and do result in disaster) it makes headlines and television specials from border to border.

In some thirty years as a practicing aviator and nearly as many as an aviation writer, my relations with the FAA and before it the CAA (I don't quite go back to the Bureau of Air Commerce days) always have been cordial. During this entire period, however, it seems that a majority of my fellow pilots and others directly involved in aviation expressed little respect for the agency. In fact, more often than not, they entertain one or more complaints—albeit some of them somewhat vague—and look upon the men and women of the FAA in the same light as they look upon the police officer—"the fuzz," hardly a term of respect or endearment.

Examining this apparent paradox, I arrived at a conclusion that the general unpopularity of the FAA with large segments of the flying public is to a large degree the result of traditional antipathy toward regulation itself; a massive lack of understanding with regard to the many roles played by the men and women of the agency quite above and beyond that of enforcer; and a monumental lack of exposure for those roles in the public press.

Eighteen months ago, I elected to find out for myself (and indirectly for the flying public who, I hope, will read this book) whether or not my assessment of the situation is correct.

From the outset, I was faced with the absolute necessity of convincing not only FAA top management but also the men and women in the field that I was not out to wield a carving knife (in the form of the pen) on them. They are understandably gun shy. Being completely frank not only with management but also with the working level men and women, I specified in no uncertain terms that, although I was disposed toward the agency in general, I was out to prove the accuracy of my assessment and in no way would this book become a "puff job." In other words, my personal opinion notwithstanding, the name of the game was and is tell it like it is. It was agreed the manuscript would be submitted to the agency to be reviewed "for technical accuracy only." I have been happy to find that the FAA Office of Public Affairs was as good as its word—the review has been exactly that.

Although, from the very beginning, I had planned to interview the Administrator and top FAA management representatives as well as the men and women at the operational level, it quickly became clear that this would not necessarily serve the ultimate objective—to develop a "people" story of the FAA. Certainly the administrator and FAA top management representatives are people and, in most instances, they are no less dedicated to the purpose of aviation safety than are those at the working level. However, in most cases they are not in a position to offer their personal convictions with regard to the agency or their individual responsibilities. They are bound, at least morally if not legally, to support the public position of the agency—the bureaucracy, if you will—as opposed to voicing opinions based on their own best judgment supported by their years of practical experience. Two things immediately were clear: (1) in many instances they would be forced to picture the agency in terms quite different from those expressed by men and women in the field and (2) this not only would be counterproductive in terms of what I, as the author, was attempting to accomplish, it also would place many conscientious, dedicated men and women now working at higher levels in an unfair light.

My research approach thus became one of consulting primarily men and women at the working levels of the FAA; as a rule of thumb, those who interface directly with the flying public; in a few instances those whose responsibility directly affects the aviator and his flying machine but where an eyeball-to-eyeball relationship is not present.

As for me, I can state unequivocally that the past 18 months have given me a better appreciation of these men and women. Now when I point the nose of Cherokee Seven Six Nine Six Whiskey toward a new destination, I fly with an even greater confidence that I will hear those welcome words at the end of the flight—"cleared to land."

FRANK A. BURNHAM

Rancho Palos Verdes, CA
July 1, 1976

ACKNOWLEDGEMENTS

Producing a volume that leapfrogs through 170 years during which men and women first dreamed of flight and then translated those dreams into reality and which then crystalizes a half century of dedicated action on the part of a particular group of those men and women could not have been accomplished without the unstinting assistance of a considerable number of people who were generous with their time and their expertise.

It would be impossible to list them all here but there are some who must share in whatever recognition this book may bring.

First is Gene Kropf, Public Affairs director for FAA's Western Region and a close friend of many years. Gene's casual remark one day, "Gee, I wish the FAA had a book like the FBI's", got all this started. Gene, his assistant, Bob Huber, and his secretary, Barbara Abel, then stayed around providing untold hours of advice, counsel and coordination.

Also generous in their help were John Leyden of FAA headquarters, and his boss, Denny Feldman. Then there were Mark Weaver at the Aeronautical Center, Lou Lombard, Neal Callahan, Bob Fulton, Len Samuels, Wally Ward and George Miyachi representing other FAA entities. And, of course, the hundreds of FAA men and women who patiently let me sit at their elbow learning first hand how they performed their jobs and how they felt about it all.

A couple of American aviation greats who took time out from incredibly busy schedules to talk with me must be publicly assured of my gratitude — Lt. Gen. James H. "Jimmy" Doolittle and, a friend of long standing, William P. "Bill" Lear.

Special thanks must go to Dale Heister, who, although retired from the FAA, has become the unofficial historian of the national airways system.

When it came to amassing photography to accompany this manuscript, many of these same FAA people helped, but due to Federal administrative practices there were critical gaps. Joan Osaka of the Air Force Office of Information in Los Angeles, Linda Cole and Helen M. Halbe of Western Air Lines, and Susan Tanigawa of Flying Tigers provided invaluable assistance in filling those gaps.

A very personal note of thanks to my faithful manuscript typist, Mary Jewett, who patiently waded through my undecipherable editing notes and abominable typing.

Last, but far from least, is my wife, Hazel, critic, confidant, editor, copy and proof reader, indexer, and a lot more.

TABLE OF CONTENTS

IN THE BEGINNING 1

"Aerial navigation will form a most prominent feature in the progress of civilisation."

So wrote Sir George Cayley—who since has been hailed as the "true inventor of the aeroplane and one of the most powerful geniuses in the history of aviation"—in 1809. Ten years earlier, Cayley, then only 26, formulated the basic problem of mechanical flight in these words engraved on a silver disc still preserved in the British Science Museum:

"to make a surface support a given weight by the application of power to the resistance of air."

With these two statements, Cayley identifies himself both as a scientific marvel and as one of the world's most accurate predictors of things to come.

Mankind, however, is inherently timid when it comes to facing the unknown. Obviously, there are exceptions—history is liberally punctuated with them. And, of course, man regularly shows great courage when facing known yet apparently unconquerable dangers. Still, the history of homo sapiens indicates he shuns that which he knows little about and does not understand.

Thus, it took roughly another 100 years and two Ohio bicycle builders—Wilbur and Orville Wright—to translate Cayley's theories into both hardware and powered flight.

Beginning with the historic events at Kill Devil Hill on December 17, 1903, the Wright Brothers went all the way during the next five years becoming the first to:

build and fly a "fully practical" man-carrying airplane;

make powered, sustained and controlled flights landing on ground as high as that from which they took off; and

make and fly a practical passenger-carrying airplane (one that could carry an individual other than the pilot).

Not to impute either the courage or motivation of those who, in history, have penetrated the unknown, it is perhaps interesting to note what Orville Wright himself had to say 10 years after those first flights at Kitty Hawk.

Reflecting on that day he wrote:

"I would hardly think today of making my first flight of a strange machine in a 27-mile wind, even if I knew the machine had already been flown and was safe. After these years of experience, I look with amazement to our audacity in attempting flights with a new and untried machine under such circumstances."

How many aviators since have recalled a situation in which, if they had it to do over again, they would have proceeded differently or not at all? This essentially is the essence of experience. But, in retrospect, it is perhaps fortunate for aviation that there have been those who proceeded forthrightly—though carefully—with only confidence in themselves to carry them through.

Through 1907, aviation in the United States revolved primarily about the Wrights. In that year, however, an organization founded by Dr. and Mrs. Graham Bell and Glenn Curtiss—the Aerial Experiment Association based at Hammondsport, New York— gave this struggling new technology a shot in the arm. The Association completed the first of a series of biplanes early in

11

CLEARED TO LAND!

1908, the first one designed by Lieut. Thomas E. Selfridge and called Red Wing. (Later that year Selfridge became the first to die in an airplane crash during the demonstration of a Wright Flyer for the Army Signal Corps at Fort Meyer, Virginia.)

Red Wing made two flights before crashing. It was abandoned. The second Association aircraft, White Wing designed by F. W. Baldwin, made five flights in May, the longest over 1,000 feet. It also was the first U. S. airplane to be fitted with ailerons. Glenn Curtiss designed the third of these craft, the June Bug, also with wing tip ailerons, and subsequently won the Scientific American Magazine's prize for the first, official, public flight in the U. S. of more than one kilometer. The last of the 1908 aircraft developed under the umbrella of the Association was J. A. D. McCurdy's Silver Dart. The success of these pioneer airplanes led directly to the line of Glenn Curtiss machines which took shape in 1909 and became the principal competition for the Wright airplanes.

While much of the earliest pioneering work in the area of airships, balloons and gliders was accomplished by Europeans, with few notable exceptions, little if any interest in powered flight was shown until the initial reports began filtering in from Kitty Hawk and Dayton. In fact, Charles H. Gibbs-Smith—one of the world's foremost aviation historians—says that the "true revival of aviation and the birth of practical flying in Europe was due directly to the Wright Brothers." He observes that the Wrights precipitated this European revival in two phases, each directly reinforcing the other, i.e., two parallel development programs for the biplane by four Frenchmen and later the development of the monoplane resulted.

Capt. Ferdinand Ferber, a French artillery officer influenced earlier by the gliding experiments of Lilienthal, received a reprint of a 1901 lecture given by Wilbur Wright. Noting that Wright did not use the tailplane a la Lilienthal, Ferber immediately affected the Wright design and shortly built a crude Wright-type glider, the first in Europe. About the same time a wealthy attorney-sportsman, Ernest Archdeacon, created the Aviation Committee in the Aero-Club de France to promote heavier-than-air flight with the goal of beating the Wrights to this achievement.

In 1904, Archdeacon built a reproduction of a Wright glider which flew briefly with only minor success. One of the pilots was Ferber. The second was Gabriel Voisin, who later was to become one of France's foremost airplane designers. Still another copy of a Wright machine was built, this one also inspired by Archdeacon. The builder was Robert Ensnault-Pelterie. He later built an improved version substituting for the wing warping mode of control used by the Wrights a set of crude ailerons.

Generally speaking, French aviation enthusiasts (and theirs was about the only development in Europe at this time) had what Gibbs-Smith called the "chauffeur's attitude" toward aviation. Essentially, he explains, this means they saw the airplane as a machine that could be driven off the flat layer of earth and through a slightly less flat layer of air. Simply, their engineering approach was one of brute force to cause the airplane to fly with a maximum inherent stability of the craft and minimum pilot control. They also demonstrated a lack of persistence, or perhaps it was a lack of understanding of the need for long-term research, development and test.

12

IN THE BEGINNING

Despite the fact that at least three of these European aviation pioneers built a reasonable copy of the Wright glider and, in at least one instance, added an innovative method of control, a full year after the Wrights demonstrated the practicability of powered flight at Kitty Hawk, only four primitive gliders had been built and flown in France.

Little expertise or new technology was added by the French the following year, 1905. It was during that year that the Wrights with their Flyer III demonstrated the capability to move through the air at will flying for over a half hour at a time, banking, turning, circling and doing figure eights. Also in 1905 and despite the failure of the French to duplicate the achievements of the Wrights, the Federation Aeronautique International (FAI) was formed to regulate sport flying and aviation meetings and thus to "advance the science and sport of aeronautics."

Predating the establishment of the Bureau of Air Commerce in the United States by some 21 years, French aviators foresaw the need for such regulation even though at that time all the real technical advancements in aviation were occurring in this country.

By late 1906, no European had yet flown a power airplane. There were two, however, which showed promise. One was a tractor monoplane powered by a carbonic acid motor built by a Transylvanian, Trajan Vuia, and the other, an odd-looking biplane built by Santos Dumont, a wealthy Brazilian living in Paris. The Vuia made several "hops" between March 1906 and March 1907 but none were spectacular, the longest being only 24 meters. Despite the weird appearance of the Santos Dumont craft— like two box kites connected by a third—this aircraft became the first powered flying machine to be officially recognized in Europe. On October 23 it won the Archdeacon prize for flying 25 meters and on November 12 went on to make several flights of 220 meters, thus winning the Aero Club's prize for the first flight of 100 meters or longer. The year 1906 also saw a French development that probably did more for European aviation than the much heralded Santos Dumont flight. This was the final stage development by Leon Levavasseur of his Antionette aero-engine. Begun earlier in the new century, these engines became the chief European aviation engine from 1906 to 1909.

During the next few years old names became more securely ensconced in aviation history—Ferber, Voisin, Wright, Curtiss—and new ones were added—Henri Farman, Louis Bleriot, Hubert Latham, Paul Tissandier, A. V. Roe, Samuel F. Cody, Louis Breguet, Ambroise Goupy, A. Calderara, Geoffery de Havilland and C. P. Rogers.

It was in 1911 that the airplane began to take on a real significance in the context of war. The first Concours Militaire—for the display of aircraft that could be utilized in combat—was held at Reims. In the United States, Eugene Ely made the first flights off a warship at sea and, at San Francisco, the first bombs were dropped by the Army from a Wright biplane. Shortly thereafter the first bomb sight was developed by Lieut. Scott Riley. Elsewhere, rifles and machine guns were being tried out on aircraft. One of the first was a two-place Nieuport carrying a single machine gun.

The airplane first saw actual war service in October 1911 with the Italians. A reconnaissance flight was made from Tripoli over Turkish positions near Azizia. Aircraft in general, military types in particular, continued to proliferate through 1914 when hostilities broke out and World War I began.

CLEARED TO LAND!

At the outset of the war, the Allies had approximately 210 such airplanes, the Germans about 180. Although this country proved to be the industrial base for the Allies by war's end, its air arm had less than 250 aircraft of all types and only 131 officers (most of them pilots) when it entered the conflict on April 6, 1917. In all the United States there were only 40 flight instructors.

1913 Wright Pusher (as reconstructed by the Camden County Vocational School in 1934) typifies the design philosophy that dominated the first decade of flight.

By this time hundreds of excellent aircraft were in European skies—Fokker, Albatross, Phalz, Aviatik, Rumpler, Gotha, Spad, Sopwith, Nieuport, Salmonson, Bristol, Junkers, Short, de Havilland. Many of these manufacturers already had gained long experience and had turned out large numbers of aircraft. On the other hand, in the United States when we entered the war Curtiss and the Wright-Martin Co. were the only manufacturers with any kind of track record. Yet, when the Army Signal Corps placed orders for 334 airplanes immediately after war was declared, they went to 16 different companies for 32 different designs. No more than six of these companies had ever built more than 10 aircraft.

No American-built airplane got into combat in any quantity. With the exception of the venerable Curtiss JN-D "Jenny," no American-built airplane even saw any substantial war service of any kind. Hundreds of Liberty engines, which were designed and built in record time did, however, see service primarily with foreign-designed aircraft. The foremost of these was the de Havilland DH-4, which became the most famous light bomber/reconnaissance plane of the war. It also was quantities of this airplane which provided the foundation for the beginnings of commercial aviation in this country in the years immediately following the first "great war."

Despite the fact that U. S. aircraft manufacturing during World War I was shot with scandal, corruption, kickbacks and chicanery, the nation emerged from World War I with a lot of aviation capability and know-how it lacked before the war.

—The United States had only two large training fields before the war. Now it had 48.

—Where there had been literally a handful of aviation-trained officers (and

14

this also went for non-military pilots), now there were more than 20,000.

—With only 1,300 mechanics and trained ground personnel to support aviation before the war, we now had 175,000.

—The capability to produce aircraft increased from a rate of 224 planes a month to a potential of more than 17,000 by war's end.

—The U.S. had produced the finest airplane engine in the world up to that time—the Liberty—in huge quantities.

Also by war's end Glenn Martin was building an American equivalent of the British multi-engine Handley Page bomber. Grover Loening had designed and built (but it did not see service) what for its time was the fastest fighter airplane in the world. A new name was added—Chance Vought—and the company was building advanced trainers (these also were too late for war service).

In his book, *Airways*, first published in 1942, H. L. Smith described the immediate post-war period like this:

"Peace was a devastating blow to an industry geared for the waste of battle. Aircraft plants were overexpanded to meet the emergency . . . surplus equipment filled the warehouses and the few commercial operators who started up after the war were not interested in buying new planes as long as the cheap surplus stock was available. War-time equipment was scarcely the way to lure the public to air travel, since battle planes were inefficient for civilian use and so costly to operate that rates were of necessity sky-high."

By the late 1920s what we know today as general aviation had begun to catch on. Although the airplane is named "Yankee Doodle," this one was German designed and built and imported by its owner. It was based at Curtiss Field, Long Island, in 1928.

In those days, a war-trained aviator who chose not to return to the drabness of non-flying, civilian pursuits could buy a surplus Jenny (or the Canadian-built JN-4 called the "Canuck") for as low as $300 "complete." Curtiss OX-5 trainers went for as low as $100. In some areas, flying schools advertised a

CLEARED TO LAND!

"brand new Jenny plus flying lessons" for only $500. This combination of conditions gave birth to a new breed of aviator—the barnstormer—itinerant pilots (and mechanics) who wandered from small town to small town, wherever they could rent a level pasture for a few dollars, putting on impromptu airshows and carrying passengers for a pittance a head.

These were the men who in reality pioneered cross-country flying. They learned their way back and forth across the country by eyeballing the landmarks, and they became pretty good at it. So good, in fact, that many of them gravitated to the new air mail service and the embryo airline operations that began to emerge in the early 1920s. It was this expertise, this capability to fly airplanes in instrument weather even before they had the most basic instruments, that permitted the first airmail service to get off the ground.

Most of the earliest passenger air carriers were involved in operating off shore. It was considered "safer" since the cumbersome flying boats could land anywhere en route. Pacific Marine Airways, operating from Wilmington, Calif., to the resort island of Catalina, was among the earliest.

On the subject of weather flying, the experience of two British military airmen in 1919 speaks eloquently of the perils faced by airmen who pushed beyond the then established frontiers of flying in an attempt to prove its commercial potential. Capt. John Alcock and Lieut. Arthur Whitten Brown departed from St. John's, Newfoundland in a 1918 Vickers-Vimy bomber on June 14—destination, Ireland, 1,932 miles across the cold, stormy Atlantic. After 10 hours of smooth cruising above lower clouds, the pair ran into trouble—weather trouble. Later Brown recalled it this way:

"At about sunrise—3:10 A.M. to be exact—when we were between 3,500 and 4,000 feet, we ran into a thick bank that projected above the lower layer of cloud. All around was dense, drifting vapor, which cut off our range of vision, even the machine's wing tips and the fore end of the fuselages.

"This was entirely unexpected and separated suddenly from external guidance, we lost our instinct of balance. The machine, left to its own devices, swung, flew amok and began to perform circus tricks.

IN THE BEGINNING

"A glance at the instruments on the dashboard facing us made it obvious that we were not flying level. The air speed crept up to ninety knots, while Alcock was trying to restore equilibrium. He pulled back on the control lever, but apparently the air speed meter was jammed, for although the Vickers-Vimy must have nosed upwards, the reading remained at ninety.

"And then we stalled—that is to say our speed dropped below the minimum necessary for heavier-than-air flight. The machine hung motionless for a second, after which it heeled over and fell into what was either a spinning nose dive or a very steep spiral.

"The compass needle continued to revolve rapidly, showing that the machine was swinging as it dropped but, still hemmed in as we were by the thick vapor, we could not tell how or in what direction we were spinning.

"Before the pilot could reduce the throttle, the roar of the motors almost doubled in volume, and instead of the usual 1,650 to 1,700 revolutions per minute they were running at about 2,200 revolutions per minute. Alcock shut off the throttles, and the vibration ceased.

"Apart from the changing levels marked by the aneroid, only the fact that our bodies were pressing tightly against the seats indicated that the machine was falling. How and at what angle it was falling, we knew not. Alcock tried to centralize the controls, but failed because we had lost all sign, and saw nothing but opaque nebulousness.

"The aneroid, meantime, continued to register a height that dropped even lower and alarmingly lower—three thousand, two thousand, one thousand, five hundred feet. I realized the possibility that we might hit the ocean at any moment, if the aneroid's exactitude had been affected by differences between the barometric conditions of our present position and those of St. John's, where the instrument was set.

"A more likely danger was that our cloud might stretch down to the surface of the ocean, in which case, Alcock, having obtained no sight of the horizon, would be unable to counteract the spin in time.

"I made ready for the worst, loosening my safety belt and preparing to save my notes of the flight. All precautions would probably have been unavailing, however, for had we fallen into the sea, there would have been small hope for survival. We were on a steep slant, and even had we escaped drowning when first submerged, the dice would be heavily loaded against the chance of rescue by a passing ship.

"And then while these thoughts were chasing each other across my mind, we left the cloud as suddenly as we had entered it. We were now less than a hundred feet from the ocean. The sea surface did not appear below the machine, but, owing to the wide angle at which we were tilted against the horizontal, seemed to stand up level, sideways to us.

"Alcock looked at the ocean and the horizon, and almost instantaneously regained his mental equilibrium in relation to external balance. Fortunately, the Vickers-Vimy maneuvers quickly, and it responded to Alcock's action in centralizing the control lever and the rudder bar. He opened up the throttles. The motors came back to life, and the danger was past."

Alcock and Brown cheated death. They continued, landing near the radio station at Clifden, Ireland, but nosed over without injury to themselves in the soft ground. Many other pilots and crewmen flying in those days were not so lucky and, in fact, for many years laymen remained unconvinced of the airplane's utility because it could not fly regularly in other than clear skies. It remained for another group of pilots, the air mail pilots, backed up by a growing system of airways to disprove this contention.

The early airmail and air transport pilots had more than a little help from other quarters. Sperry was working on the development of an artificial horizon and a directional gyro. Kollsman developed the sensitive altimeter. Sperry, with the Radio Frequency Laboratory and the U. S. Bureau of Mines turned out a bank and turn indicator. Others were improving the new wireless technology increasing the power and reliability of ground stations while at the same time developing small, lighter radio sets (these still could communicate only in telegraphic code) that could be carried aboard aircraft.

About this same time a small-of-stature but big-on-guts Army lieutenant stationed at the Army's old McCook Field, Dayton, Ohio, was getting himself fired from his test pilot job by his boss, Col. John F. Curry (later Major General Curry of the Army Air Force), because, as the colonel put it: "You are too irresponsible to be chief test pilot when you fly in the weather you fly in."

That lieutenant was named Jimmy Doolittle and he later became a lieutenant general in the Army Air Forces leading the now-historic B-25, carrier-launched raid on Japan in World War II.

About being fired from his test pilot job and transferred to engineering, Doolittle recalls he was "too proud to tell him that the reason I could fly in this weather was because I had practiced practically a mile at a time over each piece of this area—under good weather, under fairly good weather, under medium weather, under bad weather, under very bad weather— until I could fly in weather where other pilots couldn't."

"I had a reputation for flying in bad weather," Doolittle told me in a recent interview at his Los Angeles office, "and the reason I had it was because I would practice flying different places under increasingly difficult weather. I could fly in weather where better pilots could not because I had memorized every piece of the terrain—where the farms were, where the windmills were, the streams, roads and villages. From the very beginning, I had the urge not to be tied down by the weather and was too impatient to wait around until we had things like the turn and the bank indicator."

Doolittle, however, was quick to take advantage of new blind flying instruments when they came along. He was one of the first to use the bank and turn indicator. That was in 1922 when he made the first transcontinental flight in under 24 hours with an old DH-4. For this flight he "borrowed" an experimental bank and turn indicator then under test at McCook Field.

The long experience this maverick Army airman had with weather flying was largely the reason he was selected to head the Full Flight Laboratory established by the Daniel Guggenheim Fund for the Promotion of Aeronautics in 1928. He was loaned by the Army to Guggenheim. It was during his short term with Guggenheim that Doolittle made the first true instrument flight for which he was awarded the 1930 Harmon Trophy, but that story is better told later.

At the same time Doolittle was pushing out into weather, feeling his way, learning to fly low to the ground around and under the worst of it, others were doing the same. But these men, the early mail pilots, weren't doing it as a research project or proceeding at their own speed as a matter of developing their individual proficiency. They were doing it as a matter of necessity. The name of the game was "get the mail through regardless" and that didn't permit them to put in much time on the ground waiting for the weather to break. Their meager instruments were a compass, an altimeter (and not a very good one) and an airspeed indicator. They navigated by sight, becoming familiar with a route in good weather so they could determine their position while dodging the worst storms in bad weather.

Ernest "Allie" Allison, one of the pilots who participated in the first transcontinental "thru" mail operation with airplanes flying both day and night in 1921, tells how he learned the route.

"There were no beacons, no maps, no nothing," he recalls, "and the first trip you made 'in trail' behind a more experienced pilot on the route. You took notes—the course and flying time between prominent landmarks. If you were lucky, you got two trips behind an old timer. If not, and I wasn't one of the lucky ones, you got just one."

A group of pioneer airmail pilots pose with one of the de Havilland DH-4s they flew. (L to R) are Fred Kelly, Jimmy James, Al DeGarmo, Maurice Graham and Corliss Moseley.

Later the notes from various pilots were collected, put into shape and published by the Post Office Department for the use of all the men flying the mail. A portion of the resulting document—covering the route from New

CLEARED TO LAND!

Initial airmail flights were just that—they carried only mail—but soon the carriers began reacting to public demand and small cargo was accepted on a space available basis.

Bold airmen in fragile aircraft like these Stearman 4Ds at Cheyenne, Wyo., set the precedent for today's all-weather flight without the benefit of radio, electronic navigation, sophisticated instruments or even warm, comfortable flight decks.

IN THE BEGINNING

York to Bellefonte, Pennsylvania, over what came to be known as the "pilot's graveyard"—looked like this:

United States Air Mail Service
PILOT'S DIRECTIONS NEW YORK—SAN FRANCISCO
ROUTE
Distances, Landmarks, Compass Course, Emergency Landing
Fields,
with service and communication facilities at principal points
enroute.

Post Office Department,
Office of Second Assistant Postmaster General,
Division of Air Mails.

These flying directions and the ground information were prepared with the cooperation of pilots and supervisory officials of the Air Mail Service and with the assistance of the postmasters located within 5 miles of the line of flight. All employees of the Air Mail Service will be required to familiarize themselves with the information relating to the section of the route with which they are concerned.

Otto Praeger,
Second Assistant Postmaster General,
Washington, D.C., February 20, 1921.

I.
NEW YORK TO BELLEFONTE

Miles.

0. Hazelhurst Field, Long Island.—Follow the tracks of the Long Island Railroad past Belmont Park race track, keeping Jamaica on the left. Cross New York over the lower end of Central Park.

25. Newark, N.J.—Heller Field is located in Newark and may be identified as follows: The field is 1-1/4 miles west of the Passaic River and lies in the V formed by the Greenwood Lake Division and Orange branch of the New York, Lake Erie and Western Railroad. The Morris Canal bounds the western edge of the field. The roof of the large steel hangar is painted an orange color.

30. Orange Mountains.—Cross the Orange Mountains over a small round lake or pond. Slightly to the right will be seen the polo field and golf course of Essex Country Club. About 8 miles to the north is Mountain Lake, easily seen after crossing the Orange Mountains.

50. Morristown, N.J.—About 4 miles north of course. Identified by a group of yellow buildings east of the city. The Delaware, Lackawanna & Western Railroad passes the eastern side of Morristown.

60. Lake Hopatcong.—A large irregular lake 10 miles north of course.

64. Budd Lake.—Large circular body of water 6 miles north of course.

78. Belvidere, N.J.—On the Delaware River. Twelve miles to the north is the Delaware Water Gap and 11 miles to the south is

CLEARED TO LAND!

Easton at the junction of the Lehigh and Delaware Rivers. The Delaware makes a pronounced U-shaped bend just north of Belvidere. A railway joins the two ends of the U.

111. Lehighton, Pa.—Directly on the course. The Lehigh Valley and Central Railroad of New Jersey, running parallel, pass through Lehighton. The Lehigh River runs between the railroads at this point. Lehighton is approximately halfway between Hazelhurst and Bellefonte. A fair sized elliptical race track lies just southwest of the town but a larger and better emergency landing field about 100 yards west of the race track. The field is very long and lies in a north-south direction.

114. Mauch Chunk.—Three miles north of Lehighton and on the direct course.

121. Central Railroad of New Jersey.—Two long triangular bodies of water northwest of the railroad followed by eight or nine small artificial lakes or ponds about half a mile apart almost parallel with the course but veering slightly to the south.

148. Catawissa Mountain Range.—Appears to curve in a semi-circle about a large open space of country directly on the course. To the north of the course may be seen the eastern branch of the Susquehanna. Fly parallel to this until Shamokin Creek is picked up. This creek is very black and is parallelled by two railroads. Chamokin Creek empties into the Susquehanna just below Sunbury.

168. Sunbury, Pa.—At the junction of the two branches of the Susquehanna River. The infield of a race track on a small island at the junction of the two rivers furnishes a good landing field. The river to the south of Sunbury is wider to the north and is filled with numerous small islands. The two branches to the north have practically no islands. If the river is reached and Sunbury is not in sight look for islands. If there are none, follow the river south to Sunbury. If islands are numerous follow the river north to Sunbury.

170. Lewisburg, Pa.—Two miles west of Sunbury and 8 miles north.

174. After leaving Sunbury the next landmark to pick up is Penns Creek, which empties into the Susquehanna 7 miles south of Sunbury. Flying directly on the course, Penns Creek is reached 6 miles after it joins the Susquehanna 7 miles south of Sunbury.

178. New Berlin.—Identified by covered bridge over Penns Creek.

185. The Pennsylvania Railroad from Lewisburg is crossed at the point where the range of mountains coming up from the southwest ends. The highway leaves the railroad here and goes up into Woodward Pass, directly on the course. A white fire tower may be seen on the crest of the last mountain to the north on leaving the pass.

202. The next range of mountains is crossed through the pass at Millheim, a small town. A lone mountain may be seen to the south just across the Pennsylvania tracks.

IN THE BEGINNING

> 217. Bellefonte, Pa.—After crossing another mountain range without a pass Bellefonte will be seen against the Bald Eagle Mountain Range. On top of a mountain, just south of a gap in the Bald Eagle Range at Bellefonte, may be seen a clearing with a few trees scattered in it. This identifies this gap from others in the same range. The mail field lies just east of town and is marked by a large white circle. A white line marks the eastern edge of the field where there is a drop of nearly 100 feet.

One of two pilots who, in their open cockpit DH-4's, departed from Hazelhurst, New Jersey, at dawn on February 21, 1921 on the first leg of the westbound mail flight, Allison was the only one to get through that morning and he nearly didn't make it.

"Our job (Allie and Elmer Leonhardt in the other DH-4) was to get the mail to Cleveland by way of our intermediate refueling stop at Bellefonte, Pennsylvania. Weather that morning was marginal as we headed towards the Allegheny Mountains to the west. Both of us reached Bellefonte without mishap, however, and refueled. When I got ready to leave my DH-4 developed engine trouble and the mail was transferred to a spare aircraft kept at the field.

Night operations were risky at best. Only the largest terminal airfields had any kind of adequate lighting. The small emergency fields along the routes had none as a rule and the airmail pilots depended on powerful parachute flares for illumination.

CLEARED TO LAND!

"On this one, the Liberty turned over all right but I had not progressed very far before I found that the huge, wooden propeller was unbalanced. It made the plane vibrate like a dog shaking off water. As Bellefonte disappeared farther behind me, the weather worsened. The clouds were about 2,500 to 3,-000 feet and I found myself flying in freezing rain. Ice began to build up on the wings. The airplane slowed and lost lift. It looked as if I would have to make an emergency landing. About this time the intense vibration caused by the prop came to my rescue. It caused the plane to shake off the ice and it kept shaking it off as fast as it froze. By flying extremely low over the Allegheny River I was able to navigate and finally made it into Cleveland. Later I learned that Leonhardt had not been so lucky. He went down near DuBoise, Pennsylvania."

The next day Allison, on his return trip to New York, turned in the final leg of the first day/night transcontinental airmail movement west to east. It was during this now famous operation that the legendary Jack Knight made his historic night mail flight between Cheyenne, Wyoming, and Chicago, Illinois.

Even in good weather the lack of reliable communications, weather forecasts, emergency landing fields and a real feeling of confidence in the aircraft made flying the mail a hairy experience. William V. "Bill" Morgan, another of those pioneers, tells of a day flight originating at San Francisco destined for Reno, a route with which he was totally unfamiliar.

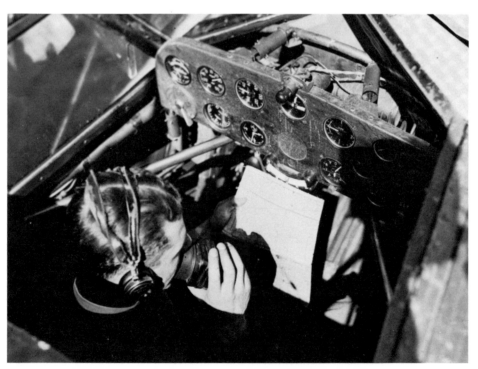

Air-to-ground radio, when it came along, was incredibly primitive and in open cockpit aircraft like this Fokker Super Universal it was all the pilot could do to communicate critical information. Still, it represented a major breakthrough for flight operations.

"I flew the second airmail plane on the transcontinental route from San Francisco at the very beginning of coast-to-coast service on September 11, 1920," he wrote, "flying that early run in weather with good visibility over the high Sierra Nevada mountains. After leaving the San Francisco Marina and

24

The Kruese radio was one of the earliest pieces of airborne equipment. It was crude, heavy, cumbersome and required an equally cumbersome power source, but it worked.

crossing the waters of the harbor, I was over the Sacramento Valley headed for Reno. I soon discovered that my compass was not adjusted to any degree of accuracy, but while I had never flown the route before, I knew that the Southern Pacific railroad would be a guide to Reno.

"Upon reaching the city of Sacramento, I was careful to follow those tracks while passing over Roseville, Auburn and Colfax. Now in mountainous country, I was constantly studying the ground for a landing place in case of engine failure. There was no place I could have landed safely. The American River and its tributaries flowed in a westerly direction from the high mountain summit in deep narrow gorges.

"There was little habitation and as I reached the high summit even the railroad tracks disappeared at times as they entered tunnels or passed through snow sheds. The highway was narrow, a crooked dirt road with almost no vehicles traveling, and already there was some snow on the highest elevations.

"It was a relief to pass the Emigrant Gap station, the summit and the lake at Donner Pass. I was flying at near 8,000 feet and there was no comfort in the open cockpit of the Army-type DH-4 airplane."

Another of the early mail pilots, Paul F. Collins, contributes a little humor to an otherwise testy situation.

"It was my first flight with the mail," he says. "Hours late after a forced landing many miles off the course, I had just floundered through fog and snow from Chicago to Minneapolis in a cranky old DH ship. As I hurried away to renew my war risk insurance at the nearest post office, a young fan trailed me. 'Say mister,' he asked, 'what does it feel like to be a regular mail pilot?' 'Son,' I said, 'it feels like a terrible accident looking for some place to happen.'"

Collins tells another tale about a friend and fellow pilot, Lloyd Bertaud:

CLEARED TO LAND!

"Bert's experience started soon after he took off from the Municipal Airport at Cleveland. Crossing northern Ohio he found himself caught in the nastiest kind of winter weather. Under a very low ceiling he had about as much visibility as a fly in a bottle of ink. To make matters worse, his ship began icing up rapidly. Bert bucked it blind for the greater part of an hour. Then he managed to locate our emergency landing field just beyond the Ohio state line at Mercer, Pennsylvania. Conditions there were too thick for the beacon to light him safely down. Pulling up his ship to 800 feet, he dropped a parachute flare.

"On all night flights in the mail service flares of this type are hung in slots beneath the ship. A lever within immediate reach of the pilot releases them. Each flare consists of a generous charge of magnesium suspended from a silk parachute. The magnesium is highly combustible. Ignited by the releasing device, it shines with incandescent brightness as it falls through fog or rain or snow. Its 50,000 candlepower glare gives us a four-minute chance to glide down and land.

"The magnesium is supposed to go out before it nears the ground. As it falls 500 feet a minute, it has time ordinarily to spend itself. Bert, however, was only 800 feet up when obliged to release the flare. He sat down as neat as you please within the boundary markers of the field, but just as he climbed from his ship to congratulate himself on such a fine forced squat without the

The early days of the airmail operation were glamorous days for aviation. The airmail pilots were public heroes and the crowds came out to see their heroes and the "crates" in which they flew. Looking back we find some of the crates—these Douglas M-2s, for instance—were pretty substantial airplanes and represented a lot of technology in their day.

A lot of it was "show biz", but pioneering airmail flight brought out the wheels like Harris M. "Pop" Hanshue, first president of Western (in shirtsleeves) and Los Angeles Postmaster P. P. O'Brien (weighing the mail). The pilot (white overalls) is Maurice Graham.

Western Air Express (now Western Air Lines) was one of the nation's pioneer commercial carriers. Western made its first flight over the contract airmail route between Los Angeles and Salt Lake City on April 17, 1926, with Fred Kelly at the controls of the DH-4. That first airmail pouch certainly didn't tax the payload capacity of the big de Havilland.

Celebrities were among the first to take to flying as passengers. Will Rogers wanted to be a "first passenger" so badly he went to the post office (as the story goes), bought enough stamps to ship himself from Los Angeles to Salt Lake City with pilot Al DeGarmo at the controls.

slightest mishap, down came the flare, still alight, on the roof of a nearby barn.

"Then Bert's woes began. The barn blazed merrily. It was full of hay. The farmer who owned it came scrambling outdoors straight from his bed. Bert dashed to the scene, pitching headlong over stumps and barbed wire fences in the dark.

"'Save the stock, help me save the stock!' yelled the farmer.

"The farmer's first thought had been for his horses. He led two husky Percherons from their stalls and tried to hold them. They were terrified.

"'The cows, the cows!' he howled at Bert. 'Get the cows out of the barn.'

"Bert raced for the cows. By tracing the noise of their complaint, he discovered the farmer's 10 Holsteins locked in their rustic boudoir. No doubt, amid the scenes of tranquil dairy life, they were gentle cows of proper matronly deportment. But a midnight rumpus was not in their line.

"Smoke and din drove them out of their ladylike wits. By the time Bert came to their aid they weren't themselves. They were all unstrung: hysterical.

"When he set them free they charged through their gate, knocked him down and trod on him.

"'Talk about your thundering herds,' he told me afterward, 'those cows did me more harm than anything I've gone up against in 12 years of flying.'"

All the action wasn't in the skies during that first part of the 1920s. The earliest tests had proven conclusively that the airplane did have commercial application. So an army of men and women on the ground now set out to make this demonstrated potential a functioning reality.

With improvements made on the Liberty motor, such as heavy stub tooth gears, drilled pistons and improved oil pump, it could be considered as reliable and dependable as any motor of that time. If not more so. A number of de Havilland planes were also obtained from the War and Navy Departments, and when remodeled and rebuilt into mail planes, they were speedy, reliable, long lived and capable of carrying a mail load of 500 pounds. Experience had also proven they were a comparatively safe plane to operate. The Air Mail Repair Depot was located at Chicago, and was used for repairing, remodeling and rebuilding of planes, overhauling of motors, etc.

When the service first began to use Liberty motors it was not an uncommon occurrence to have delayed and uncompleted trips due to motor trouble. However, by developing and perfecting rigid inspection, servicing and overhaul methods, actual forced landings on account of the failure of the plane or plane parts became almost unheard of.

During the spring and summer of 1923 work on a lighted airway between Cheyenne, Wyoming, and Chicago, Illinois, was pushed forward with a view to carrying out experiments to determine whether cross-country night flying on a regular schedule was possible, and whether a through transcontinental air mail service between New York and San Francisco could be regularly maintained. This was certainly a huge undertaking, as up to that time very little night flying had been done and, of course, there were no lighted airways in existence.

Meanwhile, the Army Air Service had carried on some experiments and developed certain necessary equipment, but had attempted very little regular scheduled cross-country night flying. The Army obligingly placed at the disposal of the Post Office Department all the knowledge they had obtained from their experiments.

Cooperation was had at the hands of manufacturers of illuminating equipment of various kinds. The General Electric Company, the American Gas Accumulator Company and the Sperry Instrument Company were particularly helpful. Beacon lights were installed between Chicago and Cheyenne, planes were equipped with landing lights, emergency fields were prepared, lighted and marked, and terminal fields lighted. Pilots were given an opportunity to make practice night flights.

All arrangements completed as planned by August 1923, a regular schedule was flown between New York and San Francisco for a period of four days, that part of the route between Chicago and Cheyenne being flown at night. The best time eastbound on any of the four days was 26 hours and 14 minutes, and the time best made westbound was 29 hours and 38 minutes. It was found that better time could generally be made on eastbound trips due to the fact that the prevailing winds are from the west. Results of the tests were so satisfactory that operation of a transcontinental service on a similar schedule, the first 30 days to be a trial, was scheduled.

It was also decided to charge air mail postage at the rate of eight cents an ounce for each zone transported, the route being divided into three zones, namely, New York to Chicago; Chicago to Cheyenne; and Cheyenne to San Francisco. Heretofore, no extra charge had been made for the transportation of air mail, although when the service was first established in 1918 special stamps were issued and the rate was 24 cents per ounce. This was later reduced to 16 cents per ounce, then to six cents, and due to lack of patronage was finally discontinued in 1919. The regular standard domestic rate of two cents an ounce went back into effect.

The remainder of 1923 and the first half of 1924 was spent in preparing for the inauguration of a regular transcontinental service. This was begun on July 1, 1924. The 30-day test was so satisfactory the service was continued as a regular operation. A typical schedule required departure from the initial terminal in the morning and arrival at the end of the route late in the afternoon of the next day.

Later on, a considerable demand emerged for air mail service between New York and Chicago on a schedule which would deliver mail of one business day to the opposite terminal in time for the first carrier delivery the next morning. To meet that demand an overnight service between these points was established on July 1, 1925.

This summary of the work done in connection with the inauguration of night flying gives some idea of the undertaking. In the last half of 1923 and the first half of 1924 these things were accomplished:

289 flashing gas beacons were installed between Chicago and Cheyenne;

34 emergency landing fields between the same points were rented, equipped with rotating electric beacons, boundary markers, and telephones;

5 terminal landing fields were equipped with beacons, floodlights and boundary markers;

17 planes were equipped with luminous instruments, navigation lights, landing lights and parachute flares.

In addition to this the necessary organization to handle operations both in the air and on the ground was brought up to a high degree of efficiency.

In later years Charles I. Stanton, one of the air mail pioneers who later became the Administrator of Civil Aeronautics, made this observation:

"We planted four seeds in the early days of the scheduled airmail service. They were airways, communications, navigation aids and multi-engine aircraft. Not all of these came full blown into the transportation scene; in fact, the last one withered and died, and had to be planted over again nearly a decade later. But they are the cornerstones on which our present worldwide transport structure is built, and they came, one by one, out of our experience in daily, uninterrupted flying of the mail."

THE EARLY DAYS 2

As Charles Stanton pointed out, the seeds of today's massive air transportation system were planted in the days of those early air mail pilots and ground technicians.

But while these seeds were being planted and nourished, often by the blood of the men doing the flying—12 airmail pilots were killed in 1921, for instance, and in the period of several years the Post Office flew the mail, 31 of the original 40 pilots met their death—other events were taking place here and abroad which would have profound effects on the development of commercial aviation and, ergo, the need to foster and regulate it.

During the period between 1914 and 1925 passenger movement by air also began to develop. In the United States it was sporadic, often hit or miss, with the impetus being provided by private enterprise alone. In Europe, however, the governments of France and England and even that of Germany (severely restricted by the onerous provisions of the Versailles Treaty, which particularly limited aviation development) seized upon what they recognized as an opportunity—accepting along with it the monetary obligation—to actively foster aviation development, especially air transport. In providing for government support of this development, they also saw to it that a suitable regulatory system was established.

Even before World War I a few visionaries saw the potential in harnessing the speed of the airplane to move people from one point to another for a fee. In the 10 years beginning in 1914, a number of U. S. air transport companies emerged, among them St. Petersburg-Tampa Air Boat Line, Aero Limited operating from New York to Atlantic City, Aeromarine operating from New York to other resort cities along the Atlantic Coast, West Indies Airways flying from Key West to Havana and Long Island Airways (forerunner to Pan American), also operating along the Atlantic Coast. By 1925, one American entrepreneur, Henry Ford by name, pioneered the establishment of an air freight operation between Detroit and Chicago.

These were but a few of the many air transport operations to be born—usually quickly to die—in the U.S. during that troubled period. They ranged from one-plane, pilot-owner operations to well-organized business enterprises having several aircraft. One thing they all had in common—they all bucked the tide with little or no support of any kind from their government.

In Europe, early development of air transportation began along the same lines. For instance, by 1921 Germany had two airlines—the German Airline (Deutsche Luft-Reederei) and Lloyd Eastern Airways (Lloyd Ostflug). Here also efforts at commercial air transport proliferated and by 1924 some 38 airlines had sprouted in Germany since the end of World War I. By the end of 1924, however, only two had survived. They were Aero Lloyd and Junkers Airways, and it wasn't long before the German government took positive action to insure that its national interests in aviation were not imperiled by competitive initiative. Late in 1925 these air lines were ordered merged into Deutsche Lufthansa, the German state airline, which in the ensuing years before World War II became a near dominant factor in world air transportation. In fact, had it not been for that war, Lufthansa could well have become the world's biggest airline. The progress it made through 1939, particularly with regard to its penetration of the southern European nations, South America and the Soviet gave it great momentum; momentum enough to probably nose out the growing British and French state airlines which were conducting parallel development, had it not been for Germany's military ambitions.

Looking at air transport in the 1925 time period, aviation historians today compare "orderly development abroad" with a "chaotic situation" here in the United States. And, they seem to agree that the key to the problem was the reluctance of the U. S. Congress to accept the necessity to subsidize the development of commercial aviation.

This is not to say that the U. S. government did nothing to support this development during the early days. As early as 1915 a rider was tacked on the Naval Appropriations Act creating an "advisory committee on aeronautics." Although funded under the Navy, this National Advisory Committee on Aeronautics (NACA) was considered an independent agency. (This was, in fact, the forerunner of today's National Aeronautics and Space Administration.)

Almost immediately NACA made three recommendations: (1) begin an airmail service, (2) establish a procedure for cross-licensing of patents, and (3) develop a series of "three-year" plans for aircraft production.

During U. S. involvement in World War I, NACA undertook a major effort to improve military aviation resources. It fostered the mass production of the Liberty engine and it worked on the important relationship between meteorology and aviation.

NACA soon became involved in coordinating most of the important aviation decisions in this country. As it studied the U. S. attitudes about aviation, it learned that despite the fact the airplane had been born in this country just a few years earlier, both the U. S. public and the Congress demonstrated a real reluctance to see the United States assume world leadership in the air.

Shortly after the Armistice, NACA recommended legislation to control commercial aviation. The powerful U. S. Bureau of Standards added its voice. But their recommendations fell on deaf ears despite the knowledge that Great Britain and the other major foreign powers had publicly revealed broad plans to both control and subsidize civil air development.

In 1919, NACA attended the International Convention on Air Navigation, representing this nation and coordinating U. S.-agency positions at a time when the United States didn't even have laws for domestic regulation.

A year later, NACA's principal recommendation was a new call for regulation. This was fully backed by the embryonic aviation industry itself. This was and still is an unusual circumstance in the relationship between business-industry and the government. Normally, business-industrial interests work diligently to avoid or at least water down government regulations. Here industry spoke loudly in support of aggressive action on the part of government to institute regulation and for good reason. The aviation industry in America was, as historians describe it, in chaos. There were no standards for pilot competence, no standards for aircraft design and construction, no business or monetary standards which would weed out the fly-by-nights or the unscrupulous, no standards for passenger comfort or safety, no cohesive thrust to U. S. aviation development as a whole.

THE EARLY DAYS

The reason for this huge void? There was one, and only one—a Congressional refusal (which the members attributed to a public apathy) to assume the financial obligation that would go along with government regulation. And there is a direct parallel here (in the same time period) with the refusal of our military leaders to spend the money needed to develop a military air capability despite the fact that World War I proved beyond any doubt that the airplane would become the world's most potent military weapon.

One would think that the advent—and the relative success of the new air mail service which made great strides between 1918 and 1924—would have sparked public support particularly since air mail was "free." But, no such thing. The new free government service, fostering faster written communications across the nation and up and down the eastern seaboard, and even the support of the press, who began to tell the story of the heroic air mail pilots and the odds against which they pitted their frail planes, did not elicit any ground swell of support.

In 1925, three things occurred which ultimately speeded up a turn-around in the attitude of Congress (some small support had begun emerging as the result of editorial support provided by many of the nation's newspapers). First, the Kelly Act was passed. This authorized the Post Office Department to let civilian contracts for air mail routes. Second, the trial of General Billy Mitchell and the wide exposure it received further awakened the public to the potential of airplanes, not just as weapons for war but also as instruments of commerce. Third, Calvin Coolidge, then the nation's chief executive, established the "President's Aircraft Board." In retrospect, much of the credit for this executive action must be given to then Secretary of Commerce Herbert Hoover.

In the Congress a variety of thorny issues were debated in the context of arriving finally at some sort of regulatory legislation. That august body—at least a significant portion of it—finally had accepted the prerequisite to regulation, expenditure of tax dollars. But there were a number of strongly diverse views about how to go about it. There were those who saw no reason why the War Department shouldn't control both military and civil aviation. There were those who opposed placing the responsibility for regulating aviation in the Commerce Department—some for purely political reasons (they did not want to add additional power to Hoover's already broad authority and growing stature). There also was the ever present "state's rights" consideration—did the Federal government have the right to regulate the use of the airspace above the states or the airplanes flying from their terrain? Not the least of the perplexing questions was, "How much?" How many dollars to appropriate? One early version of a bill called for the United States to fund the new regulatory requirement (and this included the monies to foster the growth of aviation) at $250,000 for the initial year. This, when informed sources pointed out that Great Britain was spending $1.75 million and France and Germany each were spending at the rate of $2.5 million annually.

On May 20, 1926, President Calvin Coolidge signed into law the Air Commerce Act—23 years after the Wrights' historic first flight, eight years after the beginning of the air mail service and 10 years after the establishment of the NACA. One thing is obvious from the historical records of that event, in no way did the American Congress provide for anywhere near the level of support granted to air transport operations in European nations. It is interesting to note that the Committee on Civil Aviation (a fact-finding body working within the Department of Commerce prior to the enactment of the Air Commerce Act) delivered a report recommending substantial financial support including cash subsidies. It was determined that this report be kept secret because of the possibility that it might stampede Congress in the opposite direction. Even in those days, however, the strategy of leaks was used to advantage. "Rumors" of the report did get to Congress and served to accelerate passage of the conservative legislation favored and thus pre-empted administration and industry pressure for a more generous approach.

UNITED STATES OF AMERICA
DEPARTMENT OF COMMERCE
OFFICE OF THE DIRECTOR OF AERONAUTICS

PILOT'S IDENTIFICATION CARD

This Identification Card, issued on the
6th *day of* April *, 19*27*, accompanies*
Pilot's License No. 1

Age 39
Weight 200 *Color hair* Brown
Height 6'1½" *Color eyes* Blue

Pilot's Signature.

FORM R-19   U. S. GOVERNMENT PRINTING OFFICE: 1926

Licensed pilot Number 1 in the United States was Bill McCracken, who also became the first director of the newly formed Bureau of Aeronautics in the Department of Commerce. Orville Wright was offered the first license but he declined in favor of McCracken who had been named to head the new regulatory bureau.

Under the authorization contained in the act an Aeronautics Branch was created within the Department of Commerce and William P. McCracken, a long-time booster of aviation, was named Assistant Secretary of Commerce for Aeronautics. McCracken had worked long and hard behind the scenes during the framing of the final legislation.

The nation's first body of aviation regulations (carefully worked out in close coordination with the industry) became effective on December 31, 1926. As late as November of that year the new Aeronautics Branch still had no aircraft and no inspectors. In fact, during its first fiscal year the Aeronautics Branch was able to bring aboard only 15 inspectors and set a goal of 35 for the second year. It proved difficult to find men who had the combination of long experience and above average qualification as pilots and the necessary knowledge of aircraft and engines.

A former Royal Air Force pilot, R. G. Lockwood, who also had been a civilian test pilot with the U. S. Air Service at McCook Field, became the first supervising inspector and conducted the first inspection of a new airplane, one destined for export to Canada, on Dec. 7, 1926. On the same day the first of the new Federal airways beacons (the facilities of the lighted airways established by the Post Office Department would be turned over to the Depart-

THE EARLY DAYS

This is the way it was in those days. Airfields were grassy meadows. Airplanes were things of wood, cloth, metal and rubber. The sounds of aviation included the whine of winds through the flying wires and the smells were those of castor oil.

Signs of the times in 1926—a Ford Model T mail truck and a lineup of Douglas mail planes. Several of the aircraft are the famous Douglas M-2s. The site—Vail Field.

Only the old-timers in aviation today will remember this striking silhouette—the Boeing Monomail, first all-metal, low-wing, cantilever aircraft to enter regular service. This one belonged to Wyoming Air Service and is preparing to depart Wardwell Field, Casper, Wyo.

One of the early attempts to carry passengers on a regular basis along with the mail was made possible by introduction of the Boeing 40-B-4. While the passengers were carried in the "relative comfort" of the cabin, the pilot still functioned from an "air-conditioned" open cockpit.

ment of Commerce Lighthouse Service the following July) was commissioned. It was designated Beacon 71 and it was situated on the Chicago-Dallas route some 15 miles northeast of Moline, Ill. Ten more beacons were soon added to this route and a month later the first night flight along the lighted airway from Chicago to St. Louis was made.

With a Fiscal Year budget of only $550,000 for the first 12 months, it is fortunate other Federal agencies were given certain responsibilities to support the Aeronautics Branch. Research and development was provided by an Aeronautical Research Division of the Bureau of Standards. The Lighthouse Service assumed responsibility for the navigational aids. An airway mapping section was established in the Coast and Geodetic Survey.

Initially, a major omission was made in the appropriations. No funds were allocated for travel expenses. Even after this was corrected, Aeronautics Branch inspectors rarely were able to take advantage of the superior speed of the airplane in making their rounds. They found themselves bound to the ground in autos or trains until June 1927 when the Branch got its first five planes. The first of these was, of course, a weary DH-4 transferred from the Post Office Department.

Immediate targets for enforcement of the new regulations were such things as lights for night flights, weather and distress signals, minimum altitudes, dropping objects from aircraft, stunt flying over congested areas and "rules of the road"—right-of-way, crossing the path of other aircraft, passing and the priority of non-powered aircraft over those with engines.

The first license structure provided for private, industrial, limited commercial and transport categories. A minimum age of 18 years was set and U. S. citizenship was made a requisite. Fifty hours of solo flight were required for all but the transport license, which called for 100 hours.

Maneuvers required in the first flight examinations were few and relatively simple for those experienced airmen now required to be licensed. The airplane was to be flown at 800 feet in a figure-eight pattern (no less than five times) around two pylons set 1,500 feet apart and the pilot had to make three "satisfactory" landings to a full stop. This sufficed for the first three classes of license. For the transport license the pilot, in addition, had to make spot lan-

You might see this as a commuter airline circa 1931. The fleet of Stinsons belong to Wyoming Air Service and the scene is Denver.

dings with and without his engine operating, demonstrate ability to perform sideslips and recognize and to recover from stalls.

McCracken, himself, was given the first airman's license although he wished to waive the physical requirements now in effect and bestow License Number 1 on Orville Wright. Wright declined, however, in favor of the new Assistant Secretary. Soon many already famous aviators qualified for the low numbered certificates. Among them were Jimmy Doolittle, Charles Lindbergh, Phil Love, Amelia Earhart and C. S. Jones.

When, on July 1, 1927, the Department of Commerce took over responsibility for the facilities developed and maintained by the Post Office, it acquired 2,612 miles of transcontinental airway, all of which was lighted except the portion from Salt Lake City to San Francisco. It also acquired the aeronautical radio service—small though it was—developed to support the mail service. This aggregate acquisition included:

> 17 fully-equipped radio stations with 44 operating personnel;
>
> 68 emergency landing fields (with caretakers in charge);
>
> 21 emergency landing fields (automatically operated);
>
> 21 electric beacon lights (with caretakers in charge);
>
> 79 automatically-operated electric beacon lights;
>
> 405 automatically-operated acetylene gas rotating beacons;
>
> 102 airway operating personnel (approximate).

Most terminal airport facilities operated by the Post Office Department were transferred to the municipalities in which they were situated while at Chicago, Omaha and San Francisco, where the facilities were located on Federally-owned property, they reverted to the department involved.

The Air Mail Service's newer Douglas mail planes were sold to civilian contractors while the old DH-4's were transferred to other agencies of the Federal government.

By August 31, 1927, the Post Office Department was completely out of the flying business. It was at about that time that Edward A. Keogh, in his brief history of the air mail wrote:

"Of course, weather that was considered impossible to fly through in the early stages was easily flown through during the last few years, but fog still remains the greatest enemy of the pilot and the cause of practically all serious delays and uncompleted trips. Short areas of fog are flown through or over, but it is not practicable to fly through or over large areas of dense fog, requiring designated landings to be made therein, with our present equipment and instruments."

Keogh essentially put into words the major challenge that was to occupy the Aeronautics Bureau (and the agencies that succeeded it) for the next 20 years. Fortunately, this was not a challenge the Bureau had to face alone. It was uppermost in the minds of virtually all facets of aviation—military, civil, private—and its eventual solution came from many sources.

One of the new technologies which offered the greatest potential was, of course, radio. The first plane-to-ground radio contact had been made before World War I by E. N. Pickerall on August 4, 1910. Just three weeks later J. A. D. McCurdy duplicated this contact (both were with unwieldy equipment using telegraphy) in a flight at Sheepshead Bay, N.Y.

By 1914 two-way, plane-to-plane, radio telegraph communications were conducted by Lieutenants H. A. Dargue and J. Maeuborgne at Manila and during 1919-20 tests using radio navigational equipment were being performed using a five-kilowatt transmitter and loop-type antenna at New York, Bellefonte, Pa., Cleveland and Chicago to transmit directional signals to specially-equipped twin-engine aircraft. About this same time additional experiments were being conducted between stations at College Park, Md., and Philadelphia with aircraft operating out of Washington. Radio became an integral part of the airway structure under the Post Office Department and development spurred by the requirements of the air mail operation gave the new Aeronautics Bureau a head start when it took over.

At best, however, these stations were crude affairs, in most places little more than tar paper shacks crammed with apparatus which today would appear like some of Rube Goldberg's weirdest contraptions. Heart of each station was the two-kilowatt "Federal" type arc transmitter looking all the world like a short, steel barrel with a lid and sprouting from the top and sides an assortment of knobs, wires, tubes, pipes and other hardware. The wall nearest the transmitter was a maze of electrical wiring, coils and switches supported on large black insulators. One or more radio receivers—usually at least one for long wave and one for short wave—a set of ear phones and an "all capitals" typewriter completed the station. The station staff consisted of one man.

The next improvement was the introduction of "vacuum tube" transmitters. The first ones were designed and built by two of the pioneer operators themselves at their own expense. Art Johnson at Salt Lake City and Hadley Beedle at Reno both used quarter-kilowatt tubes. Beedle's design proved more efficient and ultimately was adopted for general use. Johnson and another operator, Phil Coupland, earlier had developed a method of increasing the power of the old arc transmitters.

Operationally, the radio network established to support the mail service was devoted to passing weather reports from place to place and handling arrival and departure information. It provided no navigational aid. In the 1925-1926 period, still under Post Office Department auspices (aided by the Bureau of Standards, NACA and the military) intensive research was being conducted primarily at College Park on developing practical radio beacons. This work was continued under the Bureau of Aeronautics using the first of the Branch's aircraft—appropriately enough designed N-1. Shortly, a second aircraft was equipped to support this program and almost daily flights were made. One of the principle research objectives was to combine into a single radio set the two receivers which, up to that time, were carried—one to receive messages and one to receive beacon signals. Soon reliable communications and radio navigation were being conducted by the Bureau's aircraft ranging as far as 50 miles from Washington and the College Park facility.

By mid-1927, six radio beacons had been established or were under construction. Two were in being even before the Bureau took over. These were situated at McCook Field, Dayton, Ohio; the Ford Motor Company field, Detroit; the Ford field at Chicago; Hadley Field, New Brunswick, N.J.; Bellefonte, Pa., and College Park. The Bellefonte and College Park facilities also served as laboratories in the further development of the concept. This network of stations also supported two of the nation's pioneer passenger operations—Pitcairn, operating between New York and Atlanta, and National Air Transport, flying between New York and Chicago.

CLEARED TO LAND!

It wasn't long before radio telephone capability (voice) and a series of marker beacons were added, positioned 25 miles apart along the airway serving as mileposts. Thus, the radio telephone could provide up-to-date reports of weather en route and at destination airports; the aircraft could navigate using the directional beacons and by means of the marker beacons could judge its progress along the route. Also, for the first time, various radio facilities were remoted from the landing fields and/or visual beacon sites and controlled from the nearby airport. This marked the beginning of "remote control" of radio aids by a "center." At Bellefonte, for instance, the operator also had hard wire connections with other stations and airports and thus could coordinate activities between several ground stations and landing fields and aircraft in flight.

By 1928, the Branch had made plans and drawn up specifications to establish a series of these radio control stations beginning with a facility at Key West, Fla., to serve an overseas route to Havana proposed to open late that year. Also standardized was the type of radio beacon to be used—the equi-signal, radio range type, transmitting two interlocking signals which established a steady "on course" signal where they overlapped. The two signals were in code—A (dot dash) and N (dash dot). Except where they overlapped providing a constant tone, the pilot would hear either the A or the N. These first radio ranges provided only two courses. Later versions, basically the same types used in the U. S. through the 1960's and still used in some parts of the world, provided four courses.

A parallel area of development was the method displaying these course signals to the pilot. At that point in time it was felt that it would be "too fatiguing" for the pilot to depend on just an aural indication—the sound of the

The "big attraction" both for the public and for men in aviation at the Western Aircraft Show, November 1929, was this Fokker Super Universal which featured, for the first time, a reversible pitch propeller.

The introduction of the Curtiss Condor, 18-passenger "People Carrier", gave air transportation a big boost. The aircraft was a departure in terms both of capacity and comfort. This is the first Condor preparing for a test flight at Roosevelt Field, Long Island, on July 21, 1929.

A mainstay of the early passenger-carrying airlines was the Fokker Trimotor or F-10A. This one belonging to West Coast Air Transport is being serviced at Seattle, Wash.

CLEARED TO LAND!

A, N or on-course in his headphones. The Bureau of Standards devised a visual indicator consisting of two vibrating reeds placed side-by-side in a panel-mounted instrument with the ends visible. When the aircraft was on course, the reeds would vibrate with equal amplitude tracing out what would appear to be two white lines of equal length in the instrument. Ultimately, it was found that the aural method was preferable and a visual cockpit indicator disappeared until the advent of the radio direction finder (RDF) which had a single needle on a compass rose which could point directly at the station being received. Subsequently, this was used to "home in" on a variety of radio signals—commercial broadcast, radio beacons, radio ranges where the course signals were obliterated by static.

At first, the RDF's were of the same type developed for use aboard ship. A loop antenna on the craft could be rotated mechanically to obtain a bearing to the station. Then the pilot took up the indicated course. The loop was again rotated until the needle pointed straight ahead and the pilot followed the needle. Or with a fixed loop the pilot could turn the aircraft until the needle pointed straight ahead. Later the automatic direction finder (ADF) was introduced. In the automatic mode the needle always pointed to the station regardless of the direction the aircraft was pointed. Thus the pilot always knew his relative bearing to a given station. Taking bearings on two or more, he could find his position by simple triangulation almost immediately. The ADF also gave the pilot an immediate indication when he passed over the station, the needle swinging to the reciprocal heading.

Like many of the developments which over the years have improved the reliability and safety of air transportation, the ADF came from industry. It was the brain child of Bill Lear, the same Lear who in recent years gave aviation the Learjet and who, earlier, designed and built the first small, lightweight aircraft radio receiver permitting private pilots to take advantage of the weather broadcasts and other flight information then available only to the airlines and the military.

Lear, who began flying himself in 1922, tells three stories about the development of that radio and the ADF which provide an insight into those formative days and into the attitudes of aviators who weren't always ready to accept new technology when it was offered.

"Frankly," Lear relates, "I got tired of trying to fly around the country with nothing but a compass. The airlines knew what the weather was on the other side of the mountains. They also had radio ranges to fly. They knew what was going on. What was the use of the radio range to private pilots? Private pilots—we call them general aviation pilots today—didn't even know they existed."

Lear and Paul Galvin formed Motorola Company and offered private aviation a receiver which would let them use the radio ranges and get the weather.

"I tried to sell one to Harry Dobhurst who was the pilot for Harry Richmond," Lear recalls.

"He said, 'I don't trust 'em.'

"I asked if he didn't listen to the beacon band.

" 'No,' he replied, 'there's just a lot of dots and dashes on it.'

" 'Well,' I countered, 'don't you get the weather on it?'

" 'I don't trust 'em, I don't have 'em get it,' was his reply.

"You know, I didn't make the sale."

THE EARLY DAYS

In those days, Western Electric, General Electric and RCA had a lock on the patents involved in manufacturing radio circuitry. As Lear recalls it, you had to get a license from them if you wanted to manufacture an aviation radio and, "if they didn't want you in the business, you didn't get a license." Lear went ahead anyway. When threatened with prosecution for patent violation, Lear threatened to take the story to the newspapers. He quickly got his license and negotiated a "$5 penalty" for his earlier transgressions.

When it came to the ADF, Lear hit another roadblock. RCA offered to grant him a license if he could "prove there was such a thing as an automatic direction finder."

"So," Lear says, "I flew down to their main engineering office at Camden and took up all their engineers—over 15 of them, one at a time. The deal was, if my direction finder worked they would give me a license and buy the ADF from me for a substantial sum.

"From Newark I could tune as far away as Cincinnati and all up and down the coast. I got good bearings demonstrating to them that there was such a thing as an ADF. When we came down, I interrogated each one separately asking, 'Do I have an ADF or not?'

"They all agreed I did. I asked the boss man if I would get my license. He said, 'We'll have to talk about it.' I had a friend who was one of those engineers. He later told me what went on after I left.

"When the engineers got back in the office, he told me, the chief told them, 'I don't want to hear any more about the fact there ain't no such thing as an ADF . . . so get the hell to work and make one.'

Crude by today's standards, this company operations facility with both radio and telephone capability was a real asset in 1930 in keeping track of Western Air Express aircraft and crews.

CLEARED TO LAND!

"I got my license eventually. RCA also got in the ADF business. I had to threaten again to go to the press, however, before my license was granted."

Like the Motorola aircraft receiver, Lear encountered resistance selling the ADF to the aviation industry.

"Like when I tried to sell it to Eastern Air Lines," he explains, "I knew Eddie Rickenbacker real well. He sent me down to Miami to see Charlie Frantz, the operations manager. When I tried to sell Charlie on the idea he asked what it weighed. When I replied, '55 pounds,' he balked saying, 'That's 55 pounds of payload I could be carrying Miami to New York and New York to Miami.' That, he indicated, he couldn't afford.

"I countered with, 'Wouldn't you like to have a backup in case one of your pilots gets confused on the radio ranges?' I guess it was the wrong thing to say. He immediately got his nose out of joint. 'Are you inferring that an Eastern

1928 team of weather observers in action. Actually, the theodolite and weather balloon being used are not dissimilar to those still in use today.

With a growing demand for transportation of passengers along with mail came the requirement for on-time operation and all-weather flight. Weather stations were linked by teletype into a reporting network across the nation.

By the mid-to-late '30s, airways communications already had taken on an aura of sophistication.

CLEARED TO LAND!

Air Line pilot would get lost?' he challenged.

" 'You mean, they don't get lost,' I said.

" 'No, sir!' he replied."

At the time Lear had no way of knowing that Charlie Frantz was going to have to eat his words.

"About two weeks later," he recalls, 'an Eastern Air Lines plane got lost on a southbound flight. At that time the company frequency was 4,000 to 5,000 kilocycles—good for long distance communications. You could hear from Maine to Rio what was going on.

"Everyone was calling him trying to help out. Plus that, he was getting a lot of precipitation static. He was just about ready to run out of fuel after touring about for four and a half hours when he called in saying he knew where he was and was landing at Charleston. When he landed he called saying he was just 'outside the Charleston administration building.'

"Now remember everybody could hear this. The Charleston operator told him there was no one outside. 'I'm right outside,' he said, 'I'll come right in and talk with you.' Now everyone was hanging on their receivers, all over the east coast, waiting for the next chapter in this mix up.

"The pilot finally came back on the air. He had found he was at Tallahassee, not Charleston. This whole thing became a subject for the Congress and was written up in the Congressional Record to demonstrate the need for better navigation capability.

"I couldn't resist the urge to send Charlie Frantz a telegram. I said, 'Dear Charlie, It was a good thing your pilot wasn't lost.' Of course, this was the reason I never got any business from Eastern."

Needless to say, the ADF became one of the more important aircraft navigation systems. It was especially valuable during World War II. It still is carried as the principal back up to modern very high frequency omni range (VOR) navigation equipment and is particularly valuable navigating to a destination not serviced by VOR.

Another area of critical concern in those days was instrumentation which together with radio would permit aircraft to take off, fly to their destination and land despite the fog (or other obscurations) Keogh pinpointed in his air mail history.

One of those who played a major role in this area was Jimmy Doolittle.

Instrument flying as such—keeping the aircraft straight and level and making gentle banks and turns—had been going on for some time. It has been reported, although not verified, that some early pilots suspended an object by a string in the cockpit and by judging the angle of the string to a known vertical plane in the cockpit were able to keep their wing level. And it was pointed out earlier that as early as 1922 Doolittle with a "borrowed" bank and turn indicator (one still in the experimental stage) flew coast-to-coast, some of that distance "on instruments."

In the context of making aviation a safe, reliable medium of public transportation, this kind of instrument flying didn't hack it. It was obvious to everyone that to achieve its full potential aviation would have to offer a service that began on the flight line and ended on the next flight line in all kinds of weather. That meant instrument takeoffs as well as instrument landings.

It was in 1928 that Doolittle was borrowed from the Army to head the Guggenheim-funded Full Flight Laboratory. The first thing the laboratory did was to analyze all the work conducted up to that time in the areas of blind landing. The British had experimented with a system of tethered balloons lined up with the landing field. This worked as long as the fog was not too deep and if another factor such as blowing snow did not obscure the balloons. In both Britain and France, a "lead-in cable" idea was tried out. An electrified cable circled the field and "led" to the landing area. In the aircraft extremely sensitive sensing devices detected the presence of the electrical field. The sensing devices, however, were not reliable and the system required precision turns at very low altitudes. This system even caught the notice of the U. S. Navy and some experiments were conducted in this country. Still other concepts tried and discarded were dragging a weight suspended from the tail and even long tailskids. It was intended that the object or skid would give an indication to the pilot when to arrest his rates of descent and flare out for landing.

As a corollary to these studies, the laboratory actively experimented with a method of dissipating fog with high levels of man-made heat.

"We heard from the owner of a gravel pit who also had an interest in aviation," Doolittle recalls, "that he noticed when he used a huge blow torch to dry sand and gravel the heavy fog prevalent in his area would thin and dissipate. Since mechanical, electrical and chemical means to disperse fog had been considered, it was logical also to consider heat. One of the gravel pit operator's heaters was brought to Mitchel Field, Long Island, and set up. For several months we waited for a good, heavy fog. When it finally came one September morning we found we had a dismal failure. What hadn't been taken into consideration was the fact that the fog drifted under the persuasion of the wind. If it stood still, the heat would dissipate it. With it moving, new fog immediately took the place of that dissipated by the heater."

Although the fog dispersal experiment failed that morning, another experiment conducted at Mitchel Field was a resounding success. For many months, Doolittle, in the laboratory's Consolidated NY-2 and Vought 02U-1 Corsair, had been pushing the state-of-the-art in instrument flying. Early in the program he worked with Elmer Sperry and his son, Elmer Junior, on the design and construction of a directional gyro and an artificial horizon.

"Young Elmer worked with me on the flying end of it and then worked with his Dad on the instrument end," Doolittle recalls, "and for more than a year we did a lot of flying together. In fact, young Elmer and his wife lived with us at our house more than they did in theirs. The Sperrys had the engineering brains. I knew what I wanted—what the dials should look like and what they should tell me. They put my ideas to work."

Today's horizontal situation indicator (HSI) almost debuted there in 1928. At first Doolittle wanted the horizon and directional gyro combined into a single instrument. Sperry said he could do it but advised against it saying that two separate instruments would be simpler.

"You know," Doolittle reminisces, "The instrument I drew for him is almost exactly like the HSI used in aircraft today."

Equipped with blind flight instruments—bank and turn, directional gyro, artificial horizon and one of the very first sensitive altimeters (sensitive to within 10 feet), Doolittle had practiced for many months. A radio range section and two beacons also had been constructed at Mitchel Field and Doolittle had perfected his landing techniques.

CLEARED TO LAND!

"The radio range gave me the course to the field. I homed on one beacon at the far end of the field and the second told me when I was at the near edge. My sensitive altimeter in the cockpit was synchronized with a second on the ground (by radio I got this information). I had a mark on the throttle quadrant that told me what power setting to hold during the descent. The airplane had big wings and landed very slowly. When I passed over the first beacon I pulled back the throttle and just flew the airplane into the ground. The landing gear absorbed the shock of the impact and when my angle was just right the airplane didn't even bounce."

By that September morning when the fog experiment fizzled, Doolittle was impatient to try the real thing. Our long range plan called for a safety pilot in the other cockpit on the first blind flight. Doolittle would have his head in the cockpit observing the instruments. The safety pilot would observe the ground as the airplane broke out of the fog and prevent an accident.

"The morning the fog dispersal failed," Doolittle says, "the conditions were just right for a blind flight. The fog was heavy and down to a couple of hundred feet of the ground. Something just told me the time was now. I didn't want to wait for the safety pilot. Besides, Mr. Guggenheim might not have agreed this was the right day. So I just had them roll out the plane and off I went. There was no fear. I didn't really worry, even a little. I had done this so many times before in good weather, I had full confidence in myself and the technique we worked out.

"It went like clockwork. After the flight, I called the safety pilot and Mr. Guggenheim and suggested that we should make the flight that day. I didn't tell them then that I already had. It wasn't until that afternoon and a second flight with the other pilot that I told Mr. Guggenheim the whole story."

Doolittle was awarded the Harmon Trophy for his work, work which represented a major advance in the realm of flight. From that point on, the development of instrument flight moved rapidly ahead.

With radio communications, radio navigation, blind flight instrumentation and methods moving along and with the numbers of aircraft and aircraft operations increasing by leaps and bounds, the next requirement was for a system of airport traffic control and beyond that air route traffic control.

Despite the fact that the Air Commerce Act had established a regulatory body and the Aeronautics Branch had made great strides, the nation was well into the first administration of President Franklin D. Roosevelt before Federal control was broadened to encompass air traffic control.

On the other hand, Britain had made great strides in this regard and its system of control at London's Croydon Airport was considered the model for the world. A signal light system was employed there with great success. It is significant that at this same time, 1928, signalmen using flags still were controlling traffic at a rate of 70 to 80 landings and departures a day at Chicago's busy field.

It must be remembered that radio communications with aircraft still were in their infancy and primarily were involved with weather information. Signalmen also didn't really fill the increasing need. It remained for the "light gun" to mark the first real breakthrough. This essentially was a handheld, high-intensity light projector which could display steady or flashing red, green and white lights observable in daylight up to 10 miles. Light guns still are used today when radio equipment fails.

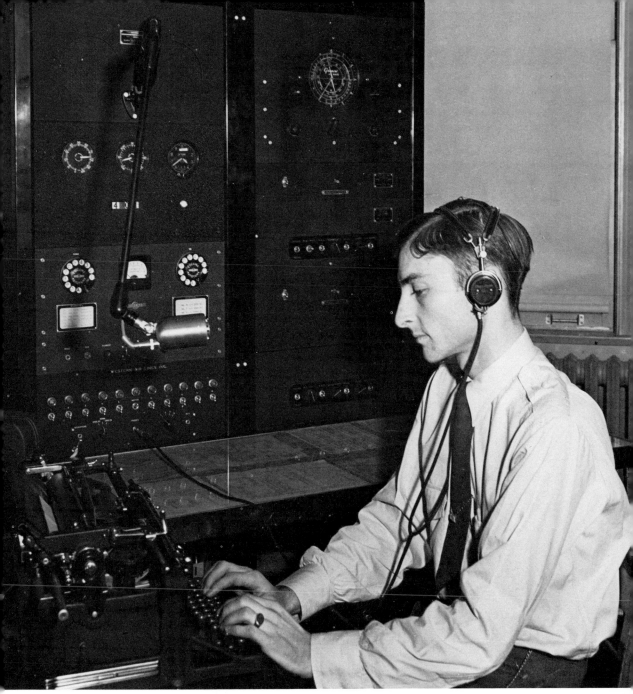

Communications equipment like this on the ground and also in the aircraft was more powerful and took up less space by 1942. Long-range point-to-point links still depended on transmitting information via the old dot-dash and code operators like this young man were in great demand.

Organizationally, the granddaddy of today's Federal Aviation Administration also was undergoing evolutionary changes. In 1933, the air navigation facilities operated by the Lighthouse Service were transferred to the Aeronautics Branch and that agency assumed a more accurate title—the Bureau of Air Commerce. Over the next four years additional changes and realignments took place so that by 1937 the Bureau was organized into seven divisions: airways engineering, airways operations, safety and planning, administrative, information and statistics, certification and inspection, and regulation and enforcement.

As the activity increased, the Bureau of Air Commerce established seven regional offices—Newark, Atlanta, Chicago, Fort Worth, Kansas City, Los

49

The first women broke into air traffic control during World War II. This is Los Angeles Center in 1944.

Angeles and Seattle. Air route traffic control responsibility largely had been delegated to the air lines until 1936 when the Federal air route traffic control centers (ARTCC) were established by the Bureau.

These first Federal ARTCC's were established July 6, 1936 at Chicago, Cleveland, New York, Detroit and pittsburgh. Three more at Los Angeles, Washington and Oakland came into being the next year. By December 7, 1941 when the Japanese attacked Pearl Harbor a total of 15 ARTCC's were in being. The fifteenth—at Boston—was commissioned as the strike against the Hawaiian Islands was in progress.

In 1938 a further investigation took place and the Civil Aeronautics Authority replaced the Bureau of Air Commerce. Integrated into the new agency was the Bureau of Air Mail transferred from the Interstate Commerce Commission. In 1940, still another reorganization took place creating the Civil Aeronautics Administration (CAA). This agency continued as the nation's aviation regulatory agency through World War II and the post-war period up through 1958.

From 1926 when it had a total of 234 men and women assigned, our aviation regulatory agency grew to a strength of 6,019 in 1941. Its budget increased from the $550,000 appropriated for its first fiscal year to $103,000,000 in 1941. Its scope of activity increased to include active research and development, Federal aid to municipalities attempting to establish or improve airports and responsibility for fostering overall aviation development in addition to its traditional assignments.

For the next four years, its civil responsibilities would take a back seat to its responsibilities in support of the military training and domestic operational requirements.

The tower as it appeared in the 1940s. Except for major terminals and military air-dromes, control towers remained few and far between for another two decades.

3 YESTERDAY, TODAY, TOMORROW

Nineteen hundred forty one—nothing would be the same again. World affairs would change dramatically. A second world war would usher in the nuclear age upsetting traditional military and diplomatic considerations and tactics. That same war would give aviation a giant boost. It would trigger the jet age. It would increase career opportunities in aviation a hundred fold. It would force the ultimate maturity of air transport. Nowhere, however, would the impact on aviation be felt as strongly as in the management of our national airways system—specifically, air traffic control.

World War II brought about the development of very high frequency radio communications—a high-reliability, line-of-sight, air-to-ground link that for the first time was not vulnerable to meteorological disturbances and "skip" propagation, and radar, which for the first time would let the controller see exactly where the traffic he controlled was in relation to other traffic, known geographic features and the departure/arrival airfields.

Air traffic control, certainly in comparison with what we have today, was sketchy at best in 1941. Air-to-ground communications were carried on by high frequency radio over a number of parallel circuits. Civil Aeronautics Administration towers and airways communications stations in some instances communicated directly with airline, military and private aircraft giving weather information, accepting flight plans and flight progress reports. Airlines also had their own ground stations and in many instances handled their own flight plans and progress reports relaying the information to the CAA air traffic control center by telephone. In a similar manner, the military had its own air-to-ground communications links and also, under certain conditions, handled this information. In all cases, this vital and time-sensitive information had to be relayed from CAA, airline and military ground stations to the ARTCC by radio (telegraph code) or by leased telephone lines. Teletype, also using leased phone lines, gradually (but very slowly) replaced the code and voice methods.

It was a ponderous system. In retrospect, it is difficult to understand how the system accommodated the tremendous upsurge of air traffic brought on by the war. One way, of course, was to commission more centers and more airways stations manned by more people. To meet the challenge, CAA undertook a massive recruiting drive and, as a matter of fact, opened this field to women applicants.

One of those was an attractive, dark-haired, young lady named Louise Anselmo. Louise intended to be a teacher but on graduation from college found there were only three teaching vacancies in the state—and California is a big state. She finally found employment in the prescription department of an optical company.

Louise, it now appears, also was one of the few women who, at that time, had strong feelings about "equal-pay-for-equal-work" when it came to women employees. When she assumed the duties of assistant manager of the department and the company refused to pay her on the same basis as the assistant manager she replaced, a male, Louise said "to hell" with them. She became a trainee air traffic controller for the CAA at the "huge" annual salary of

These aircraft continued to be a familiar sight even into the post World War II era. TWA and American Ford Trimotors take on passengers side-by-side. The Boeing 247D was the next big step. This one was operated by United.

CLEARED TO LAND!

$1,800. She became one of a relative handful of women among the 3,000 controllers recruited and trained by CAA to meet the requirements of traffic control during the war years.

"I got four weeks of broad brush training in meteorology, communications and traffic control and worked a few traffic control problems," Louise recalls, "before walking into Los Angeles Center cold.

"The center was at Burbank Air Terminal, now Hollywood-Burbank Airport, on the second floor of the American Air Lines building. In the control room there was a semi-circular bay with a raised platform, about a foot high, with the control boards on the outside of the circle and a rail on the inboard side separating the controllers from the communications positions. For each control position there was a girl with a typewriter and a telephone. She took the flight plans being phoned in from the various INSACS (interstate airways communications stations). She would hand the typewritten information to the controller who would post it on the boards."

Louise asked what she was to do.

The reply, "Just watch the other girls and do what they do."

"So this was what a controller does," she asked herself, "nothing more than a specialized typist."

Louise was assured that this was just the starting point and those that did well would be advanced to "the boards," first as an assistant and finally as a full-fledged controller.

"It was generally considered among the men," Louise says, "that women

The Douglas DC-2 (pictured here) and its successor, the DC-3, dominated the U. S. air transportation picture for many years.

were out of place in this field. That they wouldn't go any further than the telephones and typewriters. It was an uphill battle but sheer persistence finally paid off. After two years I finally got on the boards."

Louise admits that the lengthy period on the phone/typewriter position augmented by those periods when controllers plugged in an extra set of headphones and let her listen to the "real world" gave her a strong foundation for air traffic control.

"Burbank, in those days," she remembers, "had three sectors. The center sector was the tough one. It covered the area from Newhall on the North of Los Angeles to Riverside on the east. This was where most of the action took place. Ordinarily there was one controller per sector. In extremely bad weather when the work load was up we had two in the center sector. Only when we had extra people available did the other sectors get an assistant.

"Information came in by teletype from other centers (on traffic for other than the air carriers) and by telephone, to be typed, within the region. Information on air carrier flights came from airline communication stations directly by voice/phone to the controller at the board. The controller kept the board up while the assistant, when he had one, ran estimates. We had to pick up the aircraft at the last fix out of our area and, knowing airspeed, winds, course, work our own estimates. We were dealing primarily with Douglas DC-3s and DC-4s and Lockheed Connies in airline service and soon got to know their capabilities almost as well as the pilots, at least in terms of their performance characteristics. As the military traffic workload increased we got a lot of unfamiliar aircraft types and it became more difficult. We had to depend more on the accuracy of the information provided by the pilot."

Louise recalls occasionally having a "bit of trouble" with the military. Air traffic control was rather new to them. In fact, the military didn't conduct a great deal of instrument flight prior to World War II.

"They were used to flying pretty much on their own," she says, "and didn't entirely understand our role. One day when San Gorgonio Pass east of Los Angeles was closed by weather I got a flight plan from Palm Springs to Long Beach requesting 6,000 feet through the pass. Now the floor of the pass is over 3,000 feet and it is only a few miles wide bordered by peaks towering as high as 10,000 feet.

"I gave the aircraft 14,000 feet through the pass. There was a general on board who sent back word he would not be satisfied with any altitude assignment other than what he requested. In my reply I said that I didn't control with respect to terrain, I only controlled with respect to traffic. I told him I had no other traffic in the area and he was cleared to Long Beach tower at 6,-000. He hung up but immediately called back and cancelled."

There is another story about Louise Anselmo which can be pieced together from information provided by those who have known her for many years and some fragments she, herself, provides. It is an important story because it reflects a general attitude of controllers with respect to their jobs—an attitude still found almost universally in today's huge air traffic control system. That attitude is marked by deep concern for the safety of the men and women aboard those aircraft for which they must provide guidance.

By the 1946-1947 time period, Louise remembers, thousands of miles of new airways had been opened and the traffic flow had swelled beyond anyone's imagination. Yet there were too few controllers, too few navigation

CLEARED TO LAND!

aids; full-scale implementation of very high frequency communications was dragging; and a post-war Congress was turning a deaf ear to the CAA.

"I just reached the point where I couldn't take it any more," Louise says, "it just wasn't worth it. I didn't want to become part of a disaster I couldn't prevent. I turned in my resignation."

It wasn't as simple as that. Louise had established an outstanding track record as a "sharp, dependable, reliable controller." While on terminal leave, she was asked by her supervisor to "come in and talk about it." She did. When she explained her reservations she was assured that regardless of what occurred she would not legally be liable.

"I don't care about the legal liability," she told him, "I couldn't live with myself. I'd rather be selling ribbons in a department store."

Louise's boss backed her up. He also told her that many of the male flight controllers had the same misgivings. They, however, were reluctant to say or do anything for fear of losing their jobs and thus depriving their families of support. She agreed to put her feelings on the subject in writing:

December 9, 1946

Chief, Air Route Traffic Control Section 6-91
THRU: Chief Air Route Traffic Controller - Los Angeles Center
Louise A. Anselmo - Controller, Los Angeles Center
Reason for Resignation

As per your verbal request, I state the following reason for resigning from my position as Air Traffic Controller in the Los Angeles Center.

In my opinion, conditions in the Center at present are such that a Controller, upon assuming the duties of his position during IFR conditions, is placing himself in constant jeopardy of becoming involved either directly or indirectly in a tragedy which might prove fatal to fifty or more persons. This is an eventuality which I cannot face when such a tragedy would be due, not to any deficiency on my part, but rather to two factors beyond my control: primarily, lack of facilities with which to adequately handle the tremendous increase of traffic, and secondly, insufficient personnel complement to accomplish the same task.

I sincerely regret that to insure continued peace of mind I have no alternative but to resign from a position which was entirely to my liking and in which I feel I had conducted myself satisfactorily.

Louise A. Anselmo

Louise Anselmo's letter got action. It found its way to the Washington headquarters of the CAA (gathering a lot of supporting comments along the way) and, as she says, "all hell broke loose!"

It is generally agreed today that the Anselmo letter played an important role in setting the wheels in motion to double the complement of controllers the very next year.

Today, by the way, Louise is in an important supervisory position with the Western Region headquarters. As a veteran air traffic control specialist, she is involved in "obstruction evaluation"—studying the impact of both man-made and natural structures on airways facilities and aircraft movement in the system.

A simple increase in the number of controllers was not, however, the answer to the CAA's problems in the post war era. The war had brought new technology to light but full-scale adoption of this technology was moving like

YESTERDAY, TODAY, TOMORROW

"molasses in January." On the other hand, aviation activity was surging upward. After a brief post war period of comparative decline, light planes (today we call them general aviation aircraft) doubled between 1949 and 1958. Practical business and executive aircraft were introduced—and widely accepted—in significant numbers. More and more airman certificates were issued as interest in personal and business flying increased substantially. For instance, the number of private pilots doubled in the first decade following World War II.

In some areas the Federal agency charged with flight safety attempted to keep pace with the growth of American aviation. In 1946 "streamlined inspection procedures" intended to prevent bottlenecks in the production of civilian aircraft were adopted by CAA.

The agency and the military services adopted a common manual establishing standard procedures for the control of civil-military air traffic. The Federal Airport Act was enacted providing for Federal funds on a matching basis with local funds for construction and/or improvement of airports. The first radar-equipped control tower for civilian flying was commissioned at Indianapolis. The following year a modified precision approach control (developed by the CAA from the military ground control approach - GCA - equipment) was installed both at Washington National and Chicago Municipal airports on an operational test basis.

In 1948, the Radio Technical Commission on Aeronautics (RTCA) completed work on a special study of air traffic control. RTCA is made up of the top technical experts of both government and industry in the field of aeronautical telecommunications and as such its findings ordinarily represent a national consensus. This RTCA report called for establishment of a VOR airway system and the adoption of distance measuring equipment (DME) in the bargain. (VOR airways, of course, are those where very high frequency, omni-directional radio range stations having 360 possible courses are used in lieu of the old-fashioned low frequency, four-course, radio ranges. DME—distance measuring equipment—electronically provides a cockpit display which tells the pilot exactly how far he is from the station he is monitoring.) The report was accepted by the Congress and all major users of the U.S. airspace and won for RTCA the coveted Collier Trophy the following year.

Also in 1949 more realignments were made within the CAA aimed at giving the directors of major program offices in Washington greater authority over the execution of their programs in the field. An Office of Aviation Development was established and charged with the responsibility "for promoting civil aviation, particularly in the fields of aviation education and airmarking and the encouragement of private flying."

The week of October 15, 1950 was a landmark period for U.S. aviation. During that week the first VOR airways were commissioned—4,380 miles of airways connecting such major terminals as Kansas City, Denver, Albuquerque, El Paso, Omaha and Oklahoma. Actually there were already 271 VOR stations in the U.S. but this marked the first time these and new stations commissioned were organized into a controlled airway.

Radar departure procedures were inaugurated at the Washington ARTCC early in 1952 with radar approach implemented in this area on July 1. Thirty days earlier CAA marked the commissioning of additional VOR airways—then called "victor airways"—bringing the nationwide total to 45,000 miles. It also began to decommission low frequency radio range stations on the 70,000 miles of low frequency airways. However, it was 1974 before the last of the low frequency ranges finally ceased to transmit its familiar N and A signals.

Increasing air traffic continued to call for expanding the use of the available radio frequencies and in 1957 CAA began the change-over to "narrow-band" equipment which would effectively double the number of channels available for VHF communications by halving the channel width (100 kilocycles instead of 200 kilocycles). New teletype equipment capable of transmitting at 100 words per minute was introduced speeding up the distribution of weather information. At its Indianapolis experimental facility, CAA leased a computer to evaluate its capability in air traffic control.

On August 23, 1958, the Federal Aviation Act was signed into law. For the first time it treated "comprehensively" the Federal government's role in fostering and regulating civil aeronautics and air commerce. The act repealed the Air Commerce Act of 1928, the Civil Aeronautics Act of 1938, the Airways Modernization Act of 1957, as well as those portions of various presidential reorganization plans then dealing with civil aviation. It created the Federal Aviation Administration and the Civil Aeronautics Board, freeing the latter from its administrative ties with the Department of Commerce. Retired Air Force Lieutenant General Elwood "Pete" Quesada was named the first FAA administrator.

What the FAA and Pete Quesada inherited in 1958 is described this way in a current short history of the agency:

"When FAA came into existence in 1958, the airways were crowded, the air traffic control and communications systems obsolescent and overworked, and the usable airspace—once considered limitless—had reached definite limits.

"FAA's first task was to ensure maximum utilization of the airspace by civil and military users alike. Restricted areas, once forbidden to civil users, were cut back and large tracts of airspace restored to public use. Other airspace, restricted at times for tactical reasons, was made available for civil flights when military operations were not being conducted. The immediate effect of this was to enlarge the usable airspace and permit civil flight in skies formerly out of bounds.

"The second task, a lengthy and more difficult one, was to modernize the airways. U.S. technical knowledge was far ahead of its application. By accelerating the purchase and installation of electronic equipment, by developing new traffic control procedures, by training large numbers of air traffic controllers and improving the communications system, aeronautical services began to meet the growing demands being put upon them."

One of the immediate technological developments that offered a new potential was automation of the "bookkeeping" phases of air traffic control by employing the electronic computer. UNIVAC off-the-shelf computers were acquired and installed in the ARTCCs at New York, Washington, Pittsburgh, Cleveland and Boston. General purpose computers, these would be used to prepare flight progress strips (which previously had been prepared by hand), exchanging information between centers and assisting in other paperwork functions. The following year, the FAA let a research contract to MITRE

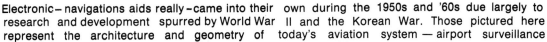

Electronic – navigations aids really – came into their research and development spurred by World War represent the architecture and geometry of own during the 1950s and '60s due largely to II and the Korean War. Those pictured here today's aviation system — airport surveillance radar (ASR) antenna at O'Hare International, Chicago; a long-range air route surveillance radar (ARSR) at Flint, Mich.; the "frangible" approach light system at O'Hare; and a typical very high frequency omnidirectional radio range (VOR) like those which dot the country.

CLEARED TO LAND!

Corporation for advanced experimentation on computer automation of air traffic control. The cost of the project was shared by the Air Force.

More and more war-developed technology began to take its place in the nation's airway system. Early in 1961 the first multi-point, high-speed, weather teletype network was commissioned. It introduced a new automatic data interchange system (ADIS) and equipment capable of transmitting aviation weather at a speed of 850 words a minute. This represented a major advance in automating aviation teletypewriter communications taking the place of the outmoded "message division system" which, in turn, had replaced in 1948 the even more archaic "torn-tape" method of weather relay. DME was introduced on the entire jet fleet of a major trunk airline in 1961 and FAA began using DME traffic control procedures for the first time on a nationwide basis. Prior general use had been limited by the small number of DME-equipped civil aircraft.

That same year action was taken to better organize U.S. airspace—in the context of providing air traffic control in an environment of increasing operations. A "three-layer" airways system was established. The floor of the continental control area was lowered from 24,000 to 14,500 feet and a new intermediate altitude system was established between 14,500 and 24,000 feet designed primarily to provide "express" airways for long and medium-haul operations. More stringent weather minimums for visual flight rule (VFR) traffic operations above 14,500 feet were established.

Also in 1961, the president requested FAA to conduct a "scientific, engineering review of U.S. aviation facilities and related research and development" and to prepare a long-range plan to insure efficient and safe control of air traffic. Project Beacon was established and late that year issued its report. While finding that the air traffic control system was "being expertly operated by a highly skilled organization," the report concluded that "substantial improvements" were needed to meet the future growth of aviation. Among other things the report recommended an air traffic control system based on the use of radar beacons—now known as transponders—as opposed to the so-called "3-D radar" then under consideration.

As a direct result of Project Beacon more new technology was integrated into the airways system over the next few years. In 1965, automated terminal radar and computer data processing were introduced on an evaluation basis. Automated equipment was installed at Atlanta to determine its terminal approach control capability and at Indianapolis to evaluate its enroute capability. These field tests essentially were part of the program to replace the existing manual system with an automated one. Between the time when these first field tests were started and the mid-1970's, ARTS (automated terminal radar system) went through a number of evolutionary iterations finally becoming ARTS III joining a companion system known as RDP (radar data processing).

The next major step was the installation at Jacksonville, Fla., in 1966, of a "model" semi-automated system for enroute traffic control Jacksonville became the proving ground for this system which replaced what essentially was a manually-operated system made up of radar, general purpose computers, radio communications and controllers whose main deficiency was the requirement for hand written data. The existing system also was only "two dimensional" in that it provided information only as to range and bearing. It

Heart of today's air traffic control system are the centers—there are 27 of them—like these at Leesburg, Va., (exterior) and New York's Islip-MacArthur Airport (interior).

depended entirely on radio communications with the pilot to obtain altitude and identity information. The controller had to print identification and altitude information on a plastic marker (called a shrimp boat due to its shape) which was manually moved across the radar display marking the progress of each individual aircraft. To do this he had to make frequent reference to his flight progress strips alongside the radar display—diverting his attention from the display itself. In contrast the semi-automated system would perform these bookkeeping chores and perform them faster and more accurately than the controller. It is significant to note that the system that went on the line in September 1966 at Jacksonville would require more than a decade to implement fully throughout the U.S.

CLEARED TO LAND!

By 1975 ARTS III was in place at 61 terminals across the nation while ARTS III combined with RDP was serving 20 ARTCCs. This system, which will be with aviation for some time to come, simplifies and accelerates handling of air traffic taking a huge bookkeeping task from the shoulders of the controller while at the same time substituting the accuracy of computer logic for human actions in those areas not requiring judgments to be made. An enroute program calculates and distributes aircraft position data to the controller; receives and processes flight plans and transfers data to other centers and/or airport approach controls as the flight progresses relieving the controller of these functions permitting him to focus his full attention on controlling.

One of the newest electronic aids is the computer-driven, cathode ray tube (CRT) display providing current weather from a variety of sources like this one in use at the Chicago Flight Service Station.

Flight plans are received from FAA Flight Service Stations (FSS) or from military operations desks and immediately are entered into the computer. Airline schedules are stored along with the associated routings in the computer and automatically are printed out at a pre-determined time prior to the proposed departure. The computer distributes the information to all controllers along the flight route. Each controller, when he handles the flight, uses a keyboard to enter new information up-dating the information on that flight. The computer assimilates this, integrates it with original data on that flight and passes it along to other sectors/centers along the route.

The control program operates with transponders aboard the aircraft to provide each controller with a real-time read-out on his display showing a symbol for the flight (for an airline, initials denoting the line and a flight number are used—for instance, AA 161 meaning American Flight 161), the

"N" number of the aircraft for other civil aircraft (such as N1234) or either a "tail number" or special flight number for military traffic. Along with the symbol which accompanies the radar "blip" across the display is information as to the aircraft's altitude and airspeed. A third bit of information reflects the transponder code assigned to that aircraft.

By means of the keyboard the controller can cause the computer to carry out special actions with regard to a target. For instance, the image, letter and numbers can be enlarged, ranges can be varied, information from another display can be called up or the controller can command his display to show only certain aircraft. When an aircraft moves from one controller's area to another, he can automatically—with the push of a key—cause the information

ARTS III (the latest iteration of the automatic terminal radar system) combined with computerized radar data processing instantly provides the controller with a wealth of new information.

The computer room at the Chicago Center is living evidence of the manner in which air traffic control is exploiting the advantages of fast-moving computer technology.

The look of tomorrow today. That's the visual impact of the new control tower at Denver's Stapleton Airport.

to be transferred to the next controller's display where it will blink attracting attention until he, in turn, presses a key to signify he has assumed control.

Notwithstanding the impact of new electronic technology in simplifying and streamlining air traffic control during the years after World War II and particularly subsequent to the creation of the FAA in 1958, a critical problem still was developing in the area of air traffic control— the area which had the greatest effect on flying safety and which also was under the closest public scrutiny. The problem was people—not the quality of people nor their dedication to the job, but the numbers of people compared with the job to do, the hours worked, the extreme psychological pressures associated with the job and, to a significant extent, the quantity and quality of training.

The Air Traffic Controller Career Committee (popularly known as the Corson Committee) was created and assigned the task of closely studying the system in the context of the interface between the job and the personnel assigned. Its final recommendations were stated emphatically. Among them were: reduce the overtime work required of controllers in high-density areas; reduce the "consecutive hours" spent by controllers on operational positions as well as the total hours per day on such positions; detail qualified journeymen controllers to high-density facilities where critical manpower shortages exist; develop a "more mobile" controller work force so that the needs of the system, rather than the preferences of controllers determine assignments; develop incentives to attract the most talented controllers to the most difficult positions and accelerate and improve the training of developmental controllers. The FAA immediately took action to up-grade training of developmental controllers and to insure experienced journeyman controllers were assigned to facilities where manpower was critical.

By November a new training program was in effect. Its objectives—shorten the term of controller training; reduce high attrition rate among trainees; make more efficient use of training resources. Where new controllers previously had been sent to the FAA Academy for nine weeks of indoctrination and then put on-the-job at an active facility for from two to three years, the new approach called for them to be first assigned to a facility for "indoctrination and pre-control"—become familiar with the overall aspects of the job, especially the non-control functions—then to the Academy for nine weeks of control training and finally to an active sector for "qualification" training.

Within a matter of months positive results from this new program were evident. Over the next few years many of the other recommendations of the Corson Committee were implemented. More important, the agency developed a new sensitivity to the human element in the system with the result that total system improvement was achieved.

Air traffic control not only is the most publicly visible activity of the FAA, it also qualifies—insofar as the press, television and the motion pictures are concerned—as the most "exciting, dramatic and glamorous." Therefore, it garners the lion's share of attention from reporters, magazine writers and authors. Also, it must be recognized that controllers make up 46 percent of the FAA's 54,000 employees. But it would be a serious error to leave the impression that in the years since the second world war this is the only area in which progress has been achieved. In fact, progress was mandatory since aviation—air transport, military, general, agricultural, private—grew like Topsy.

CLEARED TO LAND!

Just how much aviation grew is evident from a quick look at a few vital statistics. Calendar Year 1958—the nation had 93,189 civil aircraft registered with the Federal government, 67,153 of them active. Of these the scheduled airline fleet consisted of 1,814 aircraft. Fiscal Year 1958—general aviation figures are sketchy (actually what we call general aviation today—incorporating business, industrial, agricultural and private flying) didn't get much attention in those days. However, airline operations (departures) totalled 3.3 million and 44.2 million passengers were carried. By the following year, 1959, more comprehensive statistics had been developed by the FAA. In that fiscal year, for instance, instrument operations (departures) totalled 3.4 million, a 13 percent increase over the previous year with the largest increase shown in general aviation—seven percent. There were 26.8 million aircraft operations handled by FAA towers and approach control facilities—including an 11 percent increase in general aviation operations.

Let's take a look at some more recent figures for comparison. As of January 1975 there were 156,207 active civil aircraft registered with the FAA, 2,749 of them air carrier types. There were 714,607 pilots (active) and 187,908 student pilots on the rolls. Across the United States there were 12,700 active airports—only 609 served by the scheduled air carriers. General aviation aircraft alone flew three billion miles during the preceding 12 months.

Instrument operations for Calendar Year 1973 stood at nine million departures with aircraft handled by control towers at 56.5 million—a 264 percent increase in instrument departures between 1959 and 1973; a 210 percent in-

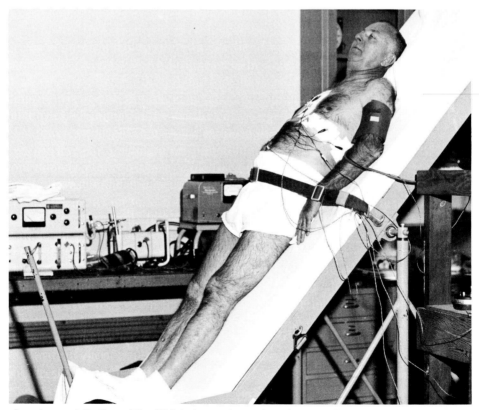

A major contribution of the FAA today and certain to increase in importance in the years to come is the work being conducted at the Civil Aeromedical Institute (CAMI), Oklahoma City. This subject is participating in the cardiovascular research program.

66

crease in the number of aircraft handled by control towers over the same period.

Even by 1958 aviation had established an enviable safety record. The number of air carrier accidents, 91 that year with 14 of them fatal (160 individuals) appear on the surface to be high. But, when taken in the context of the number of accidents and fatalities for each million miles flown they are extremely low—.083 for accidents and only .012 for fatalities. General aviation aircraft had a considerably higher number of accidents, 4,584 with 717 fatalities, but it must be remembered that there were, even then, many more general aviation aircraft flying many more hours. Even these resolve to rates of 2.8 for accidents and .2 for fatalities per million aircraft miles flown.

Neither the FAA nor the aviation industry was satisfied with the 1958 record, however, and in many areas efforts were put forth to improve safety of flight. By 1973, the air carrier rate was down to .016 accidents and .003 fatalities per million aircraft miles flown (46 accidents with 227 fatalities) and the general aviation record stood at 1.14 accidents and .19 fatalities (4,251 accidents with 1,411 fatalities).

Again it must be pointed out that between 1958 and 1973 overall air traffic increased by well over 200 percent—an astronomical increase in aircraft directly associated with a decrease in aviation accidents.

Intensive research is on-going to develop fire protection devices like this "smoke" hood being tested in the CAMI Protection and Survival Laboratory.

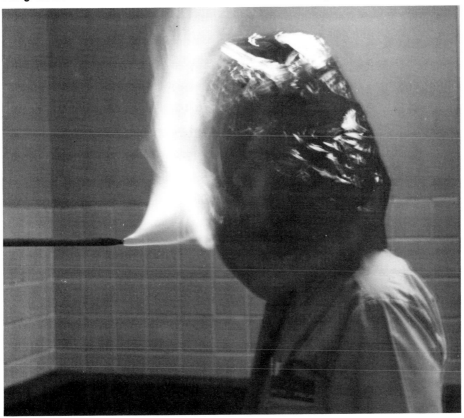

CLEARED TO LAND!

Ditching tests at CAMI involve both improving the means and procedures for crew as well as passenger evacuation in a water environment.

YESTERDAY, TODAY, TOMORROW

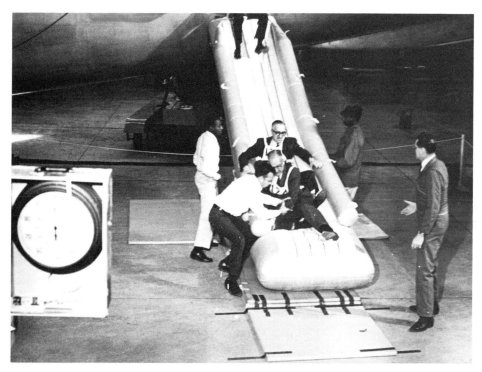

Inflatable evacuation slides now in general use by commercial air carriers were exhaustively tested at CAMI.

Sometimes FAA's steps to keep pace with the growth of aviation have been "cut-and-try"; sometimes carefully planned. There have been in the opinion of many observers all too many missteps; but in most instances these missteps have resulted either from political pressures applied by both the executive and legislative branches of the government or from their failure to heed the considered, professional opinions of the "experts" and support critical efforts with legislation and funding on a timely basis. Often that support has been too little and too late. In the aggregate serious students of U.S. aviation agree that the FAA and its predecessor agencies have done well over the past 50 years of flight.

Major steps have been taken to insure that U.S.-built aircraft meet an exhausting set of design and manufacturing criteria. U.S. pilot proficiency constantly has been upgraded consistent with the demands of more crowded skies and the increased requirement for more positive air traffic control. In other words, pilots today are better trained than they were even 10 years ago. More attention has been paid to the physical condition of America's pilots. In some critical areas physical requirements have been made more stringent while in others practical concessions have been made in areas where it has been proven that no hazard would result to the pilot or his passengers. Much greater attention now is paid by the FAA to insuring that every aircraft currently flying is perfectly airworthy so not only does the FAA assume overall responsibility in the design, manufacturing and certification stage but it also sees that the aircraft is properly maintained so long as it continues to fly.

Millions of tax dollars and man hours of FAA technical genius have gone into advanced research and development of airframes, engines, instruments, communications equipment, traffic control systems and procedures. All this

CLEARED TO LAND!

during a period in aviation history when powerful new concerns emerged—noise abatement, air pollution control, aviation security—concerns which consume FAA's budget at a tremendous rate.

The first hijacking May 1, 1961, triggered a major new problem both for the agency and for commercial aviation. The first aerial hijacking saw a gun-wielding passenger force a Florida pilot to detour on his Marathon-to-Key West flight by way of Havana. Three more occurred that year beginning a rash of hijackings that in the next 10 years was to impose a heavy new work load and financial responsibility on not only the FAA, but also on the air lines and on the municipalities operating major terminals across the nation.

To accomplish its charter, the FAA—perhaps as a necessity—has grown into a giant among Federal bureaus. There are some who feel strongly that it has become too large, too unwieldy, too wasteful. That, however, is the way of bureaucracy and so it has been since time began. One fact of life which the FAA's critics fail to recognize, or at least acknowledge, is the larger and more important any government agency becomes the more vulnerable it is to being used as an instrument of politics by whatever administration is in power as well as by members of the Congress on a continuing basis as they go about their traditional game of handing out "pork barrel" to their constituents. Also, the more important the agency becomes the more coveted it is to higher level bureaucrats playing the game of empire building.

Virtually everyone in aviation and many informed citizens outside of this huge, multi-billion dollar industry feel that the FAA and its entire program to foster and effectively regulate aviation received a major setback when President Lyndon Johnson decided in 1966 to transfer the agency to the cabinet-level Department of Transportation. Not only did this increase the FAA's vulnerability to politically motivated pressures, both from the presidential level and from the Congressional level, but it also imposed over the professional, aviation-aware men and women of the FAA a superstructure of bureaucrats who traditionally had dealt with automobiles, trucks, railroads, trains and steamships—modes of transportation having absolutely nothing in common with airplanes or aviation except the fact they carried people and goods. As one wag was wont to put it:

"It's like sending a turtle herder off to manage a family of jack rabbits."

The analogy may be a trifle vague but the point is well taken.

Notwithstanding the political pressures brought to bear, the gamesmanship played with its budget, the onslaughts mounted by its critics, the lack of real understanding on the part of the general public either of its role or that of aviation in our twentieth century economic and social structure, the FAA continued to do a creditable job.

In addition to its management, enforcement and inspection structure, augmented by training and research facilities, the agency today operates and maintains—

    27 air route traffic control centers
    85 air route surveillance radar facilities
   377 remote air/ground sites
1000 VOR/VORTAC facilities
 300 non-directional radio beacon facilities
 390 air traffic control towers

YESTERDAY, TODAY, TOMORROW

   21 combined Flight Service Station/Towers
  154 airport surveillance radar facilities
  474 instrument landing system facilities
  320 Flight Service Stations
   54 remote communications facilities
  161 Doppler direction finding facilities

These serve 133,000 miles of VOR jet routes and 177,000 miles of low-altitude airways in the 48 conterminous states and Alaska.

Its 54,000 men and women—give or take a few—do one hell of a job for the American pilot in spite of the weaknesses which are inherent in the huge bureaucracy it has been necessary to construct to get that job done within the framework of our form of government.

4 THE TOWER

The vintage Ercoupe—1946, in fact—tooled along through the Florida skies its 65-horsepower, four-banger giving out a comforting rumble. It was homeward bound to Tallahassee with a nice, fresh annual inspection under its belt and a clean bill of health for another year. The 27-year-old pilot/owner had had a relaxing weekend at Daytona Beach after getting the new inspection completed and looked forward to arriving home that Sunday evening.

When the weather briefer reported "ceiling broken at 2,200, visibility seven miles, thunderstorms in the area" it didn't seem too important. That kind of weather isn't too unusual for Florida in December and you find you usually can dodge the storms, especially with reasonable visibility.

Nearing Perry, some 200 miles from his point of departure and still 25 miles from home, the weather began to look threatening. The storms seemed to have joined up into a squall line. The pilot decided to land at Perry, refuel and check with the weather again. On paper, the forecast actually showed an improvement. Now it was "ceiling scattered at 2,000, visibility seven miles or better, thunderstorms moving out of the area." In a few minutes Ercoupe 99166 was in the air again. The pilot expected to complete his trip in the next 15 minutes landing with the last of the fading daylight.

One thing about the Florida Gulf Coast weather, it can change rapidly especially during the winter when the warmer ocean air from the Gulf moves eastward over the land creating "instant" fog and low-lying clouds and that's what it was doing. When the Flight Service Station had given the current Tallahassee weather the forecast had been accurate. Within the next two or three minutes pilots flying in the area reported denser cloud formations. The FSS specialist tried to raise Ercoupe 166 by radio to report the change but to no avail.

Meanwhile, the pilot decided to fly due north from Perry and then dogleg west to his home base in order to dodge the reported thunderstorm activity. As he made his turn, he found the Ercoupe being pushed lower and lower to remain clear of the clouds. He was not instrument rated and, moreover, the little Ercoupe was not equipped for instrument flight. At 1,100 feet the Ercoupe now was under a ceiling close to being overcast and the last light was fading rapidly. Suddenly, the pilot lost visual contact. Immediately he tried to call Tallahassee Radio. No luck. He tried Tallahassee Tower. Still no luck. He found himself in the clouds and had to descend to 900 feet to stay clear. Below he could see no light nor identify any landmark. He seemed to be constantly turning to avoid fingers of cloud reaching down for the little plane.

As his distress became acute radio reception improved and he was able to contact Tallahassee Tower. Controller Richard Gardner advised him that Tallahassee now was IFR with broken clouds at 800, more broken clouds at 2,000 and seven-mile visibility. Gardner asked the Ercoupe pilot what he intended to do since at this point he knew nothing either of the capability of the pilot or the aircraft.

"I don't know. I'm getting a little confused up here and I can't see the ground. I think I'm over some kind of swamp."

The picture now quickly came into focus for the controller. He had a pilot obviously near panic and apparently not equipped to handle the situation in which he found himself. First, Gardner tried to calm the Ercoupe pilot. He quickly issued instructions to other aircraft in the air to stay clear, put approaching aircraft into safe holding patterns and directed others ready to depart to remain on the ground. Tallahassee does not have radar. This presented still another problem. Gardner contacted the FSS asking the specialist to get a DF (direction finding) bearing on the Ercoupe. The bearing revealed the Ercoupe was northeast of the airport but DF equipment, unlike radar, cannot provide distance information. Gardner needed a more accurate fix on the Ercoupe if he was to get it home safely. It also was apparent the pilot could not execute the precision maneuvers that would be necessary to obtain that fix by DF. Gardner elected to give the pilot a heading that should lead him to the brightly lighted capitol dome. When the pilot reported over the dome, it would give Gardner a starting point from which to work.

Observing continual changes in the DF heading the FSS specialist reported the pilot appeared unable to hold a heading. Further, he had indicated by radio that he had "something wrong with the instruments." He reported they had been functioning properly on departure. His magnetic compass was "spinning wildly," he said, and neither the aircraft's directional gyro nor turn-and-bank indicator were operating as they should. He indicated, however, he was confident of his altimeter. Thanks for small favors, Gardner thought to himself.

By this time, the controller, who also is a pilot and instructor, had pretty well figured out what the instrument problem was in the Ercoupe. He was sure the spinning compass was due to erratic, circular flying by the now thoroughly-disoriented pilot. Quietly, he instructed the pilot to keep his wings level, stay clear of clouds and try to get some ground reference.

Fuel was not an immediate factor. The tanks had been topped at Perry. The weather, however, continued to deteriorate. The Ercoupe came down to 800 feet, then 500 feet, still circling blindly with no lights in sight. The pilot now had a thought—climb above the clouds and then fly away from the area until he was in the clear. He inquired about the cloud tops and made the suggestion to Gardner.

The controller's first inclination was to shout a loud and emphatic "No!" Reasoning that it might further shake up the pilot, he calmly asked three questions:

"Are you instrument rated? Can you read your directional gyro? Does your turn-and-bank indicator appear to be working?"

The reply to all three was "negative." The pilot had answered his own questions about attempting an IFR climb through the clouds. Now when Gardner recommended against it there was no argument.

Repeatedly, with help from the FSS DF operator, Gardner tried to get the Ercoupe set up on a course back to Tallahassee. No dice. It continued to fly in circles dodging clouds. Almost an hour had gone past when the tower received a telephone call from a plantation owner near Bradfordville, about 15 miles northeast of the airport. The man said he had been hearing a small aircraft milling around over the plantation for some time. Gardner told the man to turn on every light he had available, including automobile lights. Then he called the Ercoupe:

"Ercoupe 166. Will you look down carefully and see whether there are any lights on the ground below you now? Can you see anything?"

"I think so," came the reply.

"Can you see some automobile headlights now?" Gardner asked.

"Maybe." The reply was speculative.

"Good," Gardner continued, "there's a lighted house and some open field behind it. Can you see them, Ercoupe 166?"

"No, just some lights," the pilot answered.

"All right, now we know where you are. I'm going to give you another heading and if you follow it you should have the airport in sight in about five minutes."

It appeared Gardner and the pilot had things well in hand. But no such luck. Again the pilot could not hold the heading. Soon he lost the lights and was again circling in the darkness. Another 15 minutes dragged by. The Ercoupe was down to 400 feet. The pilot could still see no ground reference. Now gasoline became a concern. The little, two-place Ercoupe doesn't hold much fuel as it is and flying at minimum altitudes there could be no attempt to lean it out and conserve the precious fluid.

With the situation going from bad to worse the pilot reported seeing lights and simultaneously the tower began receiving telephone calls from Woodgate Estates, a housing development about 10 miles northeast, that a small airplane was circling, apparently looking for a place to land.

Gardner told the pilot where he was—just five miles from the lighted capitol dome. With the dome in sight the runway lights would be just beyond. Now it was a "no sweat" situation. He advised the pilot to use the housing development as a reference, pull himself together, steady the compass, take up the heading Gardner would assign and fly it home.

The radio reply was unresponsive. DF indicated the aircraft was continuing to circle the housing development. It was as if the pilot was drawn to the lights like a moth to a flame, mesmerized by a fatal fascination that would ultimately draw him to his death. To Gardner it was clear the pilot could not navigate the plane to the airport no matter what kind of directions were given. The next step—find an emergency landing spot for him and try to get him down. Also, get fire equipment, ambulances and the police in the area—just in case.

Despite his panic, the Ercoupe pilot hadn't given up. He continued to strain his eyes for sight of something, anything on the ground, that might help. Suddenly, out of nowhere there they were; lights and what appeared to be a four-lane highway—indistinct, ghostly—but there.

Now—a real time relay to the state police, by telephone to the trooper's station, by police radio to the cars in the field. First, have the cars check out the stretch of highway—completed but as yet unopened to the public—for obstacles. Then, have them line up providing what in effect would be runway lights. Soon Gardner was able to tell the pilot everything was in readiness.

Skittish about the impromptu runway, the Ercoupe pilot made one, two, three and still another pass. He was not secure in his feeling that the roadway was clear. He withdrew to the friendly lights of Woodgate and began circling again, now down to 300 feet.

Gardner assured him that the police cars had traversed the section of the roadway and that it was clear. Now, the pilot became concerned that the police cars lighting the road were too close. He asked for them to be moved

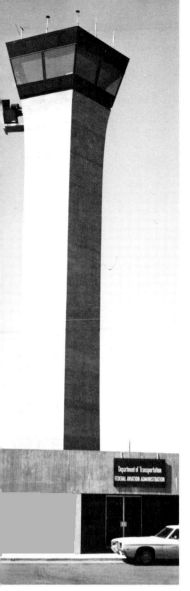

Chicago O'Hare

West Lafayette, Ind.

Plain and fancy, new and not-so-new, large and small, the control tower is perhaps the most recognizable fixture of today's large and middle-sized airports. Regardless of its size and architecture, the tower is the nerve-center for flight operations in the airport control zone and the men and women who man it are among the busiest in the FAA.

Great Falls, Mont.

Newark, N.J.

Los Angeles

back. It was not enough. The pilot asked for them to be moved farther back. This accomplished, Gardner tried for another quarter hour to entice the pilot to make a landing. Time after time he made low level passes over the strip of roadway. Time after time he made no attempt to land.

"Ercoupe 166," Gardner called, "are you going to land now? Are you ready to land?"

No reply. Try another tack.

"Ercoupe 166, we have two ambulances standing by, also fire engines in case of any trouble. Do you see the police car with the flashing light?

"Roger," was the response.

"All right," Gardner continued, "that car is going to lead you down. Just line up with the highway behind him and as you approach he will move out and lead you right down. He'll be moving faster than your landing speed so you won't have any problem. Once you start the landing, you'll probably be below the range of my radio so don't bother to call me. Just land the airplane, get it down. Ercoupe 166, do you understand?"

The pilot acknowledged in the affirmative. The Ercoupe lined up with the highway and began its descent. As it neared the concrete, the police car accelerated to 90 miles an hour keeping well ahead of the aircraft. The Ercoupe touched down, rolled out for 200 yards and came to a stop. No damage. No injuries. Two full hours had passed, two hours of unrelenting terror for the pilot and mind-bending tension for Gardner.

The controller earned one of FAA's three national awards that year, 1974, for "outstanding flight assists." The incident also motivated the Tallahassee Flight Service Station to establish an "aircraft emergency network" incorporating the state police, local law enforcement agencies, the sheriff, the fire departments, rescue squads and the local Coast Guard. Vehicles of cooperating agencies are equipped with radio receivers capable of monitoring the FSS frequencies and thus keeping them up-to-date with any emergency in progress. The network can be activated by a single call from the FSS and go into action in a matter of minutes.

During the first 12 months it was in existence, the network was activated 10 times—10 times activation culminating in a safe landing for an aircraft in trouble. The same section of Interstate 10 was the scene of one of those emergency landings just six months after the first.

You don't have to be a student novice or low-time VFR pilot to get yourself into trouble up there. Aviation is unbelievably safe, the statistics prove it. But, in an airplane you don't goof off, not even a little bit, if you want to keep it safe. Airplanes and the environment in which they operate do not go out of their way to be forgiving.

Take the experienced pilot of Mooney Zero Zero Mike Alpha. He knew what he was about when he planned his flight from Stratford, Conn., to Richmond, Va., carefully checking the distance he planned to fly against his fuel consumption and capacity, checking weather and even filing a flight plan. Good judgment dictated that he refuel at Richmond before continuing to his final destination, Columbia, S.C.

It was after he got into the air that his magnetic compass went out and in flight misjudgment forced him to holler long and loud for help.

Mooney 00 Mike Alpha made it to Richmond in good shape, so good, in fact, the pilot elected to press on. This was his first mistake. He neglected to check his flying time so far—three hours—against his fuel consumption and the amount he had on board and make allowances for any unexpected development. Shortly after passing Richmond, the unexpected did occur, only he was unaware of it at the time. His compass gave up the ghost. Now failure to continuously check on his progress and position by ground reference caught up with him.

Two hours after passing Richmond and finding himself disoriented, the pilot began checking the ground. Soon he found a town he could identify from the charts—Fredericksburg, Va., 50 miles north of Richmond and more than 300 miles north of where he should have been. Time for another mistake. Instead of landing immediately at Fredericksburg and seeing to repairs for the ailing compass, he decided to fly back to Richmond. Now his fourth error—he failed to use his radio and check Richmond weather. The field had gone IFR. The pilot was not instrument rated. Four relatively minor mistakes cumulatively adding up to one huge problem.

As you might expect, the Mooney again began to wander. It did not make Richmond due to the lack of a reliable compass and the weather now obscuring the city. At 12:21 A.M., with an estimated nine minutes of usable fuel still in the tanks Mooney 00 Mike Alpha called for help.

Fortunately, Richmond Tower controller John T. Huston and approach controller Archie G. Fincher reacted instantly to the appeal. Also, the pilot of the Mooney began to demonstrate his training and experience for a change. He immediately set the aircraft up at the best glide speed, the speed at which it could travel the greatest distance horizontally for each foot of altitude it lost. Lady Luck also stepped in. There was an airport within five miles. The pilot kept his gear up to get every last inch of glide, landing wheels up, dead stick at Northfield Airport. The Mooney sustained light damage. The pilot walked away. When Huston and Fincher later played the 20-minute tape of the incident it sounded like this: (RIC LC is Huston, RIC AC is Fincher, 00MA is the Mooney)

Time: 12:21 A.M. EST
00MA: "Richmond Radio, you come in for—uh—this is zero-zero Mike Alpha, will you come in please. Over." RIC LC: "Aircraft calling Richmond Radio, this is Richmond Tower. Read you loud and clear on one nineteen point five. How do you read me?"

00MA: "Uh—this is zero-zero Mike Alpha. I read you loud and clear. I'm lost. I think I'm due north of you and I'm almost out of fuel—uh, uh—how can you help me?"

RIC LC: "Zero-zero Mike, standby."
Time: 12:22 A.M.
RIC LC to RIC AC: "Say, Arch, I've got a 00 Mike, pick him up on one nineteen point five, almost out of fuel and lost. I'm not going to give him a frequency change. I'll alert Norfolk Search for you if you want to give him one twenty one five."

RIC AC: "November zero-zero Mike, Richmond Radar, over."
00MA: 'Uh—this is zero-zero Mike Alpha."
RIC AC: "November zero-zero Mike, what is your heading and altitude now?"
00MA: "My altitude is sixty five hundred feet. Uh—I'm near a large city but I can't identify it."
RIC AC: "Roger, zero-zero Mike, what is your heading, what is your heading now?"
00MA: "I'm due north of you, over, my heading is—uh—about north, let's see, thirty degrees (unintelligible)."

RIC AC: "Understand heading of north, okay, what was your last known position?"

00MA: "I've been flying around for some time. There's a city off to—uh—the east of me here—uh—what would that (unintelligible)."

Time: 12:23 A.M.

RIC AC: "Roger. What is your magnetic compass heading now?"

00MA: "My magnetic compass is completely out. I have two VORs."

RIC AC: "Okay, what a radial of the Rich—are you tuned to the Richmond VOR?"

00MA: "I'm—uh—due north of the Richmond VOR."

RIC AC: "Okay, is your gyro working?"

RIC AC: "November zero-zero Mike, what radial of the Richmond VOR are you on now?"

00MA: "The zero zero five."

RIC AC: "Zero zero five, for radar identification, turn right heading, one nine zero for thirty seconds then resume original heading."

00MA: "Turn right—uh—ninety degrees—uh, uh—over."

Time: 12:25 A.M.

RIC AC: November zero-zero Mike, the heading is turn right to one niner zero, one niner zero."

00MA: "Roger."

RIC AC: "November zero-zero Mike, what is the type of aircraft and amount of fuel remaining?"

00MA: "Mooney Mark twenty-one."

RIC AC: "Mooney Mark twenty-one, how much fuel remaining?"

00MA: "Uh—the gauges are, uh, down against the bottom."

RIC AC: "Okay, how many persons on board?"

00MA: 'One."

RIC AC: "I understand."

RIC AC: "November zero-zero Mike rolling out on heading of one zero now?"

00MA: "Negative, I've got a little farther to go."

RIC AC: "Okay, what is your heading?"

00MA: "Uh, I would estimate it, I can see the north star so I would estimate that it's about one six zero.

Time: 12:26 A.M.

RIC AC: "Okay, stop your turn now and start in to a left turn, start into a left turn to a heading of zero niner zero, over."

00MA: "Roger, zero nine zero."

RIC AC to RIC LC: "John, call Northfield and see if you've got any lights over there. He's—his fuel gauge is on the peg."

00MA: "(unintelligible) I see a plane off at about eleven o'clock."

RIC AC: "Do you have an airplane now at about your ten or eleven o'clock position, headed northeast bound?"

00MA: "That's correct."

RIC AC: "All right, you're radar contact twenty-one miles north of Richmond, Byrd Field, roll out on heading of one eight zero, one eight zero."

00MA: "Roger, I'll try one eight zero. I'm using the stars for the moment."

RIC AC: "Okay, we'll continue this with a no gyro, just stop your turn now and fly straight and level."

Time: 12:29 A.M.

00MA: "Fly straight and level?"

RIC AC: "Affirmative, just stop your turn, fly straight and level. We'll give you no gyro vectors to the airport."

RIC AC to RIC LC: "If you can get Northfield, John, see if they've got any lights. He says his fuel gauges are on the peg."

RIC LC to RIC AC: "Okay."

RIC AC to RIC LC: "Get the runway lights all the way up on two zero and I'll

THE TOWER

try an ASR (approach surveillance radar), we've still got—what—three hundred and five."

RIC LC to RIC AC: "All right, we'll try straight in ASR to two zero."

RIC AC: "November zero-zero Mike, Richmond Approach, do you read?"

00MA: "What was that again, zero-zero Mike Alpha?"

RIC AC: "Do you see that airplane off your left wing now northeast bound?"

00MA: "Uh, yea, uh, he's, uh, abeam of my left wing."

RIC AC: "That is correct. That is an American Flyer Constellation. He's northeast bound and you're seventeen miles north of the airport now."

00MA: "Shall I continue on my present course?"   Time: 12:29 A.M.

RIC AC: "Affirmative and this will be a surveillance ASR approach to runway two zero, the Richmond weather is measured ceiling three hundred overcast, visibility five miles, fog, altimeter three zero three nine, wind two zero zero degrees seven knots. Are you instrument qualified and equipped?"

00MA: "I have two VORs and —uh—I have about—uh—fifteen hours on—uh—instruments."

RIC AC: "Roger, do you request to make a surveillance approach at Richmond?"

00MA:"Uh, affirmative—uh, uh—vector in to—uh—visibility."

RIC AC: "Okay, you understand now, we have a measured ceiling three hundred overcast, visibility five miles, fog."

00MA: "That's okay, I can handle that."

RIC AC: "Okay."

Time: 12:30 A.M.

00MA: "(Unintelligible) I see a city, uh, on my—just off my, uh, left bow at about eleven o'clock—there goes my engine."

RIC AC: "Understand your engine is quitting?"

00MA: "That's correct. I've put on the fuel pump. I'll go to the best glide angle."

RIC AC: "Okay, there's an airport, Northfield, straight ahead, twelve o'clock five miles. See if you can pick that up."

00MA: "(Unintelligible) lights—is that it?"

RIC AC: "That airport now is twelve o'clock straight ahead, five miles. See if you can pick it up."

Time: 12:31 A.M.

RIC AC: "November zero-zero Mike, do you still read?"

00MA: "I still read, uh, but I don't—uh, uh—see the, uh, airport. I see, uh, two, no, uh, three obstruction lights, uh, almost dead ahead, uh, and the city off to my left, uh, would, uh, that be it?"

Time: 12:32 A.M.

RIC AC: "Okay, the airport is still at twelve o'clock four and a half miles. Is your engine running?"

00MA: "Negative."

RIC AC: "Okay, the airport is four and a half miles, correction, four and a quarter miles now straight ahead. I'll—maintain your present heading."

RIC AC to RIC LC: "How about getting State Police, John, to start out that way; it'll be off 301, north of Northfield Airport?"

RIC LC to RIC AC: "Okay."

RIC AC to RIC LC: "If you have time, ring Northfield again. See if we can get some lights.

RIC AC: "November zero-zero Mike, what's your altitude?"

00MA: "My altitude is forty five hundred feet."

RIC AC: "Okay, it's now three and one half miles from that airport. Hold your present heading."

RIC AC to RIC LC: "Three and a half miles."

RIC AC: "November zero-zero Mike, I do not know weather conditions or runway conditions at Northfield Airport." (An unattended airport at night.)

00MA: "How does this runway align with my heading?"

CLEARED TO LAND!

Time:12:33 A.M.

RIC AC: "The runway heading, the paved runway is runway six two four. You'll be almost in line with runway two four."

RIC AC: "If you can bear—turn left now, turn left, will advise when to stop your turn."

00MA: "Making standard turn left."

RIC AC: "Roger."

RIC AC: "November zero-zero Mike, stop turn, stop turn."

RIC AC: "November zero-zero Mike, Northfield Airport is twelve o'clock two and one half miles, advise if you pick it up."

Time: 12:34 A.M.

00MA: "Uh, I see no lights of, uh, an airfield. Uh, there is an open, uh, dark space."

RIC AC: "Roger, I do not know if the runway lights are on. I do not know if the runway lights are on."

00MA: "Roger."

00MA: "Is there any way you can telephone them and find out and alert them?"

RIC AC: "We have been on the telephone. There is no answer at the airport."

RIC AC: "Northfield Airport is now twelve o'clock one and one half miles right off your nose one and one half miles."

RIC AC: "I suggest you maintain your altitude as long as possible—and turn left, standard rate turn left."

Time: 12:35 A.M.

00MA: "Making standard left, uh, turn."

RIC AC: "November zero-zero Mike, stop turn."

00MA: "Roger. I see a string of lights off to my left that could be runway lights. Could that be correct?"

RIC AC: "Well, that airport is now at eleven o'clock, one mile—eleven o'clock, one mile."

00MA: "All right. I'll make a left turn toward what appears to be the, uh, runway."

RIC AC: "Roger."

00MA: "Would I, uh, make a landing toward, uh, Richmond or away from it?"

RIC AC: "Your choice, surface winds Richmond Byrd Field two zero zero degrees, five knots, altimeter three zero zero three niner."

Time: 12:36 A.M.

RIC AC: "What's the altitude now?"

00MA: "Altitude is, uh, sixteen hundred."

RIC AC: "Okay, the airport is half a mile away now, got it made?"

00MA: "I think so, I think I'm from the wrong end of it. What is the visibi—what is the strength of the wind?"

RIC AC: "Wind zero zero degrees, five knots."

00MA: "Roger."

RIC AC to RIC LC: "Understand the lights are on: Good show."

RIC AC: "November zero-zero Mike, just advised the lights are on, the lights are on. You're right on the northeast edge of the airport now and take over and land any runway, your discretion."

00MA: "(Unintelligible) lighted. I'm approaching it, uh, I'm approaching Richmond and will land—uh, uh—outbound."

Time: 12:37 A.M.

RIC AC: "Roger. Land any runway your discretion."

00MA: "Yes, I can see the green entry lights now."

RIC AC: "Okay, good show, and if you can get to a telephone call me as soon as you get on the ground."

RIC AC to RIC LC: "He sees the lights, John. I believe he's got it made."

RIC LC to RIC AC: "He sure has."

VFR tower controller is the bottom rung of the air traffic control career ladder in the FAA. Brand new developmental controllers begin at a VFR

80

THE TOWER

tower working under the watchful eye of a journeyman until they reach that level of proficiency and gain professional status. The next step is radar experience, usually at a tower handling both VFR and IFR traffic and having airport surveillance radar. With the radar experience under his or her belt, the controller may then move on to a center or the approach tower at one of the nation's major air terminals. Often the controller returns to a VFR tower, this time as the assistant chief or chief, and again begins the climb up the career ladder—this time in supervision and management. Many controllers, however, feel that the tower is where the real action is. Also many of them point out, it's where you "stay in touch on a person-to-person basis with the men and women flying the airplanes." There's no question but what tower controllers get more than their share of the action. The record books are full of it.

Cleveland and Burke-Lakefront, Ohio, and Erie, Pa., tower controllers team up to bring in a disabled light twin. The pilot calls over Lake Erie reporting that one of his engines is out and he is losing power on the other one. Erie and Cleveland, using very high frequency direction finding (VHF/DF) equipment quickly fix the aircraft's position. Checks of nearby airfields rule some out because of weather. Burke-Lakefront is selected and the aircraft vectored to it. It looks like a routine save. The twin is lined up for an approach to the airport when the alert tower controller sees that in the press of the emergency the pilot has not lowered his wheels. In the very nick of time, the message gets through to the pilot, the gear is lowered almost as the aircraft touches down.

A four-engine Douglas DC-6 is enroute to Miami. Still over water, his Number 1 engine conks out. Number 4 begins to run rough. Now it goes out. Number 3 begins acting up. The pilot informs Miami he expects to have to ditch. In the tower, controllers advise the DC-6 that Homestead AFB is only 12 miles away and suggest the pilot make a try for it. He can always ditch as a last resort. Coordinating the effort with Homestead controllers, the Miami tower vectors the heavily loaded transport to a safe landing at the Air Force facility.

Controllers at Bradley Field, Conn., and Westchester County Airport, White Plains, N.Y. (in early 1974) are pilots themselves. Using this additional knowledge and experience they guide a disoriented student pilot to a safe landing after he radios on the emergency frequency that he does not understand the instruments. "Extremely upset," the pilot was close to panic when the Westchester controller, a former flight instructor, took over. The controller calmed the student, explained the instruments to him and got him headed to Bradley Field. There controllers recruited an Army helicopter in the area to help them get the student safely on the ground.

There was only three tenths of a gallon of fuel left on board when Chattanooga, Tenn., tower controllers aided a "lost" pilot to orient himself with reference to ground landmarks and then vectored him to a safe landing at the nearest airport.

During 120 days in 1974, for instance, tower controllers accounted for 372 flight assists across the country. In the majority of those instances the pilots and passengers involved would have been killed or at least have suffered serious injury without the assistance given from the ground.

Tower controllers often find themselves working under unfamiliar and difficult circumstances when it becomes necessary for the FAA to establish a

There is a story in these three pictures. Controllers regularly are called upon to provide traffic control for aviation events staged at airports without towers. Such was the case for controllers operating in one portion of the hot, dry southwest. This wooden frame and canvas cover provides little real protection from the blazing sun so the controllers, headed by O. B. Cox, adopted this discarded mobile tower used by the military during World War II at a remote training field . Today the mobile tower looks like this, rehabilitated by controllers themselves, providing a first class working environment for controllers on duty at a recent Helicopter Association of America convention.

These controllers have named their tower the "Pride of Mercy Gulch."

tower capability at an airport not ordinarily served by one. For instance, the annual Oshkosh, Wisc., antique and experimental aircraft fly-in, the Reno National Air Races and the California National Air Races.

The 1975 edition of the California Nationals was held at Mojave, a former Marine Corps airfield in the so-called "high desert" some 80 miles north of Los Angeles. The area is arid desert land. In summer the temperatures range upward of 100 degrees. On this June 21-22 it was cool—only 90 to 95 degrees in the greenhouse of the abandoned World War II vintage tower structure where the FAA crew—made up of volunteers, all top journeymen from other area towers—set up shop.

Bob Newbry, an 18-year veteran from Palmdale Tower, was in charge. Other controllers included Bill Russell from Torrance Tower; Ray Joyner from Brackett Field, Pomona; Tom Huntington and Bob Starkey, both from Orange County Airport, Santa Ana; Jim Wood from the El Monte Tower and Bill Hailey from Hawthorne Tower. It is significant that Torrance and Orange County are among the nation's 10 busiest airports; that El Monte is a "high density" airport; and that Hawthorne is in the Los Angeles International control zone (LAX also is one of the 10 busiest in the United States). Only that kind of experience could begin to equip a controller to handle what begins to build as the tower opens at 7 A.M.

Russell is handling ground control. Ray Joyner is on 125.9 handling traffic approaching from the south while Tom Huntington handles traffic from the north on 118.3. Newbry keeps a watchful eye on each of them coordinating the effort and assisting where he is needed. During the next three hours and 45 minutes—until the field is officially closed for the air show and race program—Russell, Huntington and Joyner handle 520 airplanes.

"Plan C" goes into effect. Once an aircraft calls in and is cleared to enter traffic he no longer is identified by his formal radio call (such as Bonanza 411 Zulu) and two-way radio communication no longer is carried on except in event of an emergency. He merely becomes the "blue and white Bonanza" and the controller sequences him in behind another visually identifiable aircraft. Aircraft are identified as to make or configuration and color.

Joyner's rapid-fire delivery sounds like one of those Virginia tobacco auctioneers in a television commercial except that the language is pure aviation.

"Red Bellanca on short final cleared to land, please land long. Orange Citabria on mid final, cleared behind the Bellanca, land short. Red and white Cherokee continue your approach, keep the Citabria in sight. White Beechcraft on base, you're number four following the Cherokee. Yellow Cessna on downwind, continue present heading, I'll call your base. Red Yankee follow that Yellow Cessna. Blue Cessna follow the red Yankee. White Bonanza enter downwind behind the blue Cessna."

Joyner takes a big, deep breath and starts over again. It's almost unbelievable how smoothly things go until—until a pilot, "his head up and locked," approaches the field without using his radio. Ordinarily, Mojave has Unicom on 122.8 in service. Today is no exception but when an aircraft calls Unicom he is told that a tower is in operation and is given the proper frequencies for a north or south approach to the area. It is recommended procedure for all aircraft approaching a non-controlled field to contact Unicom for advisories—wind direction and runway in use—and then announce their intentions for the information of other aircraft on the frequency. Ordinary safety precautions apparently are of little concern to the pilot of this Cherokee. No radio calls. He blithely sets up an approach directly opposite to the traffic pattern in use, apparently also blind to the swarm of aircraft in that pattern. Frantically, Tom Huntington handling approaches from the north calls the red and white Cherokee. No reply. The Cherokee continues its approach.

In the operational traffic pattern, Joyner has a T-34 on short final, a Bonanza midway on final and another Cherokee on long final. Joyner calls for the T-34 to break off his approach and "offset to the left." The Bonanza and Cherokee farther out on final are advised to continue their approach but remain alert. About this time the errant Cherokee pilot apparently realizes what he is doing and abruptly begins a go-around breaking right toward the left hand pattern in use—directly in front of the T-34.

"T-34, turn right, turn right immediately!" Joyner calls.

The T-34 pilot, apparently both experienced and sharp, responds at once. He avoids the Cherokee which continues undaunted into the traffic pattern landing safely in his turn. There isn't even time to get a number on him and there are perhaps 50 red and white Cherokees on the field. Probably unaware of the chaos he caused and the lives he endangered, the pilot gets away without

THE TOWER

even the chewing out the tower crew has in mind—four-letter words included.

Are there many incidents like this at these special activities?

"No," Newbry says, "but there's always one or two in every crowd who don't get the message. No-radio aircraft present a problem but most of those pilots are familiar with light gun signals and respond accordingly. One of the biggest problems is radio discipline—many pilots try to call the tower at the same time. They talk, talk, talk, without listening enough. All-in-all, however, they're a pretty sharp bunch of people."

How about the pressure of this kind of action?

"I'd a lot rather be this busy," Huntington declares, "than sitting on my hands. That's really miserable, when you aren't busy at all."

Bill Russell joins the conversation:

"Yes, and when you aren't busy that's when you begin to worry—what if?"

"That's all well and good," Joyner adds, "but sometimes the pressure gets entirely too much. Frankly, sometimes I find it's too taxing to my youth. I'm getting too old too soon. When a 22, 23-year-old gets off shift and is so beat he can hardly make it home, you get some idea what he's been through. And that's on a regular shift at his home station, not an operation like this."

Newbry is an old-time pilot. The rest of the group all are into aviation—Russell is building himself a Thorp; Joyner and Huntington both are student pilots and are renting; Bob Starkey already has his private pilot certificate. They all can see the traffic control situation from both sides. Current observations? They agree on two:

"The increased workload isn't just the result of increased air traffic. Much of the workload is shifting from the pilot to the controller."

It's a far cry from the VFR towers at smaller, local airports across the nation to the complex, sophisticated towers required to control traffic at the major terminals. Typical of the latter is the "cab" at Newark, N.J. airport.

CLEARED TO LAND!

New York's John F. Kennedy International Airport.

"Times are changing within the ranks of the controllers. New people—'off the street' as opposed to largely coming from the ranks of military controllers—are entering the system. They have a different attitude. There used to be a bust-your-butt discipline philosophy. Now they (FAA management) just let them slide along."

It must be remembered that these observations stem from just one group of controllers, but the group represents the gamut from a short-timer journeyman—three years FAA, three years military—to an 18-year veteran and collectively the group has been involved in air traffic control for some 50 years.

Special assignments like major air races and air shows are the exception, not the rule, for tower controllers. Most of their on-duty time is spent in one of the more than 425 FAA control towers scattered across the nation. A city, by the way, becomes a candidate for a federal tower when it has air carrier service and more than 24,000 itinerant flight operations a year or if it does not have air carrier service but has more than 50,000 operations each year. Towers are categorized in four classes—I, II, III and IV—according to their operational workload and facilities. There probably is no "average" tower since the demands of every airport differ based on the terrain, prevailing weather conditions, types of aircraft operations and proximity to other airports. So, let's look at a representative tower—the Class II facility at Torrance, Calif.

Torrance is part of the sprawling Greater Los Angeles megalopolis and serves general aviation interests in an area with a population of approximately two million. The field was built in World War II as a coast defense fighter strip and now is operated by the city. More than 700 general aviation aircraft call it home. It has no air carrier service—but is less than 10 miles from LAX and Long Beach International. It has parallel east-west runways and approved instrument approaches—a localizer approach from the east and a VOR approach (off LAX) from the west. Torrance airport—thus Torrance tower—was the seventh busiest airport in the United States in 1973 and 1974 and it expects to remain in the top 10. Total operations in 1974 were 428,273. Torrance traffic runs 2,000-plus a day on peak days. Ask any pilot who flies regularly from Torrance on a weekend and he'll tell you the sky is paved with "wall-to-wall airplanes." To this, Torrance controllers say, "Amen!"

Because of its almost unique status—often handling Class III workloads but retaining its identity as a VFR tower—Torrance has unofficially become known as a "training tower." In other words, a regular parade of new, developmental controllers pass through Torrance, winning their spurs in an environment which motivates the higher-ups to observe: "If they can make the grade at Torrance, they can handle the job anywhere!" At times, the ratio of developmental-to-journeyman controllers at Torrance has been in the neighborhood of two-to-one. At Torrance the trainees learn to handle landing and departing aircraft at the rate of 250 to 280 an hour—four to five a minute. No wonder that journeyman "graduates of Torrance U" are in wide demand by tower chiefs throughout the United States.

The man currently responsible for all this is a quiet spoken Missourian of 38 years—17 of them with the FAA—who got his air traffic control start with the Navy at Pensacola's Sherman Field. Chicago Center, Long Beach Approach, El Toro Approach, a tour of FAA's National Aviation Facility Experimental Center at Atlantic City, where he worked in computer research leading to development of ARTS III, all are behind Jack Ryan. Torrance tower and especially the role in training new controllers for the system are of paramount importance to Ryan now. He tends to give the job his all and a little bit more.

Thirty-year-old John Manuszak, the assistant chief, is new to Torrance Tower, having just reported in from Phoenix TRACON. In addition to four and a half years as an Air Force controller, John served with the FAA at Oakland Tower, Las Vegas Approach and Fresno before coming to Torrance. Strictly as a hobby and "not", he assures you, for career purposes, Manuszak, who already holds an AA, is working toward his bachelor's degree in Bookkeeping.

"I'm just hung up on figures," he smiles.

Ask John how a guy gets into air traffic control and he'll tell you "by accident."

"Now I'm glad it happened," John says, "but it was a total mistake the way I began my air traffic career. I was brand new to the Air Force. Everything has the word 'air' associated with it so when they asked me if I would like air traffic control I said yes. I wanted to get in the Air Police as preliminary training for going into civilian law enforcement. I thought Air Traffic Control meant controlling Air Force traffic—you know, automobiles, trucks and the like."

In a very serious tone John adds: "For me it was a godsend. I love it. I get total satisfaction from my work. Sure, the pay is good, but it could be half what it is and I would still be here. I suppose part of it is an 'ego trip.' You know everyone could not do this and do it well. I can do it well."

CLEARED TO LAND!

"I've already had my ulcer," John admits wryly, "and that's behind me. Besides, I tend to be very intense about everything I do. I probably would have gotten an ulcer sitting on my butt in a patrol car. Then again the job gets tough. During very busy times you don't realize your guts are tensed up—you don't realize it until you relax."

Circumstances document that Manuszak really means what he says about the attachment to his job. He turned down a medical retirement and "second career" training to remain active in traffic control.

"I want to do this as long as I can—that is, as long as I can do a good job," he explains.

What are the characteristics needed by a controller?

Manuszak lists them like this: Decisiveness. Aggressiveness—not afraid to do what must be done. Team worker—must not only be able to get along with people in close quarters but be motivated to work in close coordination with them. Planner—based on what is in front of you be able to see what is developing and plan ahead. Ability to concentrate. Organized—in thinking, planning and acting.

John Price, a journeyman since 1970, transferred to air traffic control from duty as a Flight Service Specialist. Like Manuszak, Price feels that everyone cannot become a controller. Although it is a rare situation, some people just don't have what it takes.

"We had this older man," he recalls, "about 30 and who came to the Long Beach Tower from a major aerospace company. He was pretty set in his ways and couldn't take criticism. When you tried to tell him how to do something differently or more effectively he couldn't take it. It wasn't that he didn't want to learn or that he knew it all. He just couldn't accept the fact that he wasn't performing as he thought he should. We get a few like that. They have the potential but get discouraged too easily. They get on a plateau and find they are not progressing fast enough to suit themselves."

One problem which Price singled out is echoed by a large number of controllers across the nation. That is the so-called "mobility" program for controllers. In essence, it is a management philosophy that dictates a controller must either "move up or out." In other words, the controller must progress through the various steps of operational capability and be promoted to the next Civil Service pay grade. To do this he must be willing to follow the job openings, i.e., from a VFR tower to a radar tower, to an approach control, to a center, to a supervisory or management position back at a tower and so forth, since each move introduces him to a new capability and new responsibility. The philosophy as presently constituted (and it is now under study with a view to possible revision) thus makes no allowances for a controller who, for a variety of reasons, is happy with his present job, position or geographic location and does not want to go onward or upward.

"Mobility for mobility's sake isn't the answer," Price declares, "it makes for too many moves. It dictates that a controller must move whether he wants to or not. It also constitutes a problem for management. Often you have the most qualified people at a facility. They want to stay. You want to keep them. But the philosophy of 'move up or out' forces you to lose them"

A lot of controllers at various levels and not a few supervisors indicate they are pleased "the powers that be" are reconsidering the effectiveness of the mobility program. While on the surface it appears to offer some insurance that the deadwood is regularly weeded out, it also appears that the side effect of the cure may be more detrimental than the disease.

Cheri Zweiful, journeyman controller from Meadville, Pa., got her start in air traffic control with the Navy at Quonset Point Naval Air Station, R.I. She now has been at Torrance for three years. Her husband, Dave, is a controller at Van Nuys, Calif. Tower 40 miles away. Cheri commutes 110 miles a day to her job. She works two days on the 1400 to 2200 shift (2 to 10 P.M.), one day from 1000 to 1800 (10 A.M. to 6 P.M.); two days from 0600 to 1400 (6 A.M. to 2 P.M.); and then has two days off. If you're a woman looking for a career and take Cheri's advice, you'll become a controller.

"It's a terrific job for women to get into," Cheri enthuses, "the atmosphere is great and the job is so personally satisfying. You know you're doing something important. You get to work with people and the close working relationship gives you a wonderful feeling. One thing, you can't be an introvert and be a controller. And, you have to have confidence in yourself and your ability."

Does a woman get any guff from the male controllers?

"No," says Cheri, 'I never did have any trouble with the fellows. They did everything they could to help me out but still expected me to carry my end. One thing—they had to put a lock on the john. They couldn't get used to having a woman, as such, around and kept busting right in."

The flying game isn't anything new to Rod Stewart, one of Torrance's developmental controllers. Rod was an Army aviator who got shot up flying "tactical air control" in Viet Nam. That's a little different from what he's doing now. TAC in a combat zone means flying little "birddog" planes into the jaws of the enemy and directing the attack of the fighters and fighter-bombers against ground targets.

Stewart characterizes air traffic control in the same words employed by old time aviators to describe their craft: "hours and hours of boredom punctuated by seconds of sheer terror." He allows as how he might be exaggerating a little insofar as the boredom is concerned since it isn't "quite as exciting as getting shot at" but adds:

"When something gets out of kilter, it gets way out. You really have to keep completely cool to handle it."

Both Rod and Cheri agree that a lot of general aviation pilots have the wrong idea of what the controller is there to accomplish.

"Many pilots," Rod believes, "resent controllers and they let you know it from the tone of their voice."

"They think of us as airplane cops," Cheri adds, "flying fuzz. They get really defensive and even sarcastic when we try to tell them to do something differently."

Then, Torrance has a special problem shared by only a few other towers. The airport not only has heavy student pilot activity but many of them are foreign students and although English is the international language of aviation, sometimes the dialogue between Torrance Tower and these students gets a "little difficult."

Of the more than 250 controllers at all levels interviewed for this book, Dewayne Kirksey, another Torrance developmental controller, is representative of the handful who aren't really sure they are in air traffic control to stay. Kirksey, a bearded young man who describes himself humorously as an "itinerant hippy," also came into civilian air traffic control from the military—the Air Force.

"Frankly," Dewayne recalls, "the Air Force got me off to a bad start. When I was recruited, I was told 'controller is a lazy man's job.' That's why I took it. They had so many bodies floating around I had a lot of time off. I didn't begin to have enough to do and when I got out, to be truthful, I wasn't going into air traffic control again. It had proved to be pretty boring."

Subsequently, Kirksey did take the FAA exam and decided to give it a try. After two years at Torrance, he admits "it's an exciting job."

"It really keeps your interest," he says, "and it offers a lot of challenge. But I'm not sure I want to spend 20 or 30 years on shift work."

Dewayne's co-workers, however, have a different idea about him. They think he has the controller bug and will be "around for a long time."

5 THE CENTER

March can be rough in Northern California—snow, fog, low-hanging decks of stratus clouds, drizzle, ice. You name it and you get it.

Local weather can change quickly under the influence of the wet, unstable marine layer that moves in from the Northwest toward Red Bluff across the rugged coastal mountains. Often it gets trapped in the long, north-south valley that extends from the Sacramento Basin to the Oregon border between the coastal range on the west and the Sierras on the east. When it does, it stays around for a while.

To the west of Red Bluff the minimum enroute altitude is 9,500 feet and to the east the MEA goes up to 10,500. The airport itself is a low 345 feet above sea level.

In simple words—it's no place for an inexperienced pilot with two passengers aboard his single-engine aircraft; tired on a long hop from Riverside more than 500 miles to the south; shaken in his shoe tops finding himself at 2,000 feet on instruments in solid fog with zero instrument time under his belt.

But that's the way it was that March afternoon in 1963—well, let's not use his name, just call him Mooney 123.

George Baldwin, controller at Oakland Air Route Traffic Control Center responsible for the slice of sky over and around Red Bluff, sat up just a little straighter when the voice of a flight service specialist at Red Bluff Radio came over the direct phone line.

"Oakland Center this is Red Bluff Radio, we have a little problem with Mooney 123—not sure of his position. We can give him steers into Red Bluff. We want to know if you have any traffic?"

Checking, Baldwin advised Red Bluff he had traffic. "Is he VFR?" he asked.

"Oh, no, he's in the soup at 2,000," came the reply.

Baldwin advised Red Bluff Flight Service Station to have the Mooney contact Oakland Center on 118.5 or 125.7 for radar identification and steers to Red Bluff. In a few seconds the anxious voice of the Mooney pilot came through his headset.

"This is Mooney 123. Where in hell am I now?"

Calmly, Baldwin instructed: "Climb and maintain four thousand, over."

"This is Mooney 123. I read you and I am climbing out."

The pilot's lack of experience was apparent in his radio procedure. He had none of the assurance or grasp of radioese common to pilots of even average experience in using radio communications and navigational aids. Baldwin settled down to what he expected might be a hairy hour or so. The first thing, now that he was getting Mooney 123 clear of his IFR traffic, was to find out just how much time he had and just how well the pilot might be capable of responding to his guidance.

Asking if the Mooney had VOR equipment, Baldwin was told, "I don't know what I've got!"

Questions about the fuel available brought: "About a quarter of a tank—about three quarters of an hour. I don't know where the hell I'm at."

CLEARED TO LAND!

Queried about his heading, the Mooney pilot replied: "I am flying at 29 degrees."

Did he mean 29 degrees or did he really mean 290 degrees—a good deal closer to the course northbound to Red Bluff. Compass points are marked with two digits thus 29 would mean 290, but how could you be sure when the man in the cockpit is approaching panic?

By now, another player had entered the game. Capt. Milo Kopp, a United Air Lines pilot in UAL Flight 388, had been monitoring the situation as he flew above the area. He asked the Mooney pilot if he knew his position. The reply was "No!" He asked what his departure point and heading had been. The answer was, "I took off at Riverside and I have been flying for three hours and 45 minutes." Kopp asked for the Mooney's present heading and got the confused reply, "My present heading—I am going pretty near due east—due west three degrees."

It was evident the pilot was going to be of little help in the task of determining his position. Baldwin now instructed him to fly a triangular right hand pattern that could be identified on the radar scope.

"123, this is Oakland Center. On your right turn now fly one minute. Make a right turn, fly one minute on that leg and continue. We'll see if we can pick you up."

As Baldwin peered intently at his scope, the rattled pilot reminded him, "I still have no idea where I'm at."

The controller rogered, trying to give the pilot calmness with his own unflustered radio demeanor, asking for the Mooney compass heading. Again the reply was less than satisfactory.

"North 24 degrees (an unintelligible period of garbling) dead west right now."

"Is that 240—two four zero—degrees?" the controller asked.

Now, with more apparent panic than before: "I don't understand what you want—get me out of this fog up here and get me to hell out of here!"

Making his voice as reassuring as possible, Baldwin repeated his question.

"Your compass heading, can you give me your compass heading—you're flying by a compass, you have a compass in front of you there now—if you'll just take a look at that and give me the reading off it."

"We are flying due west," the pilot replied.

"Roger, roger," Baldwin said, "that's a 270—two seven zero—heading, compass heading."

Now, more panicky than before.

"I believe that's what it is—it's a fog—we're still in a fog—at 7,000 feet—we're still in the fog flying due west 20 degrees. I have no idea of what I am even doing."

The situation in the cramped confines of the Mooney cabin was worse than Baldwin had imagined. The pilot appeared to be unable to control his nerves and follow the instructions being given by the Center. Something had to be done to calm him down or he would certainly take himself and his two passengers to their death. Perhaps another pilot—a fellow airman—could help. Now, the airline captain again was called into the game.

In the cockpit of the UAL liner, Kopp turned the flying over to his first officer, picked up the mike and began a slow, comforting litany.

"Mooney 123. Okay now, just relax, we all get in a spot once in a while—if you'll just relax your hand on the wheel—just for a second, I think we'll calm down. Take your feet off the rudders for a second and then just shake your hands a bit and relax. Now go back to it and just head east which is 'E' on the indicator. East heading and hold that for a minute or so. Just nice and straight and I think we can calm down quite a bit and accomplish quite a bit, okay?"

"Yeah, I got ya," came the response.

Kopp continued: "You have a good machine under you. It's a real good machine and with a little help it will do a real good job for you."

The reply now was a little calmer: "We are going due east now at 7,000 feet."

"Very good, very good, fine," Kopp told the Mooney pilot, "just hold that now and you'll be doing real good."

Shifting his concern to his fuel, the Mooney pilot informed Kopp that he now had "less than a quarter of a tank." Not wanting to divert the pilot's attention from climbing the airplane straight into the east heading, Kopp didn't respond to the comment but continued his reassurance that things "now are going well."

"United," Baldwin chimed in, "this is Oakland. He should have a reserve of—after he goes empty—of five or six gallons—we show him now about 45 miles bearing approximately 200 from Red Bluff."

"Roger," Kopp replied, "if you could work him down in the Sacramento Valley, there's lots of airports in the Sacramento Valley which he can distinguish easily."

Baldwin instructed the Mooney pilot to continue his present heading telling him that in about 20 miles he would be out of the mountains and over the valley.

Kopp added: "123 from United. Your position is probably west of the Sacramento Valley, up near Red Bluff and the Center is going to take you east over the valley and then drop you down in the valley where you'll have a lot better weather."

Regaining a bit of his composure the Mooney pilot indicated he would continue on the east heading climbing to avoid peaks in the area.

Kopp continued to nurse the pilot along.

"That's right," he told him, "you keep that east heading now and we'll tell you when you're ready to descend. That'll put you in the valley. So you listen to him (Baldwin in the Center) and relax a little more—I think once in awhile just take your hands off the wheel, shake them a little bit and go back. It'll be pretty easy for you. Should set up a cruise now with your mixture leaned out so you can conserve your fuel."

"What altitude are you at now?" Baldwin asked the Mooney.

The report was 9,500 feet but the pilot now indicated he was having "trouble" holding his heading again. Kopp nursed him into a turn back to the right and the easterly heading. Now he was over the valley and another turn to the south would be necessary.

"Take up a heading of 180 which is south on your compass," Baldwin advised, "and maintain that heading until further advised. Be sure to keep your airspeed and, as United said, relax on your controls."

Picking up where Baldwin left off, Kopp added: "Okay, if you'll right rudder into a right turn to a southerly heading, 'S' on the compass and hold that. The Center is working you well now."

CLEARED TO LAND!

Just when both Baldwin and Kopp thought they were getting the situation in hand fear and panic again struck the Mooney cabin.

"You want—you want me to go which direction?" The voice from the Mooney faltered. "This is 123, we're having trouble!"

Now Kopp and Baldwin began alternating giving instructions with a degree of calm reassurance neither of them felt.

"This is United. Want you to go south, south. Relax, we're working on you so just relax if you can. I know it's hard but we can do it."

"This is Oakland. Settle down now, settle down. Head south, south on your compass. Be sure and keep your airspeed up, make a gradual turn, a gradual descent to 7,000—be sure and keep your airspeed above a hundred knots."

"123 from United. Just turn to a south heading now, just turn nice and easy to a south heading and hold it south, okay?"

"This is Oakland. Settle down now, settle down. Head south, south on your compass. Be sure and keep your airspeed up, make a gradual turn, a gradual descent to 7,000—be sure and keep your airspeed above a hundred knots."

"This is United. Now if you'll—when you get your southerly heading—if you'll make your descent to 7,000, you'll be in good shape."

For a moment or two the frequency was quiet. In the United cockpit, Kopp lay the mike in his lap. Baldwin relaxed in his seat before the radar console. But not for long. The moment of quiet was shattered:

"This is 123. We're way out of control!"

For a fraction of a second Baldwin sat motionless in the dimness of Oakland Center. In his mind's eye he could see the panic in the Mooney cockpit. He could see the little monoplane begin to enter a spin or, even worse, a graveyard spiral. But, only for that fraction of a second did he consider what was happening in the sky over Red Bluff. His reaction was almost automatic—

"123. Let the controls go. Just let 123 go. Release the controls. Release the controls. Just let go of them."

At least his voice was penetrating the panic.

"I got yah," came the reply.

"123. Don't worry about your airspeed picking up. Just relax, the airplane will come out of it on its own. If you have at least 7,000 feet you'll be all right in your present position—there's clear weather about 25 miles to the south. As soon as the airplane recovers try to take up a southerly heading, over."

The next call from Mooney 123 expressed increased concern over the fuel situation.

"You'll have about five gallons—five gallons will take you where you have to go," Baldwin explained, "now, has the airplane righted itself and can you tell me your airspeed?"

A moment's hesitation and the reply, "My airspeed is about 110 miles an hour."

"If you have 110, you're all right. You are all right," Baldwin said, "if you were in any kind of a spiral, it should be in excess of that if your trim is on normal. Was your trim normal when you started, when you went on instruments?"

No reply. Baldwin continued: "At 110 you should be all right. Head south, head south, just 'S' up there on your compass, your liquid compass."

The Mooney pilot appeared to get a grip on himself. He reported he was at

5,500 "going north." Now, to get him turned around headed south away from the mountains.

Baldwin continued, "You are heading now towards higher terrain. Turn right, turn right, back to south, back to south. Make your turn with your rudders. Just use a little right rudder pressure, right rudder pressure, that's all—not very much, just a little—just keep your hands off the wheel, don't use the wheel, don't pull back on it or push forward, just use a little right rudder."

For the past 20 minutes Baldwin had pondered what to do next. Sure, get the Mooney headed away from the mountains hemming it in on three sides. Get it down to a VFR situation. Get it safely on the ground at Red Bluff. But, it was going to take more than what he and Kopp could do.

Controllers who work certain positions in certain sectors for extended periods of time become familiar with aircraft—and the pilots—that frequent their airspace. Even though a controller and a particular pilot may never meet eyeball-to-eyeball, they develop a kinship based on mutual confidence and respect. Such was the case of Baldwin and Louis Pelletier who regularly used the center as he flew his Piper Aztec 4875 Papa or "Pop", as many pilots and controllers shorten the phonetic for the letter "P." Pelletier in 75 Pop was in the area today. Baldwin called:

"4875 Pop, Oakland Center. Will you give 123 a call? He's about 25 miles north of your present position, and see if you can raise him?"

In the Mooney cockpit, the pilot was still having trouble holding the aircraft straight when Pelletier responded.

"Okay 123, just steady down—just try to keep around the "S" and around 110 miles an hour. If you can descend to about 5,000 you'll break out of this bottom layer—we're at 4,500 right now between layers and we'll try to keep an eye out for you—we'll turn our landing light on."

"Oakland, 75 Pop. Do you have us both on radar?"

"I have 75 Pop," Baldwin answered, "I do not have the Mooney. That last known position of 123 was about 12 miles east of Red Bluff. If he heads southerly he should be all right."

Pelletier and Baldwin worked out a plan. The Aztec would stay in the clear between cloud layers at 4,500 feet and work its way north towards Red Bluff. Pelletier would display both his landing light and his red rotating beacon. Baldwin would continue to try to vector the Mooney toward Pelletier. If, and it was a big if, he could get the two airplanes together, Pelletier would be able to slow the Aztec down and lead the Mooney to safety at Red Bluff.

"123," Baldwin called, "Okay. Make a nice gradual descent now to about 5,000 feet, five thousand. You should have another aircraft at your 12 o'clock position, that is right off the nose, about 15 miles. Do not gain excessive airspeed in descent; the best way to do it would be just to roll a very slight amount of trim forward—just roll the trim forward a little—and let the airplane come down by itself."

The Mooney asked for a repeat of Baldwin's instructions. The controller complied again cautioning the pilot to do everything in easy stages.

Now a wait set in. Although it was not more than two or three minutes, it seemed like hours as Baldwin sat watching the scope in front of him. One little white blip moving slowly northward. Suddenly, another white blip. This one moving south. At almost the same time his headset crackled:

"Oakland Center, 75 Pop. I think I've got him. I'm going to flash my light.

123, do you see a light ahead of you?"

"Yes, I do," came the now reasonably calm reply. The sight of the Aztec had been like a nerve tonic to the Mooney pilot.

"That's us!" Pelletier almost laughed. "Come on over and we'll take you to Red Bluff."

Immediately, Baldwin cleared the Aztec and its nursling for an instrument approach into Red Bluff.

High above the soup Kopp had continued to monitor the drama. He now told Baldwin he would switch to Seattle Center and continue his scheduled trip.

"Are you completely in the clear now?" Baldwin asked the Mooney pilot.

"I believe I am," came the comforting reply.

"Okay, fine," Baldwin told him, "the lights should be on at Red Bluff shortly. Just follow 75 Pop. You don't need to talk to us any more."

The controller pushed back from the console. He was bathed in perspiration and weak as a kitten now that adrenalin was no longer pumping through his blood stream. Wearily he removed the headset and handed it to the relief controller who slipped into the chair.

Baldwin remained near the console for the next 10 minutes. While the responsibility for safely getting the Mooney on the ground now rested with

The nation's 27 air route traffic control centers and the telephone, teletype, radio and digital data links that connect them can be compared with the body's central nervous system. Just as the human nervous system coordinates the senses and the signals sent by the motor centers, so do the centers work to keep air traffic flowing smoothly and safely. Oakland Center .

THE CENTER

Pelletier in the Aztec, the controller had to know that what he had started was successfully concluded. The rest of the operation wasn't easy. Pelletier had his hands full talking, instructing, cajoling the Mooney pilot through the descent on instruments. Finally, the welcome word:

"This is 75 Pop. He's on the ground safe and sound."

George Baldwin made his way slowly to the controllers' lounge. Somehow, he felt he had earned his pay that day.

Officially, air traffic controllers' primary responsibility is to maintain separation between aircraft using the same airspace and facilitate an orderly, safe flow of aircraft along the nation's airways. That in itself is a herculean task when you consider that in 1974 U.S. aircraft—all types—flew in excess of 50 million hours and that FAA air traffic controllers handled no less than 80 million operations. However, the underlying objective of the FAA, and thus its men and women, is air safety. Often, safety considerations dictate that the controller do a lot more than merely maintain aircraft separation. Take Leon Orr, Clyde Hansen, Manley Williams and Paul Hildreth of Minneapolis Center, for instance.

They were on the swing watch. It was a cold, overcast October night. Fog had been closing airports one after another in the area between Lake Michigan and Lake Superior when the request for an instrument clearance came in from a Cessna 172 enroute between DeKalb in northern Illinois and Land O' Lakes, in northern Wisconsin. At the controls was a former Royal Canadian Air Force pilot with some 33-years flying experience—James Hebert. Finding Land O'Lakes closed, Hebert asked for an IFR clearance to Wausau, Wisc.

Orr and Hansen checked, found that Wausau also was closed and proposed that Hebert proceed to Oshkosh. No go. The Cessna's fuel reserve would not permit it to cover the 106 miles to Oshkosh. A further check of the area failed to provide much hope. Ceilings were zero with visibilities ranging from one eighth to three quarters of a mile in fog.

The two controllers, now assisted by Williams and Hildreth, got out the aeronautical charts for the area, spread them out on the floor at the center and began an inch-by-inch search for airports which would be within the airplane's diminishing fuel range and could be checked one-by-one for local weather. Calls were placed to the Chicago Center, Green Bay and Wausau Flight Service Stations for additional information.

It looked like Green Bay was the best possibility—84 miles from Hebert and the weather was holding above instrument minimum. The Cessna was cleared to Green Bay at 7,000 feet.

Normally, that would have concluded the assist, but fate wouldn't have it so. The controllers discovered that Hebert was bucking headwinds that weren't doing his cause any good. The Cessna was recleared at a lower altitude where winds were better. Still, it was no go—fighting the winds, the Cessna's ground speed was estimated to be only 60 knots. The plane was not going to make it to Green Bay.

Back to the floor, Orr and Hansen found Shawano Airport, 21 miles northwest of Green Bay, to be the most weather-free within range. They called the airport manager for up-to-the-minute weather reports and arranged for the airport beacon to be lit and police patrol cars to line up alongside the sod runway with their dome lights flashing.

CLEARED TO LAND!

Hebert was given a heading, a description of the small airport and its surrounding terrain and was guided along his way.

With four gallons of fuel left, Hebert set the plane down at Shawano, nearly three hours after his initial contact with the Minneapolis Center.

In official FAA terminology, actions like these are called "flight assists" but in fact they more often than not qualify as "saves" in every sense of the word. Take March 1974, for instance. Nationwide that month, FAA men and women—not just at centers, but at towers, approach controls and Flight Service Stations—were credited with 240 flight assists to aircraft carrying a total of 377 people. These included 137 lost pilots, 36 low on fuel, 59 involved in weather and 63 with some type of equipment malfunction.

Typical of these was the case of a pilot without an instrument rating lost at night in bad weather. This time it took the whole team—flight service station, center and approach control—to bring him home safely.

The pilot called Jackson, Tenn., FSS for help. The FSS had him contact Memphis Center where his position was fixed by radar. The aircraft was vectored toward Memphis but this wasn't enough. Low fuel and high head winds made Memphis an impossible destination. He was rerouted to Covington but could not locate the airport. Meanwhile, the FSS called the Tennessee Highway Patrol and asked for assistance in getting the lights at Covington turned on. With runway lights to identify the airport, the pilot landed safely.

Take another instance, this one in July of that year. On his first extended cross-country, a student pilot became lost in a rainstorm between Charleston, S.C., and Jacksonville, Fla. Frightened, near panic, he still had the presence of mind to use his radio and call Jacksonville Center where controller Buddy Friedlin reassured him and guided him toward Brunswick, Ga. Although the pilot wanted to land the plane "anywhere, on any available open ground," Friedlin kept him in the air constantly reassuring him. The thoughts of letting a student pilot already frightened make an emergency landing just didn't seem the way to go. Friedlin's persistence paid off. The student finally located the airport by its beacon and landed safely. This was one of the 293 flight assists recorded by FAA that month, flight assists involving some 447 pilots and passengers.

Air traffic control centers (now called air route traffic control centers or ARTCC) initially were created by the airlines in the mid-1930's. In 1936 what then was the Bureau of Air Commerce took over the original three centers at Newark, Chicago and Cleveland. One of the original government controllers who came over with Newark Center was Edward A. "Ted" Westlake. Westlake, who returned in 1968 to become a consultant to the Aircraft Owners and Pilot's Association (AOPA), remembers the early days well.

"The controller's tools," he recalls, "were a blackboard and map table but after a while we had to do away with the map table because it got too cluttered with 'shrimp boats.' We had no radar, of course, and no direct radio contact with the pilots of the aircraft we were controlling. All messages had to be relayed through airline or government communications stations.

"Crude as the system was, it usually was adequate for the volume of traffic handled. Air carrier movements in and out of New York then were only 50 to 60 a day. If a controller got 10 aircraft on the board at the same time, he really began to sweat. That was a real traffic peak." "Sometimes," Westlake adds, "it was difficult to persuade pilots what we were doing was really

THE CENTER

Chicago Center

Even though center facilities are crammed to the eaves with the most sophisticated electronic and computer hardware available today the critical factor, judgment, which no computer can provide, is contributed by hundreds of skilled, dedicated men and women.

Kansas City Center

CLEARED TO LAND!

necessary. This was particularly true when you had to tell a pilot he was number four or five to land in about an hour."

The veteran air traffic expert—he spent his last 20 years with the FAA as a specialist in international air traffic control—recalls that among those who gave him trouble was one of the "nation's most famous aviators." Since this pilot is still among us, Westlake declines to give his name.

The flier had been given instructions to maintain 13,000 feet on a flight from Chicago to a Long Island airport while over New York City. He decided for himself, Westlake says, that "this was not really necessary and let down through several layers of airline aircraft that were holding over the city on instruments awaiting clearances to land."

"Fortunately," he adds, "nothing happened. He missed them all." Such incidents were the exception, Westlake notes, and "most pilots recognized the need for air traffic control and went along with it. In fact, it was the airline operators themselves rather than the government who took the initiative in this area."

During low traffic periods, generally in the early morning hours, a center can seem almost deserted, but during peak periods this huge room with its two score operating positions is a beehive of activity.

The basic system of spacing aircraft and bringing them in for a landing in an orderly manner, Westlake recalls, was worked out by Earl Ward of American Airlines with the assistance of Glen Gilbert, also with American. Subsequently, Ward became the first supervisor of airway traffic control for the Federal government. At Ward's invitation, Westlake joined the crew at Newark in April 1936 just three months before it was transferred to the Department of Commerce. Initially, he was on a leave of absence from his job as chief radio

Center area of responsibility is divided into sectors and vertically the sectors are divided into high and low altitude sectors. Just as aircraft under control are handed off from center to center, so they also are handed off from high to low altitude sectors, and from sector to sector as they near the point they are handed off to the approach control for the destination airport.

Progress of aircraft monitored by radar is kept both in a computer and also by hand recorded on flight strips kept in plastic holders. The holders and flight strip for a particular aircraft then can be handed to the controller at the next sector in the same manner as the aircraft is handed off on radar.

operator for United Air Lines at Newark but, ultimately, stayed with the government.

It's a far cry from that first center at Newark to a circa-1975 center with its multiple radar, hundreds of channels of VHF voice communications, radio beacon interrogation equipment, high-speed teletype and, perhaps most important, third generation digital computers.

The traffic load also is a far cry from those pre-World War II days when 50 to 60 aircraft in a single day represented the peak. At Los Angeles Center, one of 21 that cover the continental United States, a daily weekday traffic load runs in the neighborhood of 3,000 aircraft. On a weekend, 2,000 to 2,500 are handled with the annual total running between 1.75 and 1.9 million. On November 11, 1974, for instance, Los Angeles Center handled 4,037 individual aircraft.

Los Angeles Center covers a huge geographical area—its borders are irregular but in essence its area begins at Los Angeles on the west; extends to Fresno, Calif., and Wilson Creek, Nev. on the north; eastward to Bryce Canyon, Utah, and Grand Junction, Colo., and southward to the Mexican border. Centers which border it are: Oakland, northwest; Salt Lake, northeast; Denver, east; and Albuquerque, southeast.

It's a hell of a big area including some of America's most rugged and desolate expanses; peaks towering beyond 14,000 feet, Death Valley—blistering hot and below sea level; thousands of square miles of high desert wasteland; hundreds of miles of sea shore. The area also includes probably more major military research and development and training areas than any other in the country—Edwards AFB, Vandenburg AFB, Pacific Missile Range, Fort Irwin, China Lake, Twentynine Palms, Yuma Test Range, Camp Pendleton, the Navy's San Clemente Island test facility. With these come myriad special problems for the air traffic controller.

John Dunham, assistant chief, Air Traffic Control, for Los Angeles Center, is one of a relatively few FAA people who has been able to "homestead" during his career. John has been with Los Angeles Center for 29 years. He has seen it grow in size, responsibility and complexity.

Today Los Angeles Center occupies a multi-million-dollar structure situated on Palmdale Airport (Air Force Plant 42) 52 miles northeast—along Victor 201—of Los Angeles International. It is staffed by some 350 people—175 of them journeyman controllers. Obviously, since Dunham came aboard in August 1946, there have been some changes.

"When I joined the FAA and reported for duty at Los Angeles Center it was a small operation housed in one medium-sized room on the third floor at 741 South Flower Street in downtown Los Angeles. As I recall, we had a chief, one secretary, three supervisors (who then were called senior advisors), 14 controllers and about 18 assistants.

"The center area was divided into just four sectors. In those days we didn't have anything like high altitude sectors and on the day shift, for instance, we would have at least one journeyman controller and an assistant for each sector. We had the capability of dividing up one of our sectors—the one covering metropolitan Los Angeles—into two sectors.

"Burbank was the principle Los Angeles terminal in those days but if Burbank was socked in we would divert the traffic to old Mines Field (now LAX). When we did this we would have to also assume approach control for Mines.

That's when we would divide up the metropolitan sector."

Communications left much to be desired in those earlier days. Air/ground communications were on high frequency and were subject to build and fade at different times of the day and to "precipitation static" during bad weather. Actually the center had little contact directly with the pilots. Radio communications with general aviation aircraft were few and far between. Air/ground communications with air carriers were primarily via company radio. Communications with military aircraft were mainly through military airways communications stations.

The centers had "drop lines"—direct telephone lines—to the airline radio stations, the military airways stations and to the CAA flight service stations—then called Interstate Airways Communications Stations (INSACS).

Say, a TWA DC-3 was inbound to Los Angeles from Denver. Approaching Las Vegas he would call his company radio station giving his altitude, estimated time of arrival over Las Vegas and other pertinent information. The TWA station at Las Vegas would contact Los Angeles Center on the drop line requesting a clearance on to Los Angeles and an altitude. Checking on other traffic in the area, the center would pass a clearance "as requested" or, if necessary, "amended," back via the drop line to the TWA operator who would relay it to the aircraft. Separation criteria were 1,000 feet of altitude or 10 minutes flying time.

"Of course," Dunham recalls, "there was a communications delay. You automatically had to take this delay into consideration. The delay varied with the situation. In good weather you didn't have any problems. If you had thunderstorms or frontal systems, you could expect more delay because of radio interference. I'd say it wasn't unusual to wait five minutes for a vacating altitude report. This wasn't too bad because you always were planning at least 30 minutes ahead—ahead of his estimate—to decide what to do with him. If you were controlling the aircraft in real time, you had a problem.

"Without radar we had to depend entirely on the crew for position and altitude. After you had been on the job for a while, you knew pretty well what the land conditions were in the sector where you were working and you knew the time between fixes pretty well for various types of aircraft. One of the first things we would do in our own area was to check the times between fixes, say between Fresno and Bakersfield. For a DC-3, for instance, taking into consideration the winds, it would take 50 to 55 minutes. So you kept real close track of the wind conditions and the weather—wind particularly, whether the airplane had a tail wind or a head wind.

"As a matter of fact, you could compute your estimates pretty well. There weren't all that many types of aircraft—the DC-3, the Boeing 247 and later the DC-4s."

Actually, according to Dunham, those early controllers had a "good handle" on the situation, even under emergency conditions.

"Suppose we had a Mayday," he says, "we had a pretty good idea of where he was. Checking his last known position, knowing his ground speed (applying known winds) and course and knowing the different aircraft characteristics you could pretty well pinpoint him. Without too much hairy estimating, you could vacate an altitude and bring him down.

"Ice was a real problem, though. Few aircraft had deicer boots and even

Controller monitors an ARTS III display.

with them if you started building up a load of clear ice, those boots didn't mean much. It wasn't uncommon for the aircraft to call me up and say 'I can't maintain altitude, I'm going down.' I'd have to tell the guy I couldn't do anything for him if, say, he was at 12,000 and I had opposition traffic at 11,-000. If they were in close proximity, by the time I could call up an INSAC and issue a clearance, he'd already be through the altitude. Coming down he might be in double jeopardy, but I couldn't reach out and hold him up. Actually, I don't recall many situations like that where there was any kind of collision."

The intense pressure on an aircraft traffic controller isn't just a figment of the screen writer's imagination. It's very real. This was recognized by the Corson Committee in 1970. What about those pressures when Dunham began his career as opposed to those controllers face today?

Second controller keeps track of aircraft progress manually with flight strips,

"I feel the pressures were just as great in the 40s and 50s as they are today," he declares, "different, but just as great. Sure the volume of traffic was less but you still faced the same problems with tools to work with that were inadequate. You also didn't have enough people. I recall many times—well, we didn't have a cafeteria or anything—so I had to bring my lunch to work and end up taking it home with me because I couldn't take time to eat it. This didn't do either your digestion or your nerves any good.

"You could tell when things began to pop and the pressure built up. The tenor began to increase; you got up out of your chair, pushed it back and used stand-up control; you got a little more tense as you got deeper into it. One of

CLEARED TO LAND!

the worst periods was when a storm began to build up. The tops (cloud tops) began to rise. You tried and tried to get top reports, to find out exactly what you had. That's when airplanes began calling in for IFR clearance. It wasn't mandatory for airlines to fly IFR in those days so they would fly contact (VFR today) until they could go no farther; then call for an instrument clearance. Now you had to get all these guys assigned to an altitude and get that 10-minute horizontal separation—all at the same time."

The situation isn't too different today when the weather goes sour. The workload is spread out timewise a little more since all airline traffic now must file IFR. This serves to maintain a constant IFR load on the center but with the heavy general aviation traffic—thousands of business and executive flights which go IFR when conditions warrant—the "clank factor" still comes into play.

From 100 to 110 men and women are required to man Los Angeles Center on each of three shifts—controllers at the scopes of the multiple arrival, departure and enroute sectors, the high and low altitude sectors and the "positive control" area, shift chiefs and supervisors, data systems coordinators, flow controllers, the "mission" coordinator who maintains a real-time liaison with military agencies using the airspace and administrative personnel.

Technicians work backstage to keep the electronics and computer systems operating properly.

THE CENTER

Sure, they are assisted by seven air route surveillance radars (ARSR) each with a 200-mile range spread out over three states—Mount Laguna, San Pedro, Boron and Paso Robles, Calif., Las Vegas and Tonopah, Nev., and Cedar City, Utah; "Big Blue"—the huge computer complex that assimilates data from these radar sites, digitizes it, stores it and displays it on command at any control position; and the national radar data processing system that automatically transmits flight plan and position data on enroute aircraft from center to center. But, when you get right down to the nitty gritty of it all, it's men and women who must issue the control instructions and assume the final responsibility for those instructions. And, one fact of life that can't be avoided—they are just that, ordinary, everyday men and women, with the normal human penchant for not always being perfect. They can and do make mistakes and they know it. It is this grim realization that makes the air traffic controller strive even harder to make every shift error-free, often driving him to the breaking point—"burning him out" at an early age.

Sid Curry is a journeyman controller with a total of 13 years experience—four in the military and nine with the FAA. Notwithstanding the pressure, he likes what he's doing.

"As far as I can see it's a fantastic job," Sid unabashedly declares, "and you don't need all kinds of education for it. I only completed 10 years of school, but I'm a good controller."

Curry—as far as that goes, every controller—has his own theory about the pressures of the job. He feels that different people react differently to the pressure.

"It changes from person to person," he says, "there have been a lot of stories about controllers and the fact that they are only good for about 15 years—20 years before they burn up. Naturally, some people can't stand it for even that long. Others can stand it for a long time without having any problems. One of our guys died of a heart attack at home this morning—at 50. We've had guys collapse on the sectors; another driving out the gate; some collapsed on the way home. About 60 to 70 percent end up having ulcers after they have been in for a few years."

"I figure I'm one of the guys it slides off of," Sid smiles, "all I end up with is a nervous stomach—the next thing to an ulcer—but it doesn't affect me quite enough to get an ulcer. The way I feel about it, the pressure comes from what I consider the possibility of killing so many people—with one small mistake—you make just a small error, just the mis-statement of a number, and you could run two airplanes together and kill a whole bunch of people in one fell swoop. That's where I feel the pressure.

"Some people see the pressure from the standpoint of too much business in too short a time—a pure case of cramming a number of things in a given period of time. That doesn't bother me, that's the way I like to work."

ATC work doesn't appear to be conducive to a stable family life. Curry says the divorce rate at his center is "a little over 80 percent of them divorced at one time or another," but he doesn't attribute it to the hours—shift work—like many controllers and their wives.

"I think it's just the pressure of bad marriages," he says, "I don't believe it is the hours. I've watched a lot of people work shift work in other jobs with no problems. The problem here is the controller takes the work home. He takes the pressure of the job home and the marriage isn't sound enough to stand it."

John Cadigan, a 24-year controller, has another theory.

"I think the type of people who are attracted to this job," he declares, "are predisposed for all the problems they encounter—the ulcers and the divorces. If they worked at other jobs, they still would get ulcers. They work under pressure but they are attracted by that pressure. It's a job where the challenge is always bigger than you are—you never catch up—you never are as good as the job demands and that's what makes it attractive. We have all the personnel problems we have because we are that kind of people. We're the kind of individuals who would be bored to death spending eight hours a day at a desk or a machine.'

Cadigan, like many veteran controllers, feels strongly that for a controller to do his job he must remain aloof from any personal involvement in the work.

"You have to keep it on the level of a game," he says, "a game against the scope. You are playing a game against the birds up there and as long as you keep it as a very precise game—you do it very precisely and professionally—you're all right. You can't let it get personal by thinking about the people up there. The time you get in trouble is when you start thinking that every one of those targets on the scope involves human beings. When you become involved with humanity, you get involved in trouble."

Obviously, Cadigan admits, it is impossible not to think of the people in the aircraft under control, but that realization "must be kept in the background of the mind" with the cutting edge of the controller's faculties always focused on beating the game.

One thing about which Curry, Cadigan and Dunham—in fact all the more than 100 controllers interviewed—agree. In the final analysis, the responsibility must rest with the pilot in command of the aircraft. Controllers can issue advice, information, even directions, but it is up to the pilot, taking into consideration all the facts available to him in the cockpit, to decide what to do and when to do it.

"I know there have been cases where pilots feel their decision-making responsibility has been usurped from the ground," Dunham says, "but that is entirely the pilot's reaction to the instructions given. I don't know a single controller who wants to get his hands in the cockpit. We don't want to command that airplane. We want to give that pilot the best professional help and guidance we can, all the tools to make an intelligent decision, and then leave it up to him."

"Sometimes we sound a little rough," Cadigan adds, "particularly if we've been working a 'dummy.' Now there's nothing personal about this. That's what we call an airplane that's doing something out of phase with all the other airplanes in that area at that particular time. Even when we call him a dummy, he hasn't necessarily done anything wrong. It's just that he's giving us a problem in relationship with all the others. He doesn't know he's a problem just then; he just isn't cooperating as quickly as he should because he can't see himself in relation to the other planes.

"When that happens, we get a little upset. Especially if we're extremely busy and someone is slow to cooperate, we put a little edge on our voice. It's hard to get the edge off once it's on, so occasionally it overlaps with another aircraft. You talk to the next one and he gets the same edge even though he didn't deserve it. Most of the pilots understand, however, particularly if we're busy and take it into consideration.

"Fortunately, most people who fly today know what we're here for—to help."

FLIGHT SERVICE 6

Graveyard spiral! Aptly named because if you don't recognize it and get out of it in one hell of a hurry it usually leads to your funeral.

Although the Cessna 180 lost in an Alaskan snow storm was redlined at 170 miles per hour, the airspeed indicator on the panel read 200 and nothing seemed to slow the course of the needle as it moved around the scale. Now, the Cessna 180 is a big, husky taildragger of an airplane. It's a great favorite with bush pilots because it can take a lot of tough handling but it wouldn't be long before this 180 was reduced to fragments if its spiral plunge to earth wasn't stopped.

Although the pilot was experienced and capable, he was in over his head. With no instrument capability he had been flying in blinding snow whipped by a 40-mile wind for some time. Often he had been down to 200 feet to make the best of the limited visibility. Although marginal, the weather had been VFR when he filed for the 100-mile flight to Cordova from Cape Yakatogo. Sometimes it gets a little chancy forecasting Alaskan coastal weather. This had been one of those times. The high winds and snow had not been expected.

Halfway to his destination, the pilot called Cordova Flight Service for a DF steer (a ground-based system employed at selected FAA facilities which gives the operator a compass bearing to an aircraft transmitting on an assigned frequency). Mrs. Jo King—who had been flying since she was 13—was at the air/ground operating position. She gave the requested steer and then made several periodic checks on the aircraft's progress. Suddenly, the pilot radioed the chilling news. Jo's years of experience as an instructor and bush pilot in the Alaskan wilds immediately told her what was occurring. Whiteout—that condition when the sky and earth blend together in one unending glare of white. No horizon, nothing except the instruments to provide an attitude cue. Nine out of 10 times a pilot without instrument experience caught in a whiteout would immediately go into that deadly graveyard spiral.

This was no time to project the image of calm, cool deliberation from the safety of her communications room. Gut instincts said the pilot needed to be jolted and jolted hard.

There are several different accounts as to just what words Jo King used to accomplish her objective. One account describes her as using an "expletive" (this term became popular among writers during Watergate). Another account allows as how Jo used a couple of "hells" and "damns." It is probable, however, that the situation required even more explicit language. Thing is, Jo King was up to using whatever language was necessary—and did. Giving the four-letter words a second or two to have effect she followed them with:

"Turn loose! Now level the wings. Then bring the nose up."

Now she held her breath. It seemed like hours although it could not have been more than a few more seconds.

A frightened voice from the 180 told her the aircraft had been righted and the airspeed was coming down. Then the pilot added that when he pulled up he "bounced the wheels on the ground." It had been a squeaker, all right! But, he wasn't home free yet. Jo still had to get him to Cordova and safely on the ground.

FLIGHT SERVICE

Since the pilot indicated he now could see some trees, Jo recommended he circle until she could get a fix on his position. The DF gives a bearing from the station but does not provide any information on distance. If she could get a good description of the area from the pilot with her own intimate knowledge of the terrain and the DF bearing, she could establish a good fix and then instruct the pilot how to navigate—always keeping the ground in sight—from that point.

As the 180 circled, its pilot relaxed. He began giving Jo a feature-by-feature report of the terrain beneath him. Soon the picture formed in her mind. Along the west shore of the river delta just south of the place where the Copper River highway hopscotches its way island-to-island over a 10-mile expanse of water—that's where the Cessna was. Just to the north of the highway, glacier ridges and mountains reared to 6,000 feet.

"Don't cross the highway or bridge," she told the pilot, "and keep an eye on the bank-and-turn and artificial horizon (to prevent again falling into a deadly high speed spiral)."

Weather often seems to have substance—a malicious, implacable spirit—when it comes to unlucky airmen who fall into its clutches. It is jealous of its victims; refuses to give them up; throws the book at them. This was one of those days. Gale winds, blinding snow, the whiteout had not been enough. Thanks to his own training and the consummate skill of Jo King the Cessna 180 still was flying—and toward safety. It was time for weather to deliver the Sunday punch—ice.

The first indication—the airspeed indicator began to go squirrely. Pitot ice. Then, the telltale buildup on the wings. The airspeed now crept down. Full power and extreme nose-up trim. The Cessna staggered through the air. The pilot added flap to try and reduce the stall speed.

Just when it appeared nothing would keep the aircraft in the air, the road leading to the Cordova airport hove into sight. Gratefully, the pilot let the ice-laden craft have its way—go down. The road gave way to the runway. He gently powered it onto the concrete, closed the throttle, let it roll out and breathed a sigh of relief. In the Cordova FSS, Jo King echoed that sigh.

There can be no question but what flying in Alaska is rewarding in more ways than one. First, the dearth of railroad mileage and the weather which significantly inhibits movement by automobile and truck along the relatively limited highway system during much of the year, make the airplane a must. In more cases than not, it is the only way short of slogging overland on foot or by dog sled that man can travel to and from many parts of the state. Second, the Alaskan panorama when seen from the air is perhaps the most breathtaking in the world, certainly on the North American Continent. Thus, flying in Alaska also is esthetically satisfying. But, notwithstanding the beauty, flying in Alaska, even in the summer, pits the airman against a threatening and often hostile combination of terrain and weather.

Take that drizzly day when a charter pilot took off from Lake Hood in his float-equipped Cessna 185 with a 65-year-old passenger bound for a lake "somewhere to the west" across the Aleutian Range. As the pilot maneuvered through Clark Pass he found it closed.

Calling Kenai Radio, he worked out an alternate route with Flight Service Specialist Charles Bliss—routine for Alaskan bush pilots and routine for the FSS personnel who regularly shepherd them from point to point. For the next

CLEARED TO LAND!

30 minutes Bliss continued his watch working several aircraft providing weather, taking PIREPS (pilot weather reports on actual flight conditions) and recording position reports from aircraft on flight plans. Suddenly the speaker blared:

"I need help!"

"That's all he said," Bliss recalls, 'that's what electrified us. He didn't know where he was. He sounded quite scared. He said he'd had a little bit of float plane experience 25 years ago. I asked him how high he was and I think he said 8,200 feet. He said he could see some water through a hole in the clouds straight below."

The pilot had suffered a heart attack and was dead or dying. His elderly passenger, who fortunately had some flying experience even though it had been more than two decades before, now was in command of the big seaplane.

Bliss immediately got a DF fix on the aircraft. It was on the west side of Cook Inlet with only tossing sea below.

"I couldn't put him down," Bliss relates, "it was windy out there and that float plane would capsize immediately. I told him to circle down until I could head him for Kenai—he couldn't even read his compass—and I just kept talking to him, asking how he was doing just to keep him on the horn.

"When I saw he was flying the way I wanted him to fly, I didn't care what his compass read. 'Just fly the way you're doing,' I told him. I knew he was out there. I knew he was coming. That's all I needed to know."

Now Bliss began having the passenger-turned-pilot make gentle banks, describing to him certain landmarks.

"Pretty soon you're going to see a big bluff and to your right side the mouth of a river. Turn left there and follow the highway for a couple of miles and then you'll see a lake. Land on the lake. There'll be a state trooper and doctor waiting for you there . . ."

"I've got the bluff," the passenger told him, "I see the lake. I got the highway. Which way shall I land?"

"Look for the wind lines on the water," Bliss told him, "land into those—to the west. Put your wing flaps down about 20 degrees and watch your trim . . ."

That was the last Bliss heard from the Cessna 185. A Cessna 206 from Andy's Flying Service at Kenai watched the touchdown and radioed the news:

"Well, Kenai, he got on the water. He broke a float but he's got it to shore!"

Annette Island is on the southern tip of the Alaska panhandle. Its airport is situated on a spur of land barely five miles across. It has a single runway 7,500 feet long with approaches from either direction over open sea. The field elevation is 119 feet but only five miles away loom 3,000-to-4,000-foot mountains. It was snowing and foggy with an "indefinite 400-foot ceiling and three quarters of a mile visibility" when Henry Bayeur, then working the FSS alone, received an inbound IFR flight plan from Anchorage Center. The aircraft was Twin Bonanza 213 Delta with a pilot and a single passenger.

For an experienced instrument pilot, particularly one who is wise to the ways of Alaskan flying, the situation wasn't too hairy. Not unless you take into account that just moments before severe weather had knocked out Annette VOR and the compass locater (a low frequency, non-directional radio transmitter marking the final approach fix for the VOR approach). There was no radar or ILS available. Bayeur did have VHF/DF but under the cir-

FLIGHT SERVICE

Flight Service Station at Mason City, Iowa, is typical of the more than 340 across the country and in Alaska which provide pilots with weather and flight planning information and where Flight Service Specialists provide air-to-ground communications in some of the wildest and remotest areas of the nation.

cumstances it was almost like having no help at all.

At first Bayeur recommended alternate airports—Sitka, Alaska and Sand Spit, British Columbia. The pilot, however, had his own troubles. The light twin was taking on a heavy load of rime ice, one engine was running rough from carburetor ice and the automatic direction finder was out. At least with the ADF the pilot could have provided cross bearings along the DF track provided by Bayeur so both he and the Flight Service specialist could keep track of the Bonanza's progress. With the ice, the pilot said he could not take a chance on another airport. He was coming to Annette and had "no choice." Bayeur also had little choice—he had to get him down.

Bayeur got a DF bearing on the Bonanza and instructed the pilot to make frequent transmissions so he could continuously check the bearing. Meanwhile he kept a close check on the weather and arranged for snow removal equipment to be removed from the runways. He also continued to check with the electronics technicians on repair of the ailing navaids. Runway and approach lights were turned up to their maximum brilliance.

That old Alaskan weather devil saw the Bonanza and its two occupants slipping away so he tightened the screws and called in some more "electronic gremlins" for assistance. He lowered the ceiling to 200 feet. He increased ice build-up on the aircraft to the point the pilot said he could not climb to reach another airport "under any conditions" and probably would find it touch-and-go if he could not make the DF approach on the first try. The gremlins then put the localizer and the TACAN out of service.

Bayeur had his hands as full as those of the pilot—checking on removal of the heavy equipment, continuing to check with the technicians on status of the NAVAIDS, constantly checking weather for the latest report, checking braking action on the runway (a truck reported it to be "nil"). One eye on the clock to check the projected progress of the aircraft along the inbound bearing, Bayeur said a silent prayer that he could bring it off.

Now! The clock hand indicated the aircraft should be nearly overhead. He instructed the pilot to look over the right side for a sign of the airport lights. He waited. It seemed like forever. Then:

"13 Delta has the lights," came the call.

Two minutes later the aircraft was on the runway and despite the lack of braking action was brought safely to a halt. Before 10 minutes had elapsed, Bayeur had a grateful pilot and passenger in the FSS pouring out words of thanks. The flight service specialist extended a few words of thanks himself—to the pilot for being a "first class professional" and making the difficult approach under the "worst possible conditions."

You don't need to be flying in Alaska or be a general aviation pilot to need help. Sometimes you can be an Australian student in a Navy A-4 Skyhawk jet over Florida. That's the way it was on a quiet December afternoon in 1969.

The student and instructor were on a high-speed, low-level training flight out of the Navy's big Pensacola flight training base. A bird strike—apparently a large, heavy fowl—ripped off the canopy, smashed vital flight instruments, injured the instructor to the point he was unable to continue to command the aircraft and scattered charts and equipment overboard.

In the ensuing chaos, the pilot activated the dual ejection mechanism and punched himself out, expecting the student to do likewise. In the rear, the ejection seat jammed, trapping the student in the cockpit. Gus Kosik, Tallahassee

FLIGHT SERVICE

FSS specialist, was at the air/ground position when the call came in:
"Mayday! Mayday!"

Kosik immediately established radio contact with the student and at the same time got a DF bearing of 50 degrees on the stricken aircraft. On the hot line to the Albany, Ga., FSS, he requested a second bearing for triangulation. The two bearings placed the A-4 near the western edge of Lake Miccosukee, 22 miles northeast of Tallahassee.

To say the least, the unlucky student was extremely upset. With the canopy gone, the slipstream lashed through the cockpit area. Every directional instrument was out. The young man had no idea of the heading of his jet or of the location of the nearest airfield. But he had both the presence of mind and the courage to be concerned about the fate of his instructor who had ejected. The student refused to leave the area even when given directions until he was reassured by Kosik that the downed pilot's position was known and a search was being instigated.

Kosik, himself a veteran pilot, sized up the situation and decided the best thing would be to talk the student in. Since the pilot had no means of navigation, Kosik told him to fly directly into the sun. That would bring him within sight of Tallahassee. Once he could identify the city, he should be able to see the airport. Kosik continued to monitor the aircraft position (bearing from the FSS) with the DF and within 10 minutes the A-4 reported over the city. From there it was a "piece of cake" for the student to set the Skyhawk safely down. The student lost no time jumping from his jet into a patrol plane departing on the search for his instructor. Fortunately, and due largely to Kosik's quick action, the instructor was located from the air just as the last rays of the setting sun illuminated the landscape. Soon a ground party arrived where he was suspended in a clump of trees. Doctors at a nearby hospital completed the "save" some hours later.

Safe operation of an aircraft requires that the pilot's senses not be impaired and that he have a clear mind with the physical capability to act quickly as the mind directs. In other words, he cannot function properly under the influence of alcohol, drugs, lack of sufficient rest or—the effects of carbon monoxide poisoning.

In an aircraft as in any vehicle powered by an internal combustion engine the possibility of carbon monoxide invading the passenger compartment is ever present. Although this problem occurs infrequently, it has occurred often enough for the FAA to make a serious study of the situation—its causes as well as its effects. Results of this study and recommendations to pilots were included in an article in the October 1963 issue of FAA Aviation News. Flight Service Specialist Preston Gautier had finished reading the article just before going on shift at the air/ground console in the Alexandria, La., FSS. One paragraph in the article made a special impression on Gautier, the one describing the symptoms.

"The first symptom of carbon monoxide poisoning is a feeling of tightness across the forehead usually accompanied by a slight headache. As the poisoning becomes more severe, the headache increases and there is a throbbing in the temple. Next, there may be severe headache, general weakness, dizziness and dimming of vision. Then, there is a decided loss of muscular power, vomiting, convulsions and coma. The pulse gradually weakens and the respiratory rate slows until there is a complete respiratory failure and death."

CLEARED TO LAND!

This grim picture hovered in the back of Gautier's mind as he took a call from a 24-year-old student pilot and owner of a handsome Luscombe Silvaire. The pilot was familiar to Gautier and a regular user of the services provided by the FSS. He asked for a weather briefing and filed a VFR flight plan from Buhlow Lake Airport at Alexandria to Baton Rouge some 90 miles to the southeast. He advised Gautier he was climbing to 5,500 feet.

Specialist transmits the latest weather information to a pilot flying in range of Washington National FSS.

Some 10 minutes later the pilot reported an altitude. He also said he felt dizzy and was experiencing blurred vision. Instantly those carbon monoxide symptoms flashed across Gautier's mind. He warned the pilot to immediately turn off the cabin heater (most cabin heaters are of the manifold type where fresh air is ducted through a chamber constructed around a hot exhaust stack where it is heated and distributed to the passenger compartment), open a window and descend to 2,500 feet. Based on the Luscombe's time of departure, course and speed, Gautier estimated it was just about 10 miles short of Marksville Airport. He alerted the Louisiana State Police to have an ambulance standby at Marksville and then directed the pilot to the field. Just seven minutes after the nature of the emergency became apparent, the Luscombe was on the ground at Marksville and the pilot was on the way to a local hospital for treatment. As the situation had developed the accuracy of Gautier's estimate became more evident. When he made the approach to Marksville, the pilot complained of numbness and muscle spasms in his arms and legs and a severe pain in his left ear. At the hospital, doctors quickly confirmed that, indeed, the culprit had been carbon monoxide. Gautier's immediate recognition of the symptoms and the instructions he gave saved the young pilot's life.

On April 9, 1971, Flight Service Specialist Richard Cox on duty alone at the Parkersburg, Va., FSS, found out that there can be a lot of truth in the old adage, "It never rains but what it pours." That shift it poured emergencies for Cox.

116

FLIGHT SERVICE

Specialist in North Philadelphia FSS provides a VHF/DF steer to a pilot who isn't exactly sure of his location and that of his destination airport.

At 7:04 P.M., he got a call from a Cessna 172, lost, short of fuel and asking for assistance to get to Parkersburg. Cox took a DF fix on the aircraft, gave the pilot instructions for a course to fly and warned him to stay clear of a thunderstorm nearby. The assist progressed routinely; the pilot following instructions exactly with Cox giving minimum course corrections.

Two minutes later—another lost Cessna 172. This one had been forced off course from North Carolina to Ohio and needed a DF steer to Parkersburg, where he planned to wait out the increasingly bad weather in the area. Despite considerable interference on the radio, Cox got a bearing on the second aircraft and directed him to fly 270 degrees. The flight service specialist now had two birds to watch over.

"Mayday! Mayday! I'm lost. Help!" The time was 7:12 P.M., just eight minutes since the first call for assistance. It was a Cherokee transmitting but Cox couldn't establish contact with it. The pilot kept calling for help and in the background Cox could hear children crying.

He alerted the DF network (several stations with DF capability in a common geographic area that work as a team). Charleston FSS was able to contact the pilot and provide a bearing to that station but Cox would have to continue to monitor its progress on his DF scope. Three to keep track of.

Six minutes had gone by since the Mayday but for the busy flight service specialist it seemed like only six seconds. Now—the station clock showed 7:18 P.M.—another emergency. A third Cessna, this one a twin-engine 310, was caught in rain and turbulence. He had lost all his radios except for a single VOR. He could transmit but could only receive on the VOR frequency. Cox gave him a DF steer to the airport. Since the pilot could not talk directly with the tower, the flight service specialist—now as busy as the proverbial cat on a hot tin roof—had to relay landing and clearance information. Since the pilot was instrument rated this assist came a little easier.

CLEARED TO LAND!

There are a few areas of the United States where a pilot cannot find a voice—Flight Service Specialist ready with whatever the pilot requires even if it is just a friendly word to break the boredom of a long flight.

At 7:24 P.M. a fourth Cessna asked for weather at Akron, Ohio, but indicated no problem. Meanwhile, the first two Cessnas got safely on the ground. The 310 was okay. Only the Cherokee was still in the air. Cox relaxed, but not for long. Now the fourth Cessna radioed that he had sick children on board and needed an immediate DF steer to Parkersburg. Cox put him on the proper heading and within four minutes the pilot reported he had the airport in sight.

The Cherokee was still up there. During the last two emergencies—in his "spare" time— Cox had contacted pilots who might help the Cherokee. One of these was a Piper twin-engine Navajo. Cox arranged for Charleston Approach to vector the Navajo to the vicinity of the Cherokee. The twin located the smaller aircraft and flying wing on it escorted it to a safe landing at Charleston. Time: 9:02 P.M. One hour and 58 minutes had elapsed since the first call for help. Cox had handled five emergencies—any one of which could ultimately have caused multiple fatalities—in less than two hours. It is understood that the rest of Cox's shift "went quietly." By the next day, it seemed just "all in a night's work."

The annals of the flight service specialist throughout the history of the FAA and its antecedent organizations is jammed with accounts like these, accounts that read like the wildest concoctions of the television screen writer. FSS stories are just as dramatic, just as exciting, just as hair-raising as those told by the controllers. Thus it isn't hard to understand why the flight service specialist feels a little like a second class citizen within the ranks of the air traffic system. The grade structure (Civil Service pay grades) for the men and women who man the more than 340 flight service stations work out across the board to be approximately one grade below that of the air traffic controller at each proficiency or experience level. Traditionally, FAA management took the position that the primary duties of the flight service specialist—observing and reporting weather, communications (point-to-point as well as air-to-ground); handling flight plans and progress reports; providing weather briefings and other information affecting flight—did not involve the same level of complexity as the duties of the controller. In the broadest sense of the word, this philosophy may have an element of truth. But you're never going to sell it to the flight service specialist.

Important to the flying public is that, notwithstanding the fact the flight service specialist feels he is put upon by the system, he (and this is the "editorial he" since women have been an integral part of the service since its inception) is sustained by an impressive level of pride in his job and the manner in which he performs it. This, in great part, can be attributed to the fact that the flight service specialist knows that his particular role historically has been the backbone of the entire air traffic system.

The air traffic system began with a network of landing fields established for the airmail manned by caretakers who would set out the kerosene flares when an aircraft was inbound. Next came the intermediate or emergency fields. Then the big acetylene beacons marking the airways to be followed by the electric beacons, each with its own emergency power generator and a man to operate it. Crude radio, at first point-to-point passing weather information and airplane departure and arrival times and later providing air/ground communications, was next on the list of evolutionary developments. In the '30s the low frequency radio range came into existence and remained the mainstay for aerial navigation until the 1960s. In most cases, a flight service station—then called an Interstate Airways Communications Station or INSAC—was associated with a low frequency range. Today the "low freqa" are gone and VOR is the mode. An FSS still can be associated with each and every VOR either directly or remotely.

Dale Heister of Santa Barbara, Calif., a retired flight service expert, also is considered to be the unofficial historian of the system. In his history, which has been in the works for some seven years(he hopes to have it published soon), Dale writes of the original "Air Mail Radio Station" that "several name changes occured during the first 50 years of existence, however, one word was never changed . . . station!"

"Outwardly," he continues, "the stations bore a family resemblance . . . small, wooden, box-like buildings set on a cement slab at an airport. Wooden, lattice-work towers and poles . . . some as much as 100 feet high . . . were used for the suspension of the long-wire antennae.

"Station interiors were even less impressive than the exteriors . . . in fact, they were quite primitive. Walls were generally bare boards; there were several windows and light bulbs dangled from the ceiling. One portion of the room was set aside for use as the 'operating position.' The remainder of the space served as repository for tools and other paraphernalia required in the day-to-day conduct of air mail business.

"The operating position was usually nothing more than a homemade work bench occupying one wall . . . and occasionally extending partially along another wall. The most dominant feature at the position was a squat, ugly monstrosity resembling a short, steel barrel with a lid. Sprouting from the top and sides was an assortment of knobs, garden hose, water pipes and other articles of hardware. Despite its appearance, this was one of the most important pieces of equipment in the station along with the radio receivers. It was a two-kilowatt 'Federal' type arc radio transmitter—shipboard type obtained from the Shipping Board."

According to Heister, the "station staff" consisted of one man—a radio operator. He transmitted and received weather reports, airplane arrival and departure messages, air mail administrative traffic and often was required to handle traffic for other government agencies—like "agricultural crop reports." He also was his own carpenter, plumber, radio repairman and exterminator—rattle snakes and scorpions in the southwest, water moccasins in the deep south, wolves in the northwest and mosquitos, flies and roaches all over.

"He stood," Heister writes, "split shifts in order to be available at the airport during flight schedules. For example, he might start the day at 4:30 A.M., and work for a few hours . . . be off the remainder of the day and return at 4 P.M., for another four hours or more. A work week covered seven days and although annual vacations were 'authorized' they were seldom obtained due to lack of money to hire a relief operator. The base pay normally was less than $2,000 per annum (a lot less) . . . and there was frequent 'non-paying' overtime."

The money didn't improve much with years either. Ralph Vroman, now retired, began his air traffic career at Douglas, Ariz., as an "under communications operator" with the Bureau of Air Commerce in 1938. His salary—$100 a month. Basic requirements for entry was a passing grade on the general entrance exam and the ability to type 50 words per minute. The typing capability was, of course, in connection with the need to communicate station-to-station by teletype. If the applicant held an amateur radio operator's license or a pilot's license, he could qualify for a higher grade. At Douglas, Vroman's duties included monitoring the Tucson low frequency range three minutes out of each hour to insure it was operating properly, making hourly weather observations and "specials" as necessary, monitoring the weather and notices to airmen (NOTAM) broadcasts and occasionally handling missing aircraft notifications.

"As far as general aviation aircraft were concerned," Vroman recalls, "they rarely had equipment to fly the ranges. They usually followed the railroads and highways which also were few and far between in those days. More often than not they led the pilots right into Mexico. We had a lot of airplanes that wandered into Mexico. Some never came out."

From Douglas, Ralph was posted to Beowawe, Nev., 60 miles south and west of Elko. As Vroman recalls, this was "really no man's land."

"We had the 'K' type watchhouse," he says, "one building with family quarters—usually for the station chief—on one side, bachelor's quarters on the other and the operating room in the center room. We actually had a lot of time off. Paul Rainey and I kept a trap line. We got a lot of crows and rabbits but nary a coyote. It got cold, real cold, in that country and we had ice fogs. It would be 45 below and you couldn't see your hand in front of your face. The Indians called it the 'white death.'

"In addition to operating, we had to keep everything going. There was a lot of improvisation. At one time we had to substitute a washing machine motor for the motor that turned the discs in the range identifier. Also, we had to keep track of everything we used, every part, regardless of how small. We even had to record in the log the replacement of a three-cent fuse."

Vroman also remembers how it was when the station first got equipment for ground-to-air voice communications.

"The microphones scared us to death," he laughs. "We hoped against hope that no one would call."

Ralph finally learned to send and receive the International telegraph code at a speed of 30 words a minute. This qualified him as a full-fledged radio operator and a transfer to Ash Fork, Ariz., where, he remembers, "we had no water, cooked on a wood fire and had to saw up our own firewood from telephone poles." Vroman particularly recalls the beginnings of realtime air traffic control by radio and the establishment of the controller job position.

"With the advent of ATC," he grumbles, "a sort of super society was formed. The controller wouldn't even speak to a lowly communicator. The communicator was someone to whom he looked down his nose."

In 1952, Ralph "bridged the gap" and moved into air traffic control. From there he continued upward along the career ladder ultimately serving in several top management and planning positions at the regional level. Now in real estate, Vroman still vividly recalls how the invisible barrier between the flight service specialist and the air traffic controller began. Even in the 1950s the relative "responsibilities" faced in FSS duty versus active traffic control still seemed to justify the pay grade gap. A few excerpts from the station log from Lone Rock, Wisc., are graphic evidence of the vast difference in flight service and controller duty just 20 years ago.

"1-30-51 Record low temperature - 53 degrees.
This station was commissioned about 1932.
Station well from bottom of pump pipe: water level 4'7" down 28' to bottom of well."

"1-30-56 New stove installed in INSACS by Coast & Coast store of Richland Center. Kruse also on job and took down old stove the R/O (radio operator) had sent here earlier this fall. The new stove is a Siegler . . . The cost of the new stove was $290.00 less $50.00 for trade-in of old stove and $12.50 for not needing a new thermostat or cost $227.50 net to CAA."

"2-6-56 Field lights - N3836N pilot R. L. Mohns of Damascus Steel Products, Rockford, got to about Broadhead and due to weather had to reverse course and land at Lone Rock by aid of field lights."

"2-29-56 Station water pump failed this morning. Seems to be in pump as motor is okay. I had suggested to maintenance inspector within last few weeks pump should be checked over as it had not been done for a long time. But no action was taken. Called Greenbeck Hardware at Lone Rock to work on pump at 8:30 A.M."

"3-5-56 Rosemary Baker returned to duty today after maternity leave."

No, things were not very exciting at flight service stations even as recent as 20 years ago. But, the important thing was they were there when they were needed. Two University of Minnesota educators were extremely grateful to the men and women of Lone Rock FSS in 1964. They expressed it this way in

CLEARED TO LAND!

a letter to Gaylord Trumbel, then station chief.

> "This letter is in the form of many thanks for the help you and your staff gave to Dr. Dan Weiner and myself today. We especially want to thank Mr. Carl Waszak for his excellent directions in 'talking' us down. Without his patient handling of our distress ('emergency') we no doubt would have ended up putting our plane down in the trees on some forsaken ridge.
>
> "It takes a case of poor judgment, bad weather or something similar really to bring home the importance of stations like yours to the average pilot. This is especially important when one flies over an area like Lone Rock and the flight service stations are the only assist available to small aircraft in getting them out of a bind.
>
> "Again, many thanks to you and your staff and to the proprietor of the ground maintenance and service facility at Tri-Airport. From now on when I fly over and check in with you I'll give a '. . . many thanks, 52 Tango,' for example, and then you'll know the man who always checks NOTAMS and the Airman's G just passed over.
>
> "Sincerely,
>
> "Karl R. Kelly Nicholas, M.D.
>   Research Fellow
>
> "Daniel E. Weiner, M.D.
>   Instructor, Physiology"

A talk with Ruth Dennis at the San Diego, Calif., FSS not only sheds more light on the beginnings of the service but also provides an authoritative view of an FSS circa 1975. Ruth, who has been with the FAA (and its predecessor organizations) for more than 30 years is chief of the San Diego station, one of the busiest in the nation. She became the first woman chief of an FSS in 1971.

The "Number 2 daughter" in a tribe of five children with a widowed mother, Ruth had to think in terms of gainful employment at an early age. Originally from Boston, the family moved to California—then believed to be the "land of opportunity"—where she managed to hold down a job and still establish a creditable record in school.

"I was studying to be a laboratory technician," she recalls, "but I didn't like to take blood out of people. I saw an advertisement for CAA traffic controllers. The agency then was hiring 3,000 women. The requirements included two years of college, which I had, and it looked a heck of a lot better than sticking needles in people for the rest of my life."

Ruth's goal of being a controller didn't pan out because of a talent she didn't know she had—a talent for high speed code operation. In those days most point-to-point communications—weather forecasts, flight plans, progress reports—still went by CW (continuous wave, a mode of radio communications transmitted by dots and dashes in the International Code). Ruth turned out to be a whiz at CW so, along with two other women who also had shown an affinity for CW, she found herself on the way to Lucin, Utah, not as a controller but as a radio operator. Lucin is one place she will never forget.

"It is 60 miles north of Wendover, Utah, in the middle of nowhere," she remembers vividly, "in fact, I was so out of touch with the world I didn't know when World War II was over until the pilot of a passing airplane told me.

"Well, the other girls were Dore' Seeley and Jean Willett. Dore' had been a professional dancer attracted to the 'glamour' of air traffic and the need to serve during the war in some 'important' capacity. Jean came to the CAA right out of college. For us the glamour turned into Lucin Crossroads. Our 'government' quarters were a rickety frame building of some 600 square feet. The chief and his family lived in a separate building. One thing I remember was the heating system. We supposedly had an 'oil' furnace—one big hole in the floor where the heat came out. You could roast near the vent and freeze near the wall. And it got 10 to 20 below zero in the winter. Summer was no better. It went over 100 degrees and there was no air conditioning of any kind. You can believe that when we arrived at Lucin the tennis rackets, bathing suits and sports clothes we brought were out of place."

Ruth had another tale to tell which provides a graphic picture of the relationship those first women controllers and radio operators had with their male counterparts—particularly the supervisory level. Kiyi, Ruth's little mixed-breed terrier, had a part in this drama.

"The first thing I did on arriving," Ruth relates, "was to go over to report to the facility chief."

"I understand you're from Boston," he said.

"Yes, sir," I replied.

"I've never liked people from Boston," he declared, adding, "or women operators."

As Ruth remembers it, their relationship deteriorated rapidly from that point with Kiyi's help.

"The pup, you have to remember," she says, "had just finished an upsetting 60-mile ride in an open jeep. It was hot as hell. It was bumpy. None of us felt too well, Kiyi especially.

"I asked the chief if it would be all right if I brought Kiyi over to stand watch with me."

"Is he a well behaved dog?" he asked.

"Certainly," I answered, "she's housebroken. Wouldn't you know, that was the time the hot, bumpy ride caught up with her. She got sick and threw up all over the chief's foot."

Things finally shook down to the point where Ruth earned her chief's grudging respect. It was a location where traffic (especially military traffic out of Ogden's Hill Army Air Field and Salt Lake City's two airports serving the Army Air Force 18th Replacement Wing) was heavy filing for Hamilton Field in California and the Pacific Theater of Operations. Still things began to go smoothly. Ruth, Dore' and Jean all began to feel that "this is no big deal." Then one day a C-47 with engine trouble made an emergency landing at Lucin.

"The pilot asked if 'they' could come up for a cup of coffee," Ruth recalls, "and when 23 of them walked in suddenly, at the grand old age of 19, I realized I was in the business of saving lives. It was sort of spooky to say the least."

Ruth got a couple more "good assignments" before the war ended, including one at Baker near Death Valley. Again, except for the chief who Ruth recalls "really knew how to manage people," it was an all-woman station. They lived in quarters attached to the operating room and the single, window air conditioner kept breaking down in the 120-degree summer heat.

With the war over and the men coming home, it no longer seemed the "patriotic thing to do" so many women left the CAA. Ruth Dennis was not among them. She got posted to Los Angeles where, she says, she turned out to be somewhat of a know-it-all.

CLEARED TO LAND!

"After all, I'd been with CAA throughout the big war," she smiles, "and now was assigned to one of the really important stations. I knew everything there was to know, or so I thought.

"One day a pilot came into the station to file a flight plan from LAX to San Diego. I help him—making very sure he 'filled out the flight plan correctly.' And then I showed him 'how to read the teletype weather forecast properly.' The pilot was flying a B-25 and filed at 2,000 feet. It was Feb. 9, 1947, and the time was 9:54 P.M. I know because I still have that flight plan. I kept it as my lesson in humility. The signature on the flight plan reads: Jimmy Doolittle."

Today, Ruth supervises a staff of 28 men and women manning a station which stands among the nation's top 10 percent in terms of traffic load. There are 12 general aviation airfields, five with FAA towers, in San Diego's area of responsibility. In addition, the station has a heavy military workload generated by the Navy's North Island, Miramar and Imperial Beach air stations and the Marine Corps Air Facility at Camp Pendleton. Since San Diego is the home of the Pacific Fleet, there usually is heavy carrier training in progress off the coast. There also are some 8,000 'hometown' pilots in San Diego County who contribute their share to the 440,000 flight operations a year handled by the San Diego FSS.

Ruth's facility has one additional workload, one that isn't shared even by other key stations in critical transition areas like Miami, New York, Seattle and New Orleans. San Diego handles approximately 800 border-crossing flight plans to Mexico each month. The majority of these are to Baja California, an area rapidly developing as a major fishing and vacation mecca for "norte americanos." Traffic to this area increased by 15 percent in just 24 months and still is on the rise. Where they used to primarily constitute a winter workload, now they are consistently high year around.

One thing, according to Ruth Dennis, U.S. pilots do not realize is that a flight plan in Mexico is an administrative exercise. It is used only to record a departure and arrival of the aircraft. It is not used to determine if an aircraft is overdue or down. It provides no search and rescue alert. For this reason, Ruth has instituted what she calls a "baby sitting program." U.S. pilots bound for Mexico are urged to file a "round robin" flight plan with San Diego FSS, giving the route to be flown to and from the Mexican destination and an estimate of when and where the pilot plans to return to the U.S. In other words, he provides San Diego FSS with a "SAR time"—a time he specifies when search and rescue procedures are to be instituted (and requested of the Mexican government) if he has not reported back across the border.

"In fact," Ruth explains, "we urge all pilots flying south to Mexico to take time and stop at Lindberg Field (San Diego) and get a thorough briefing from our people before they cross the border. More and more pilots are taking us up on our offer."

Most of the regular and special services San Diego FSS provides the flying public are not unlike those provided by the other 339 across the nation. Each station—big ones like San Diego and small ones like Lone Rock—provide the basics, weather observation and preflight briefing, in-flight communications, flight plan handling and, perhaps most important, emergency assistance. From each station the pilot also can expect special types of information and assistance resulting from locally-generated programs geared to flight requirements indigenous to that area and its unique geographic, climatological or traffic characteristics.

After all, Ruth Dennis realized more years ago than she likes to remember,—"FSS people are in the business of saving lives!"

From the early days, women have found a rewarding place in the Flight Service Station.

CLEARED TO LAND!

The Flight Service Specialist doesn't always work in a sophisticated environment like this one at the South Bend, Ind., FSS. Sometimes they must make-do like these specialists manning a temporary FSS at the annual Merced, Calif., antique fly-in.

7 APPROACH

A Beechcraft Baron is two tons of sophisticated, twin-engine aircraft—a lot of aircraft for a skilled pilot to handle especially in marginal weather, weather like that in the Gulf Coast area of Louisiana the October day in 1972 when Fred Laird and Raborn Bruce were working Shreveport Approach Control.

The Shreveport Regional Airport was reporting on-and-off instrument conditions—overcast, dense clouds, rain showers. Occasionally, the weather would go VFR, but mostly remained suitable only for instrument operations.

In addition to the normal workload, funneling aircraft from the enroute segments where they were under ARTCC control into the Shreveport approach patterns, controlling departures and providing separation between the IFR aircraft and the occasional VFR bird wending its way through the control zone between rain squalls, the controllers were monitoring a new ARTS III radar computer system which had not yet been commissioned. All-in-all it was a busy day.

In the Baron's right seat when it reported 15 miles east of Shreveport was a middle-aged, non-aviator, James Crosby. At the controls was his 59-year-old friend, a thoroughly competent pilot. Baron 612 Hotel reported at 5,000 feet "in-and-out of clouds" and was instructed to descend first to 3,000 and subsequently to 1,700 for the Shreveport approach. The pilot responded that he was leaving 3,000 for 1,700.

Laird waited a moment or two then instructed the Baron:

"Turn left heading two one zero. Your position five miles north of the outer marker."

No reply.

"Baron 612 Hotel," Laird transmitted again. "Copy?"

Still no reply. The blip that was the Baron still marked the scope. It was still traveling in the right direction at the same speed. Bruce, the journeyman controller of the team (Laird then was a developmental controller), checked the communications equipment. The controllers changed transmitters and tried again. Still no reply from the Baron. Then, suddenly:

"Someone come in. Someone please come in! I'm in a Baron and my pilot just had a heart attack!"

"Is this the Baron coming to Regional Airport?" Laird asked.

"Coming into Shreveport, right," was the frantic reply.

"Do you know anything about flying the aircraft?" Laird shot back.

"I don't know anything!" Crosby answered.

The problem that faced the controllers at Shreveport Approach appeared one without a solution. There seemed to be only one possible conclusion to the situation—the Baron would soon plunge to earth taking with it the pilot and passenger and wrecking havoc on the ground if it struck in a populated area.

Laird and Bruce refused to accept this conclusion and, as it later developed, Crosby also refused to accept what seemed to be inevitable.

Over the next few minutes the controllers calmly and clearly gave Crosby a crash course on how to keep the Baron in the air, flying straight and level, and then making gentle turns. The next step—get him making easy throttle adjustments keeping his eyes on the airspeed. At the same time they carefully

asked pertinent questions. How high was he? Could he see the ground? How much fuel aboard? Crosby responded—he was at 1,600 feet, he could see the ground and there was about half a tank of fuel remaining.

Although the ARTS III system at Shreveport still was in the shakedown stage, Laird and Bruce used it to good effect. The flag associated with Baron 612 Hotel not only gave them position but, because of the computer, continually provided airspeed information. This way the controllers constantly could monitor this critical value from the ground cautioning their "student" in the Baron to give the airplane more throttle when necessary. In a short time they had to throw a lot all at once at a man who knew nothing about the airplane or what kept it in the air.

"Baron 612 Hotel, your airspeed is dissipating. Add a little more power and keep your wings level. Keep your airspeed at approximately 130 knots," Laird told him.

"How do I keep my wings level?" Crosby asked. From his speaker the confident voice of Shreveport Approach counseled:

"Okay. If you see the horizon, look at both wing tips and make sure you have the same distance above the horizon on both wings. Open the throttle up to about 130 knots. Do you know where the throttle is? That's the lever in the middle of the console. Push forward on the throttle to increase the airspeed."

In the Baron, Crosby found himself doing a slow roller coaster as he tried to keep the airplane level and expressed his concern to Approach.

"You're doing fine," he was advised. "Did you increase your airspeed?"

Crosby replied in the affirmative and at the same time Laird and Bruce saw the radar tag on the ARTS III screen indicate 130 knots. For another minute or two they had Crosby identify different instruments on the panel and their readings—RPM indicator, manifold pressure, etc. These he would have to watch during the next phase of the hoped-for rescue effort. First, they had to get the plane out of the busy Shreveport traffic area and to a higher altitude, one in relatively clear weather. They selected an open area west of Shreveport and began to vector the Baron toward it.

"612 Hotel," Laird called, "maintain reference to the ground and, if you can, begin a slow turn to your left. Keep a shallow turn to your left and I will let you know when to roll out."

He looked at the scope. The Baron was slowly changing course. He continued:

"Very good. Just remain calm and maintain contact with the ground."

Finally, Baron 612 Hotel was flying relatively straight and level in clear air at 4,000 feet in an area where Approach could keep it separated from other aircraft, at least turn it away from another target in the event a VFR aircraft not under radar control should get too near. It had been 12 minutes— perhaps the longest 12 minutes of their careers for Laird and Bruce. It was time for a change. Facility Chief Herman Reyenga assigned the responsibility for control of the Baron to Calvin Losey, supervisor of the team. Laird and Bruce now were assigned to routine—in comparison—task of controlling other aircraft approaching the busy Regional Airport. All runways and taxiways were being cleared so an attempt to get Baron 612 Hotel safely on the ground could be made. It wasn't the first time in aviation history a non-pilot had been talked down to a safe landing although most of the cases on record did not involve a hot, multi-engine aircraft. Crosby, however, had shown himself to be extraor-

APPROACH

dinarily adept at taking instruction from Laird and Bruce. In fact, he had been doing a creditable job flying the Baron with still another handicap. While many aircraft have full dual controls—controls for both a pilot and a co-pilot—the Baron had a single control yoke for aileron/elevator control with a "throw-over" wheel. A pin in the yoke could be pulled allowing the control wheel to be pivoted over to the right seat. Crosby could not identify the pin. So he had been flying the aircraft while leaning out of his seat and over the body of the unconscious pilot. The controllers reasoned that if he could do this, they had a better-than-even chance of talking the Baron down in one piece. It would help if another aircraft could be found to fly wing on the Baron so the pilot could provide Crosby with instantaneous advice during the descent. Losey selected a Gulfstream approaching Shreveport at that time. Could Crosby see the other aircraft and follow it?

"I hope and pray I can," was his answer.

It soon was clear that the airspeed differential between the Baron and the Gulfstream was too great. Losey would have to find another "seeing-eye plane" to nurse the Baron down. Meanwhile the local FAA General Aviation District Office had been alerted to the impending disaster. Accident Prevention Specialist Bennie Voss boarded a Piper Twin Comanche at Shreveport Downtown Airport and headed for the Baron to see what he could do. His Comanche would be able to fly formation with the Baron and he was more familiar with that aircraft and its flight characteristics. Since visibility was improving closer to the ground Losey decided to descend the Baron to 3,000 while Voss was enroute to the area. For the next few minutes the dialogue between Losey and Crosby and between the Comanche and the Baron sounded like this:

> Approach Control, '12 Hotel, do you know where the trim tab is located on your aircraft?'
> Baron 12 Hotel, 'Do I know where the what's at . . .?'
> Approach Control, 'The trim tab . . . trim tab . . .'
> Baron 12 Hotel, 'Ten four.' (This is a Citizen's Band and law enforcement procedural code which means the same as Roger—I have received and understand your message. Probably Crosby's familiarity with some type of radio procedure enabled him to contact approach in the first place and thus saved his life.)
> Approach Control, 'All right. If you will just slightly move the trim tab forward . . .'
> Baron 12 Hotel, 'The trim tab down—forward.'
> Approach Control, 'Yes, sir, roll your trim tab from bottom to top toward the nose of the airplane, very slightly.'
> Baron 12 Hotel, 'Is this trim tab a great big round wheel about six inches in diameter?'
> Approach Control, 'That is correct, a vertical wheel.'
> Baron 12 Hotel, 'Roll it in what direction?'
> Approach Control, 'From bottom to top, forward.'
> Fifteen miles west of the airport Losey established radio contact with Voss in the Comanche, and directed him toward the Baron. The Baron reported that clouds had formed under him, and he was unable to see the ground. Voss, from the Comanche, said he could not spot the other plane.
> Approach Control, 'Comanche, 07 Yankee, he's at twelve o'clock right now. Three and a half miles.'
> Comanche 07 Yankee, 'We're looking.'
> Approach Control, 'Your twelve o'clock position, two miles.'
> Comanche 07 Yankee, 'Roger. We have him in sight. One two Hotel, this is

129

CLEARED TO LAND!

Comanche zero seven Yankee, we'll be taking you down to the airport. Just maintain your present heading and keep your wings level. We'll be on your wing in about 30 seconds.'

Baron 12 Hotel, 'Ten four.'

Comanche 07 Yankee, 'Good, hold it right where you have it now. And, one two Hotel, it appears that you have your gear down. Is that correct?'

Baron 12 Hotel, 'The gear is down. You want the landing gear left down?'

Comanche 07 Yankee, 'Affirmative, leave it in the down position, don't cycle the gear anymore. Now increase your manifold pressure to about 22 inches. That's fine. Keep studying the gauges and stay straight and level. We're coming up on your left.'

Baron 12 Hotel, 'We see you!'

Comanche 07 Yankee, 'Good, good. Now increase your manifold pressure and stay with us, match your wings to our wings and keep them level.'

Baron 12 Hotel, 'Ten four.'

Comanche 07 Yankee, 'One two Hotel, there is a pin in the column on that control yoke right in the top. Pull that out and swing the yoke over to your side.'

At this point in the drama, Lady Luck, who this far could not have been said to have completely turned her face away from Baron 612 Hotel, gave out with a downright smile in its direction.

In the Baron cockpit, the pilot had regained consciousness. Groggy and certainly not completely alert according to his speech patterns and tone of voice, he did assume command of the aircraft and with Voss's help—staying on the Baron's tail and giving a constant flow of information about altitude, headings and power adjustments—got 612 Hotel on the ground, but not without one or two hairy last minute power corrections and one prodigious bounce. The Baron rolled out stopping on the runway. Voss, right behind, went to the Baron, took over and taxied it to the waiting ambulance. One hour and three minutes had elapsed since Laird and Bruce had heard those first desperate calls for help.

The Baron 612 Hotel incident now is but a memory at Shreveport Approach. The pilot recovered. His passenger-turned-pilot continues to fly routinely on business, convinced that with the help of an FAA team he can handle any contingency.

You don't need to have a heart attack in flight to get into trouble up there, you just have to get yourself in over your head in terms of matching your experience and aerial competency against the requirements of a given flight situation. For instance, you might be the pilot of a Cessna 182 with no experience in flying instruments who, through lack of good flight planning, finds himself lost 50 miles northwest of Baltimore's Friendship International Airport on a dreary day in February 1970—lost, in a snow storm, no instrument experience and, to top it off, the aircraft also was not even equipped for instrument flight.

Approach Controller Donald C. Legge was on duty at the radar position in the Friendship tower approach control when the pilot—who it turned out had less than 100 hours total pilot time—called in for assistance. Legge immediately gave him instructions to make a series of identifying turns so he could pick him out of the other targets shown on his scope. Once the aircraft was identified on the scope, Legge asked if the pilot could "fly a localized approach." It was immediately obvious from the pilot's response that he was totally unfamiliar either with the term or the procedure. Legge then learned

Although approach controllers like air route traffic controllers work in a radar environment, in most cases their task often is more complicated. Taking inbound aircraft on hand-offs from the low altitude sector controllers at the center, they must arrange them in sequence for landing at the terminal, always maintaining safe separation distances between them. It is a lot like pouring fluid into a funnel without spilling in the midst of a swarm of curious bees; the bees being all the local air traffic—commuters, charters, training flights, pleasure flights and other traffic common to every metropolitan area. Simultaneously, the approach (departure) controllers must keep outbound traffic moving smoothly.

that the aircraft had neither a localizer nor a glide slope receiver even if the pilot were able to use them. There would be a chance of giving him a cram course by remote control and talking him in that way. The controller now turned to the alternate means—an ASR (airport surveillance radar) approach. With his radar, Legge could continually monitor the bearing of the aircraft from the runway, the approximate distance from the airport and the manner in which the pilot managed to follow the instructions given him. He would, however, have to depend on the pilot to monitor and report his altitude during the approach. With this information, Legge could give the pilot instructions so he could set up and maintain a safe rate and angle of descent until he could see the runway. He could do all this if— if the already distraught pilot did not panic and if he would prove to be a good student—because that's exactly what their relationship would be for the next 15 minutes, instructor and student.

Calmly, Legge explained the ASR approach. Then he began issuing vectors and descent instructions. It was obvious from the movement of the target on the radar scope that the pilot was woefully inexperienced in controlling the aircraft without reference to the horizon. He was having trouble making his turns and in maintaining the vectors given from approach. The biggest danger was that the pilot would over control, bank too steeply, even roll the airplane on its back, or worse, get into an accelerated stall during too steep a turn and fall off into a spin from which he probably would never recover. There was one way to minimize this danger. Have the pilot keep his wings level and "skid" his turns, in other words, make turns only with the rudder and then with only light rudder pressure. Legge glued his eyes on the radar scope and kept up a running patter.

"Cessna 15 Romeo, we're six miles from the runway, begin your descent now, just an easy gradual descent . . . 15 Romeo, you started a left turn, now come back to the right . . . good, good, level it out for a moment at 1,500 feet, nice . . . now pick up your power . . . make the turns easy, just use those rudder pedals, don't roll in that aileron at all . . . just the rudder pedals, good. Now holding a heading that is 150. Right. Now begin your descent . . . again nice and easy . . . just give yourself about 300 feet a minute . . . good, hold that heading . . . 150 . . . you're sliding off the right now, a little left rudder, just a gradual easy left turn . . . fine, real fine."

Legge asked for and got an altitude report from the Cessna—"900 feet." He continued with the impromptu instrument flying lesson.

"Okay, that's good, you're in a good descent. You're just a bit to the right edge of the runway but your heading is taking you back, so just hold that heading. Keep that rudder pressure equal and keep that descent. You're starting to go left, a little bit on the right rudder . . . not too much, just easy . . . "

Suddenly the welcome words burst from Legge's earphones:

"I've got the runway. This is 15 Romeo. I'm on the ground."

The hands of the tower clock pointed to 11:49. It had been only 14 minutes since the first call for assistance from the Cessna. For Don Legge it had been an eternity.

In all probability the pilot of that Cessna 182 didn't forget his experience for many months to come. We know for certain he did not forget it for at least the next 30 days. His pilot certificate was suspended by the FAA for that period because it was determined that he "knowingly" put himself in the position of flying in instrument conditions without an instrument rating.

APPROACH

In approach control as in air route traffic control the computer is playing an ever-increasing role. As ARTS III continues to develop more and more major terminal approach controls are being integrated into the system with their radar data being added to the mass of information handled by the RDP system. However, it still requires highly trained men and women to make the system function and get the most out of this new sophistication.

Today's general aviation aircraft have achieved a remarkable degree of reliability. The chances of a mechanical or structural malfunction are slight. Still occasionally a pilot is faced with a situation over which he has no control. That's the way it was for a Los Angeles man with three passengers aboard his single engine Mooney on October 21, 1974. Enroute to Palm Springs, the aircraft was VFR five miles northeast of the Seal Beach VOR at 5,500 feet. It had just been "handed off" by Long Beach Approach to Ontario Approach. Eight miles west of Corona, Calif., the pilot declared an emergency, telling controller Richard E. Case he had "lost his propeller."

As Case recalls the incident, a look at the scope indicated the aircraft was equi-distant from Chino and Corona. Since Chino had longer runways and more emergency equipment, Case elected to vector the crippled Mooney to that field. Observing the aircraft's course and reaction to his instructions, it became clear that the pilot was reacting as if he had no directional gyro. Reasoning that he probably had lost the gyro instruments when the engine was shut down, Case began giving "no-gyro" vectors. Since the aircraft had "turned past Chino" and without gyro instruments would encounter difficulty executing another 360-degree turn, Case now elected to direct it to Corona. As the Mooney progressed toward Corona it became clear Case had made the right decision. The aircraft arrived over Corona with sufficient altitude for a successful "dead stick" landing despite the additional problem that the pilot had no forward visibility due to oil from the propeller governor which now covered his windshield.

CLEARED TO LAND!

The people aboard the Mooney were among the 357 men, women and children aboard 249 aircraft that encountered in-flight emergencies that same month—emergencies involving becoming lost, low on fuel, weather conditions beyond the pilot's capability to cope with or some type of mechanical malfunction.

Sometimes it takes a massive team effort to "bring 'em back alive" and sometimes it doesn't always work out quite like the situations that faced Fred Laird, Ray Bruce, Cal Losey, Don Legge and Dick Case. In January 1974, it took the combined efforts of Norfolk Approach, Washington Center, Coast Guard 1346, and a Coast Guard chopper to snatch the pilot and passenger of another Mooney from a watery death in the Atlantic.

The flight had begun as a routine return from Nassau in the Bahamas to Baltimore. The two men had been plagued by bad weather and were forced to spend one night in Florida and another in South Carolina. On the third day, the weather at Baltimore was more promising (although unbeknownst to the pilot there was a 60-knot off-shore wind blowing at 12,000 feet and before the flight was terminated in near disaster the Mooney would have to climb to that altitude to remain clear of encroaching clouds). The incident went into high gear when Norfolk Approach could no longer see the aircraft with its limited radar and called on Washington Center—with its long-range radar—to assist. An official FAA report of the rescue went like this:

> 3:29 P.M. EST
> Norfolk Approach: "I've got an aircraft east of here . . . probably off our scope. He's on (transponder) code zero one one five. Do you see anything east of Norfolk . . . more than 50 miles?"
> Washington Center: "Yes, about 90 miles out."
> Norfolk Approach: "Nine zero miles?"
> Washington Center: "That's affirmative."
> Norfolk Approach: "How about my putting him on your frequency and you working him towards Norfolk. He's VFR on top, Mooney 985, has about an hour and 15 minutes of fuel now."
> Washington Center: "Roger. Mooney 985, Washington, go ahead."
> Mooney N985: "Okay, I have a navigation problem and I'm rather east of Norfolk or, ah, east of Salisbury, somewhere in that area."
> Washington Center: "Okay, Mooney 985, understand you're squawking zero one one five. Give me an ident, please."
> Mooney N985: Squawking ident.
> Washington Center: "Okay, Mooney 985, I show you approximately 90 miles east of Norfolk, sir . . . what are you requesting?"
> Mooney N985: "I'd like to get to the Baltimore area."
> Washington Center: "I've been advised by Norfolk Approach that the winds aloft at 12,000 feet are from 270 degrees at 60 knots, sir."
> Mooney N985: "At how many knots?"
> Washington Center: "At six zero knots. Six zero knots, sir, and I show you tracking northbound. Suggest you turn westbound."
> 3:39 P.M. EST
> Washington Center: "Mooney 985, I still show you tracking northbound, sir. Do you concur?"
> Mooney N985: "Ah, indication that I'm going into the two seven oh degree radial of Norfolk."
> Washington Center: "Suggest you start a half standard rate turn to the left if you would like to go to Norfolk, sir. Understand you've got only about an hour's fuel, sir, and if you want to go to Salisbury I'll try and get you there, or Norfolk, sir—it's your choice."

APPROACH

Mooney N985: "If I can just get on that radial to Salisbury I'll be okay."

Washington Center: "Okay, Mooney, the Salisbury VOR frequency is one one four point five, and, ah, see if you can receive it suitable for navigation. Suggest a heading of about three one zero."

Mooney N985: "I've got indication now. It's, ah . . ." (transmission lost)

As it appeared that the aircraft was having trouble with radio navigation, Washington Center contacted Navy and Coast Guard stations in the area to learn what rescue aircraft might be available. Coast Guard 1346, a C-130 returning to Elizabeth City, N.C., after a routine training flight, was dispatched to the scene. The C-130 was originally routed over and above the Warning Zone that was active between Elizabeth City and the distressed Mooney (because of considerable military air activity in the Zone), but the aircraft commander estimated that the detour could mean arriving at the scene of trouble too late to be of assistance. He asked for and received clearance to fly through the Warning Zone maintaining VFR conditions.

Washington Center: "Roger, Coast Guard 46. If you want to go direct VFR we'll try and give you vectors for the Mooney."

Coast Guard C-130: "Roger. Otherwise this fellow will be in before we get up there."

Washington Center: "1346, advise me of your VFR cruising altitude."

Coast Guard C-130: "9,500. We're passing eight for that now."

Washington Center: "Okay, zero six zero heading looks pretty good for now. Approximate distance 90 miles. He's burgundy and white and he's got two souls on board. Advised he has an intermittent transmitter."

Coast Guard C-130: Okay. Mooney 985, this is Coast Guard Rescue 1346, we are level 9,500 proceeding to your direction on radar vectors from Washington Center. We'll try to join up with you and guide you into the nearest airfield which should be Oceana (Naval Air Station, Virginia Beach). Are you still at 12,000 feet?"

Mooney N985: "Yes, sir, that's affirmative."

Coast Guard C-130: "The pilot is instrument qualified—is that correct?"

Mooney N985: "Negative on that."

Coast Guard C-130: "Okay, 985, go ahead and put on your life vests just in preparation. We're coming up close on you and you should be able to see us in just a minute. What is your airspeed now?"

Mooney N985: "Indicating 135 miles per hour."

Coast Guard C-130: "Okay, we have you in sight, heading 274 now. How is your fuel state? How many minutes have you left?"

Mooney N985: "About 50 minutes."

Coast Guard C-130: "Five zero minutes, understand. Washington Center. I have a helicopter proceeding to a point 200 miles on the 090 radial of Oceana, on your frequency."

Washington Center: "Roger."

Mooney N985: "Coast Guard, how far off am I now?"

Coast Guard C-130: "You're about 60 miles off shore."

Mooney 985: "Ah, how far is it down to the water?"

Coast Guard C-130: "The cloud layer should be about 2,000 feet. Have you ever gone through an overcast before?"

Mooney 985: "Oh, a few times, but not quite that many feet."

Coast Guard C-130: "Okay, you shouldn't really have a problem coming through it. Just take your time as you go down, make sure your wings are level and don't let your airspeed get below about a hundred knots. Let me know when it looks fairly clear for you to start down, and we'll come on in behind you then."

Mooney 985: "I think I'll sit up here for a little while."

CLEARED TO LAND!

Coast Guard C-130: "Okay. If you do run out of fuel and have to ditch, we will give you a heading to turn to that will be parallel to the major swells and in that case you would fly the airplane right into the water . . . make sure you don't stall, just a nice easy flight into the water. Inflate your life jackets after you get out, and sit on the wing until the helicopter picks you up. The Coast Guard helicopter should be right on the scene if you have to ditch."

Mooney 985: "Okay, 985."

4:32 P.M. EST

Coast Guard C-130: "985, you're going to have to start looking for a hole to get down through. You should be able to break out at about 500 feet, or you may have to go down a bit lower than that. You're bucking too much of a headwind at this altitude, sir."

Mooney 985: "Okay, I'm on my way down now. What is the base of this stuff?"

Coast Guard C-130: "You should get down to about 500 or 1,000 if you can."

At this point a Coast Guard Air Evacuation helicopter, summoned by the C-130 and flying just above the surface of the sea, spotted the Mooney through a hole in the overcast.

Coast Guard Helicopter: "This is Coast Guard 1415. We see you and you look like you're coming down real good. About 25 miles off shore everything picks up real nice so you should be able to stay out of the clouds. Ease around to heading three zero zero and just hold it. How are you doing?"

Mooney 985: "Oh, pretty good. How many miles off shore am I?"

Coast Guard Helicopter: "About 45 miles. What is your altitude now?"

Mooney 985: "Ah, I think I would like to level off. I'm at 45 now."

Coast Guard C-130: Okay, the winds at 4,500 feet might be easy enough so you could make it okay to shore, just keep going."

Mooney 985: "Coast Guard, I got a jet right out here in front of me playing around . . ."

Coast Guard C-130: "Okay, Mooney, he's off an aircraft carrier down below. He should be leaving now. Just continue your heading of two seven zero and stay over the tops of the clouds. I have land in sight so you should have no problem."

Mooney 985: "Okay. I've got about, maybe, another 15 minutes of fuel."

Coast Guard C-130: "Okay, go ahead and get on down as fast as you can now to about 1,000 feet."

Mooney 985: "I'd rather stay up here for awhile."

Coast Guard C-130: "Okay, the helicopter has you in sight and he's going to fly wing on you right on down. Better secure all loose objects, in case you have to ditch, and brace yourself as soon as you hit water. Make sure you stay above stall speed going in. Any questions about ditching?"

Mooney 985: "You want me to turn to three three zero, right?"

Coast Guard C-130: "That is correct, three three zero will land you parallel to the swells. You'll have about five knots of wind on the surface, so it should be nice and easy. You are now about 23 miles off the beach."

Mooney 985: "Where am I in reference to the airport?"

Coast Guard C-130: "Oceana Naval Air Station is about 27 miles at two seven five from your position. I should mention that if you have to land in the water make sure your gear is up and your flaps down. Suggest you open the door on short final for a water landing."

Coast Guard Helicopter: "985, look down toward the surface at about your one o'clock position. Do you have us in sight?"

Mooney 985: "Ah, that's affirmative."

4:55 P.M. EST

Mooney 985: "We just ran out of fuel!"

Coast Guard C-130: "Okay, take it easy now, pick yourself a nice clear spot and come around to heading three three zero and hold it all the way down. The helicopter will be right alongside you."

Mooney 985: "Okay, I'm three three zero."

Coast Guard C-130: "Okay, nice and easy now, the helicopter is right next to you . . . when you get in the water just open the door and step out on the wing and you've got it made. Just make sure you don't hit nose low."

There were a few white caps and streaks of foam on the sea as the Mooney with a dead engine glided down, accompanied by the Coast Guard helicopter flying within 50 yards of its wing. On making contact with the water the airplane skipped up once, spun around 180 degrees and came to rest rightside up on the surface. Both the pilot and his passenger, neither of whom were wearing shoulder harness, struck their heads sharply against the windshield, enough to break out the glass on the pilot's side. Both, however, managed to scramble out on the wing and inflate life vests. They were taken on board the helicopter by means of an extended platform and a boathook. Water temperature was 49 degrees. The airplane sank within two minutes of splashdown.

The rescuees were flown to a hospital at Virginia Beach, treated and subsequently released.

After completing their studies at the FAA Academy, controllers continue to train at their operational sites in "training labs" like this one at Chicago's O'Hare Airport.

Approach control actually was the third segment of today's integrated, nationwide air traffic control system to come into being. Initially, control towers were established at airports where the amount of traffic began to require some sort of local control. In 1929, for instance, the "tower" at Lambert Field, St. Louis, Mo., consisted of a single controller who worked under a

CLEARED TO LAND!

large umbrella in the center of the field and directed landing and departing aircraft with a pair of flags. Soon elementary radio communications replaced the flags and a glass-enclosed "greenhouse" replaced the umbrella. About this same time, the initial experiments in providing enroute traffic control were beginning. The first centers were established by the airlines. In 1936 these were absorbed by the federal government and integrated with new ones being established. Through the war years following the attack on Pearl Harbor, the network of control towers, air route traffic control centers and what then were called Interstate Airways Communications Stations (INSAC) grew. Air traffic also grew to the point where a new traffic control capability was required. As more and more aircraft operated under instrument conditions and so-called all-weather operations increased a separate facility was needed to funnel approaching and departing aircraft between the point where the tower controller could visually direct the aircraft and the various points where air routes intersected in the terminal area. These early approach control facilities were established and co-located with the control towers at the nation's busiest terminals. The approach controllers' tools were the same as those then used by the centers—large maps of the area on which markers (the now legendary "shrimp boats") were moved about by hand representing the real-time position of the various aircraft being worked in the control area.

William Flener, who later became FAA Director of Air Traffic Service, was one of those early approach controllers at the Portland, Ore., tower. Bill recalls that although he could transmit on one frequency and receive on three, often clearances had to be routed through the local radio range stations or, in the case of the airlines, through the individual company stations.

"We had to depend on the pilot's word for his position, course and airspeed," he says, "and then we would estimate his time of arrival."

Aircraft separation was accomplished using altitude and time. Normally, aircraft were kept 10 minutes apart horizontally and 1,000 feet apart vertically. When several aircraft arrived in the terminal area simultaneously they would be "stacked up" in holding patterns over one or more radio fixes.

John Dunham, now assistant chief of the Los Angeles Center, remembers how it was in the Los Angeles area in those early days. From the beginning, Los Angeles was one of the nation's busiest terminal areas. What now is the Hollywood-Burbank Airport—in the San Fernando Valley on the opposite side of the Santa Monica Mountains from Los Angeles proper—then was the main air terminal. Later, after World War II, Mines Field near the Pacific shoreline at El Segundo became Los Angeles International Airport or LAX as it is known today. The approach responsibility first was assigned to Los Angeles Center (in addition to its enroute responsibility) when LAX began handling airline traffic in addition to the Lockheed Air Terminal at Burbank.

"Landing at Mines Field," Dunham remembers, "the primary approach fix was the Downey low frequency beacon. Everything would go to Downey and hold east of Downey—east of the east course of the Los Angeles low frequency radio range. Those were the days of the stacks—you just stacked them up 1,000 feet apart. Our minimum holding altitude was 3,000 feet and we would bring in the first aircraft from whatever direction he came, take him out to Downey and put him at 3,000. The next one went to 4,000, the next to 5,000, the next to 6,000 and so forth. That first one had no delay. The others had to wait their turn. As the final approach altitude was vacated we would bring

138

each aircraft in the stack down in sequence. If one guy missed his approach we just sent him right back to the top of the stack.

"Let's say the top of the stack was 10,000 feet. Starting at 3,000, you have eight birds stacked up. A DC-3 misses his approach. We climb him out on the west course of the Los Angeles range with a procedure turnout altitude assigned and a crossing altitude assigned coming back over the range station—say 11,000 feet. With his climb to 11,000 and the procedure turn the DC-3 would take 25 minutes to get back over the range east-bound to Downey. Then he would have to work down the stack all over again. In those days planes had to have a lot more reserve fuel than they do today."

It isn't hard to imagine what it would be like today to handle approach and departure control at a major terminal without radar. Simply, it couldn't be done. Currently, Los Angeles Approach handles 1,350 aircraft a day on a peak day. This actually is considerably less than was handled in, for instance, 1969 before the jumbo jets, fuel conservation and a downward economy. In 1969, a peak day saw Los Angeles Approach handle 2,160 planes.

Officially, Los Angeles Approach now is known as Los Angeles TRACON (for Terminal Radar Approach Control). In addition to handling the approach/departure chores for LAX, one of the nation's 10 busiest airports, Los Angeles TRACON also is responsible for Santa Monica Airport, Hawthorne Airport and all approaches/departures from or to the west from Torrance Airport—also one of the nation's 10 busiest airports and one of the five busiest general aviation terminals.

Administratively, Los Angeles Tower and TRACON are combined under the overall supervision of Jim Holweger, a veteran controller. Merle Nichols is deputy chief of the combined facility. Physically, the facility is divided with the tower situated at mid-field and the approach control function in a specially-built, building-within-a-building in the FAA hangars on the south side. The unique structure housing the TRACON is needed to accommodate the elaborate air conditioning required by the computers associated with the automated, radar control equipment now in use.

At full strength, the tower operates with 36 journeyman controllers on each of three shifts while the TRACON requires 52. In all, 123 men and women are required to operate the combined tower/TRACON, including management, data systems specialists and training specialists.

Merle Nichols, who began his air traffic control career with the Army Air Forces in World War II, is typical of the experience level found in major terminal approach control facilities around the nation. After the war, Merle became a civilian tower chief at nearby Norton AFB, San Bernardino, Calif., and when he joined the FAA (then the CAA) in 1946 he became an assistant controller at the old Los Angeles Tower. His experience thus bridges the original VFR tower control at LAX, the transition to combined VFR tower/radar tower operation and today's sophisticated tower/TRACON setup with fully automated computer/radar control capability. He saw the first airport surveillance radar (ASR) installed at LAX to be followed by the first precision approach radar (PAR). (Later, this civilian version of the military-developed ground control approach (GCA) radar system was decommissioned when the airlines and civilian aviation adopted the instrument landing system (ILS).) For many years Los Angeles Approach "lived" in a blacked-out room directly beneath the cab of the Los Angeles Tower. In 1974,

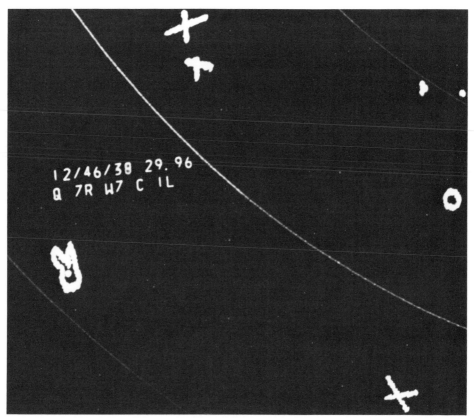

The only approach control scope in the nation to display the Playboy rabbit symbol is situated at Milwaukee, Wisc. The symbol marks the location of the Playboy airport on the scope. This type of symbol is made possible by the use of digitized radar information. The information displayed on the scope is provided by a computer. Dynamic data is, of course, taken by the computer directly from the radar antenna. Static data, like this airport symbol, can be generated by the programmer.

the TRACON moved into its present quarters across the airport.

Los Angeles TRACON basically controls the aircraft on instruments (and those VFR aircraft with transponders that request radar traffic advisories operating in the Terminal Control Area or TCA) from Ontario 40 miles to the east, to Fillmore VOR on the north, about 10 miles to the southeast and out to sea. The broad area of control responsibility is divided into two approach sectors and two departure sectors. Its primary responsibility is to handle inbound and outbound traffic from LAX which normally operates parallel instrument approaches and departures from two of four runways. A minimum of 4,300 feet centerline separation is maintained when simultaneous instrument operations are in progress on parallel runways. Along each runway centerline, three-mile separation is maintained when simultaneous instrument operations are in progress on parallel runways. Along each runway centerline, three-mile separation is maintained between any two "non-heavy" (other than jumbo jets or the so-called stretched DC-8 type aircraft); four miles between any two "heavies"; and five miles between a non-heavy in-trail behind a heavy (because of the danger of wake turbulence).

IFR operations into and out of LAX, if you could string them out evenly over a 24-hour period, would account for one every 1.07 minutes or 56.24 an hour. Of course, this isn't the way it happens. There are peak traffic periods and slack periods with the count bunching up in the peak periods. Also, Los Angeles TRACON, like similar high density areas in other parts of the country, must provide traffic control for instrument traffic between other airports in the control area. In the case of Los Angeles, heavy traffic loads are experienced through its area between airports like Long Beach, Burbank, Van Nuys, Torrance, Santa Monica and El Monte. Although Burbank and Long Beach have their own approach control facilities, most traffic between these terminals and the others with instrument approaches in the area sooner or later must pass through Los Angeles TRACON's sphere of responsibility.

How does working approach control differ from other radar traffic control jobs in the system?

Nichols puts it this way:

"Approach control must operate in a more confined area. For instance, the high altitude sectors in a center control traffic on a broad scale. As these aircraft are brought down into the low altitude sectors preliminary to a landing, control is exercised on a smaller, tighter scale—more airplanes in a smaller area. At the TRACON we must control on a very small scale, in other words on a very high density basis. We control the small end of the 'funnel'. Center feeds them into the mouth. We have to pick them up, sequence them down the funnel so that they have the proper interval when they are spit out on final approach to the airport."

Like most veteran controllers, Nichols plays the game of "keeping the blips from bumping."

"You simply can't think of those dots as aircraft carrying people," he resolutely declares, "you must remain detached from any emotional response. You have to play it as a game. It's like those doctors and nurses on the television program MASH—and that's real life, that's the way it has to be for real medics in that kind of situation—you can't let the horrendous responsibility get to you. It's like that for us."

Nichols also points out that while a controller's worst critic is himself, his peers also keep him on the straight and narrow.

"In this business when you make a mistake, it's done," he says, "you don't have a chance to make the decision over again. Your peers are always aware of what is going on. They know when you're good and when you're bad. Also, there's no laying down on the job. Your peers will never let you get away with it. If you can't hack the course there's no place to go but out. One thing, you have to be good, know you're good and have a lot of self confidence. This is no business for faint hearts."

Like most controllers, Nichols loves his job. He singles out two of the characteristics of the career field as especially attractive—"you know the job is over when you go home—and no two days are ever the same." About the "ulcer and the divorce problems" which seem to be directly associated with air traffic control, Merle isn't sure whether it is the job or the nature of the men and women attracted to the job. But the problem is there.

Recently, Nichols took advantage of an FAA program for controllers designed to give them an idea of "how the other half lives." Specifically, controllers have the opportunity to fly with an airline and to observe the air traffic control situation from the flight crew's point of view. He spent 40 hours flying with one line during which time he had the chance to observe the operations in two center areas and at two different tower/approach facilities. Among Nichols' observations are these:

"I couldn't believe the 'absolute' command responsibility the captain has in that aircraft."

CLEARED TO LAND!

"He thinks ATC is 'fantastic' and he loves the controllers until . . . until he is delayed."

"There appears to be two kinds of captains—those like the little old ladies that drive 40 miles per hour in the fast lane and the hot rods who push everything up against the pegs."

"When a controller has to slow the aircraft down, divert it to maintain separation from other traffic or in any way impede its progress on the course locked into the captain's mind, every instruction of the controller is taken personally. He seems to lose view of the fact that there are a lot of other airplanes up there with him. He is 'all alone' and every instruction which is counter to what he wants to do appears to be part of conspiracy to delay him."

Is all this necessarily a real problem?

"No," Nichols smiles, "captains and crews are just like other people, like us. There are good guys, cooperative guys. And there are grouches. The grouches, fortunately, are in the minority."

8 THE INSPECTORS - I

It was a bright, moonlit, September evening, one of those with just the slightest touch of Autumn crispness beginning to appear. The four-place Cessna turned on final to the Provo, Utah airport. To those on the ground and apparently to the 51-year-old physician/pilot, everything appeared normal.

Suddenly the aircraft began to lose altitude prematurely. Striking two 40-foot trees just a mile from the runway threshold, it plunged to earth and burst into flame. The pilot and both his passengers—his son and daughter-in-law—were burned to death.

The flight began as a "short joy ride" for the young couple who were celebrating their first wedding anniversary with the husband's family. What better way to top off a relaxed evening than with a short spin in the family plane? This one ended in disaster, however, and since there had been a celebration involved the Sunday-morning-quarterbacks immediately chalked it up to pilot error, probably due to the effect of party libations, intentional low flying, or both.

Because three fatalities occurred an immediate intensive investigation was launched by the National Transportation Safety Board (NTSB) and the FAA. FAA investigators (both maintenance and operations inspectors) usually are the first in the field, dispatched from the General Aviation District Office (GADO) or Flight Standards District Office (FSDO) having responsibility for the geographic area. They work hand-in-hand with the NTSB investigators and in the case of non-fatal accidents, usually are delegated the full responsibility for the investigation.

Ultimately, it is the responsibility of the NTSB to determine the "probable cause" of the accident while the FAA investigators are concerned with determining if violations of FAA regulations, maintenance deficiencies or other causative factors within the purview of the FAA were involved—this aimed not at pointing the finger but at developing information that might be used to prevent similar accidents in the future. Where the NTSB representative is on hand, he (or she) becomes the Investigator-In-Charge (IIC). In those cases where the total responsibility is delegated to the FAA, the senior inspector assigned becomes the IIC.

Immediately after the crash report by the FAA and NTSB, Provo police were requested to secure the area and plans were made for the IIC and FAA inspectors from the Utah GADO to meet the next morning to begin sifting the physical evidence at the crash scene and locate and interview all possible witnesses both to the accident and to the circumstances leading to it. A large part of this task involved talking with family, friends, flying associates and business/social acquaintances of the pilot and passengers. The object—turn up every possible bit of information which might provide a clue to the cause of the tragedy.

Photographs of the accident site were taken by the two investigators. Each part of the plane was carefully located and examined. A chart was made of the exact location of various parts of the wreckage. Although the plane had burst into flames, the fire had been quickly extinguished and most of the frame was still intact. Both propeller blades, however, had been separated from the propeller hub, and one of them was found 75 yards from the crash site.

Witnesses were located, and in a series of interviews they gave their recollections of the accident. The most knowledgeable testimony came from an experienced IFR-rated pilot who had been driving toward the airport in a car at the time of the crash. He had observed the doctor's plane in the sky above him as it was making its approach. He stated that everything seemed perfectly normal.

The physician-pilot's background and flying history were examined. He had an excellent reputation and, although he was only VFR-rated, he had many years of accident-free flying experience. The weather at the time of the accident was checked: it had been a cloudless night, the wind a mild six knots at 180 degrees.

When the autopsy report was received, the toxicological examination of the pilot revealed that there was no alcoholic content of any kind in the blood stream. The possibility of the imbibing pilot could now be dismissed.

Gradually the investigative picture began to emerge. An experienced, reputable pilot who had not been drinking was making a routine approach in good flying conditions. Could he have been careless in flathatting? The evidence to date did not seem to support it—the reflections of friends and colleagues argued against such behavior. The search for clues now focused on the airplane. Slowly and carefully the investigators examined each section of the plane, power plant, structure, condition of cables, etc. Some parts were shipped back to the NTSB laboratory in Washington for further scrutiny. One thing which particularly aroused suspicion was "the distance the propeller had been thrown from the airplane." All parts of the propeller assembly were carefully collected for examination.

A metallurgical inspection in the laboratory eventually turned up the first real clue. An examination of the microstructure of the threads of bolts used on the propeller governor and control yoke revealed that there was no evidence of "cold work"—that is, they had not been formed by rolling, as required by FAA approved specifications for bolts on that particular type of aircraft. Somewhere along the line someone had used improper bolts when working on the doctor's plane.

Ultimately it was determined that the probable cause of the fatal accident was "propeller and accessories failure." At a crucial moment propeller failure caused the airplane to lose altitude abruptly and crash. Shortly afterwards the FAA issued an Airworthiness Directive "to prevent loss of propeller control" on that particular type of aircraft.

The AD instructed owners and operators to have an inspection by a mechanic within the next 25 flying hours. The propeller spine was to be removed and the equipment examined to make sure that the approved manufacturer's bolts were being used. The AD cited the proper bolt number, advised the owners to test for the evidence of cracks, and to repeat the examination by dye penetrant procedures every 100 flying hours.

The investigation at Provo, by demonstrating that the pilot was not guilty of carelessness, but rather that his airplane had failed him, possibly saved other pilots from suffering the same fate.

In cooperation with the NTSB, FAA conducts an investigation of all aircraft accidents, large and small. FAA has its own network of over 3,000 "investigators" throughout the country, most of whom have been specially trained in accident investigation during a four-week course in Oklahoma City.

The thrust behind the exhaustive investigation of aircraft accidents is to prevent their repetition but sometimes the clues are so subtle or non-existent it is only after the accident repeats itself that a cause is found. Only then can effective preventative action be taken. The case of a Caribbean-based Grumman Goose presented such a situation.

In June 1971 the twin engine air taxi, with a pilot and ten passengers on board, crashed in the sea off Puerto Rico. The airplane departed St. Thomas and was two miles northeast of Puerto Rico near Culebra Island when the engines failed. The pilot tried desperately to restart but was unsuccessful. He radioed a Mayday signal and instructed his passengers to don their life vests.

The weather was fair and the sea moderate but unluckily a swell caught the left wing float on impact causing the Goose to turn tearing away the bow section. The pilot was flung out of the open bow with a force that broke both of his legs. Struggling in the water he watched the passengers scrambling out of the cabin and counted eight of them floating safely with their life vests in the 75-degree water. Two other passengers, without vests, sat on the broken wing petrified with fear, ignoring his instructions to jump. Navigating as best he could with his broken legs, he started to swim towards them, shouting at them all the while. But, before he reached the plane, it suddenly slipped beneath the surface taking the two passengers with it. They were never found. Within a few hours all the remaining survivors were picked up by Navy and Coast Guard helicopters.

The investigation was frustrating. Down in over 200 feet of water, the Goose was never recovered; there was no wreckage to examine. The captain, an experienced and qualified pilot, was unable to offer any explanation for the engine failure and the ground crew at St. Thomas testified that there had been more than adequate fuel on board for the short flight. Power plant failure was obvious. But, without access to the engines, probable cause could not be determined.

Three months later another airplane of the same type had a similar power failure near St. Croix. This time there was hope the mystery could be solved. The air taxi had taken off in the early afternoon on a flight from San Juan to Cristiansted with a pilot and three passengers on board. About 20 miles northwest of St. Croix the engines failed and the pilot was unable to re-start. This time the landing of the amphibian in the open sea was a successful one and the plane floated easily on the surface. After some minutes the pilot found he was able to get the engines started again and he began to taxi toward land. His emergency signal had been heard, however, and a nearby fishing craft took off the passengers as a precaution. The pilot taxied the plane back to the dock. He could not explain why the engines failed but he felt it was probably some contaminate in the fuel tanks.

That would not do for the FAA inspectors and although they seldom investigate "incidents" they decided to investigate this one in light of the earlier Goose accident. (An "incident," as opposed to an "accident," is an episode in which there is no substantial aircraft damage and no personal injury.) The plane was ferried to a large hangar at St. Thomas and investigators began to break it down to examine the fuel system and power plant. During the power tests the main fuel inlet pipes were found to be hot to the touch but, when the fuel crossfeed valve was turned to "off," the pipes cooled. A mockup of the fuel system was then built, using fuel pumps from the original plane. A pressure differential between the fuel pumps was noted which seemed to be causing a back flow, resulting in high localized fuel temperatures when the crossfeed valve was open—an invitation to vapor lock and fuel starvation in both engines.

The manual for this type of plane instructed the pilot to fly with the crossfeed valve open. Since the St. Croix emergency landing was only an incident, NTSB did not issue a report of probable cause, but the FAA did issue an Airworthiness Directive instructing all owners of the airplane to affix a placard near the instrument panel reading: "Cross feed valve must be closed during all flight operations except for emergencies resulting from engine pump failure." To date, there have been no further reported episodes of engine failure on that airplane. The puzzle had been solved.

Accident investigation isn't the only function of the FAA's operations and maintenance inspectors, but, according to Al Sanell, principal maintenance inspector assigned to the Ontario, Calif. GADO, it is an important and time-consuming one.

Sanell, whose love affair with the airplane engine began in 1927 when Lindbergh flew the Atlantic, knows his way around aviation. He is both a pilot and a maintenance technician with wide experience including a tour with the National Aeronautics and Space Administration (then the National Advisory Committee on Aeronautics) as a copilot and airplane/engine mechanic on the B-29 and B-50 "mother" aircraft that took part in the nation's initial supersonic research program with the Bell X-1 and the Douglas D-558.

"I guess folks really have little understanding of the role the inspector plays in aviation safety," Sanell observes, "they only see us as enforcers. They don't realize that the only reason we have for being around is to help prevent them from busting their butts."

Al cites two recent cases where investigation by FAA maintenance inspectors probably saved some lives in the future, and at least, saved one airplane owner from paying a $350 bill for maintenance performed improperly.

"A Cessna 210A lost a prop blade," he recalls, "and was busted up in the subsequent forced landing. It could have been worse, the prop blade was thrown on takeoff. We found that the blade failure resulted from a crack in the blade's threaded shank. Now, there's an AD out that applies to certain McCauley constant speed propellers installed on various single-engine aircraft which required inspection of the threaded shank portion of the blades and eventual replacement of the blades.

"We found that the blade had not been inspected during the preceding annual inspection. Also, the mechanic failed to check to see if the AD had been complied with. He told us he did not research the ADs because he was 'familiar' with the aircraft. That's no excuse. By not doing his job, he placed the lives of others in danger. The FAA had no choice but to revoke his inspection authorization. He won't get another one until he shapes up and demonstrates he can be expected to perform his inspection responsibilities to the letter and then only with prior written authorization from the FAA Administrator."

In another case, Sanell says, a mechanic paid a $300 civil penalty and the airplane owner refused to pay the mechanic's bill for maintenance performed

THE INSPECTORS - I

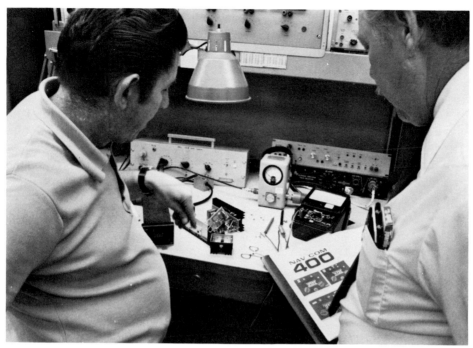

The average airman rarely sees or even, for that matter, is aware of the maintenance inspector, yet this man makes one of the most important contributions to his safety. He is the man whose responsibility it is to insure that the mechanic, the FBO and the overhaul shop follow the book giving the owner the best maintenance available for his dollar. An avionics inspector (a recent addition to the FAA inspection team) checks out an FBO electronics shop. He is concerned that the technician is trained in the equipment, that he has the proper manuals and that he has available the appropriate test equipment properly calibrated to do the job.

From the maintenance inspector's point of view, one of the most important tasks is to insure that all ADs issued on a given aircraft or powerplant have been complied with. ADs are issued by the FAA when it is determined that a deficiency is present which would have a significant effect on flying safety.

immediately prior to an accident in the Cessna 150. The accident subsequently damaged the aircraft injuring the pilot and passenger.

"When a mechanic works on your airplane he is expected to (and the FARs require that he) return it to you at least equal to its original or properly altered condition. In this case the oil was drained by one man who installed the drain plug only finger tight. A second man then put in the oil. The mechanic approved return of the aircraft to flight status without checking, torqueing and safetieing the plug. The plug came out in flight with the loss of oil and a total engine failure."

It doesn't always take an accident to bring shoddy maintenance to the attention of an FAA inspector. One mechanic paid a $150 civil penalty when an FAA spot check turned up the fact he failed to inspect the work performed by an uncertified mechanic under his supervision. That man had failed to tighten and safety the alternator bracket bolts and the propeller hold-down bolts on a Beechcraft.

Since accident investigation isn't all the maintenance inspector does, what else does he do? One "hell of a lot," according to Sanell.

Certification of standard aircraft, restricted category aircraft, experimental aircraft, limited category aircraft, mechanics and repairmen.

Inspection of major repairs and modifications; annual and progressive maintenance of privately-owned aircraft, commercially-operated aircraft and air taxi operations.

Inspection/certification of aviation maintenance technician schools, approved repair stations and parachute lofts.

Examination of mechanics for inspection authorization and for parachute riggers.

Selection, designation and supervision of mechanic examiners.

When he isn't busy with these duties, Sanell investigates service difficulties; conducts airworthiness surveillance on general aviation and air taxi aircraft in his area; provides aircraft registration advisory service to owners; authorizes special flight permits (ferry or one-time maintenance permits); certifies aircraft and components for export, wrestles with his own paperwork and supervises the technical and administrative personnel under him.

Routine—there's no such thing as routine, he declares. Every day, every week is different. Some weeks Al can't get out of the office. Then, for two or three weeks running, he is in the field and can't even get started on the mountain of paperwork that is inherent in his job.

"Let's see," he says, "there's a guy over at Perris who wants to use his plane for parachute jumping. We've got to check it out. He needs to take the door off. We need to see if this model is approved for flight without the door and if not what might be done to make it acceptable. We have to help him develop a set of operational instructions and emergency procedures. If modifications are necessary we have to approve them.

"Then, there's this owner who wants to modify his airplane—put in a different engine. On this we can go two ways. If he wants to make a one-time modification and if my people and I feel we have the experience and capability to insure the airworthiness of the modified aircraft, we can work with him and ultimately give him a field approval. If we find that the job is bigger than we feel we can handle, we help him get his request for a supplemental type certificate (STC) started through the engineering folks at region.

Another maintenance inspector checks out a powerplant mechanic on the job inquiring as to his diagnosis of the problem and the maintenance steps to be taken.

CLEARED TO LAND!

"Now, along comes a guy with a long, sad story—one that touches my heart and may, in the long run, touch his pocketbook. He's lost his airworthiness certificate and his logs. The airworthiness certificate usually is no great problem, strictly a paperwork task, but the logs are something else. It can be a long and costly thing to recreate the logs and those logs are a must, particularly if he may want to sell or trade the aircraft. First step is backtracking to the last inspection with his mechanic. Then he gets a letter off to Aircraft Records at Oak City asking for copies of everything on file there. Copies are not gratis, by the way, you have to pay for them. Then, there is the question of AD compliance. He must come up with full documentation that all ADs have been complied with even if it means tearing down the airplane and engine. Finally, there's the question of arriving at 'reasonable flying hours.' Obviously, this often must be a guesstimate but it has to be a darned accurate one because it must be notarized."

Sanell's "typical week" hasn't even begun yet and already he's snowed.

"Surveillance," he says, "isn't what it sounds like; we aren't like the FBI or the CIA. It means actually checking in the field to see if folks are doing what they're supposed to. On most general aviation aircraft—at least the privately owned ones—it is a spot check type of thing. We check 'em whenever we can. With air taxi operations, it's another ball of wax. Air taxis, I call 'em baby airlines, have a high priority because of their impact on the public. When you buy your ticket on an air carrier you know exactly what level of comfort and safety you're paying for. We think you deserve the same level of safety, if not comfort, when you take that air taxi to make connections. Therefore, air taxi operations come under close scrutiny. We check their aircraft, their records, their avionics, the maintenance base and the maintenance people."

What sort of time does this take? Sanell estimates one hour per aircraft, three hours for the maintenance base and four hours for certification of new aircraft. This must be accomplished at least once each quarter. Al figures most of the operators in his area—there are 35 of them—have an average of four aircraft and so it takes him one day each quarter (including travel time) or 35 out of the 60 work days in each quarter.

Sanell admits it doesn't leave much time to conduct surveillance on private aircraft. They must be spot checked when time permits.

"Often," he says, "we check private aircraft on the basis of a hunch while we're going to or from another job. A good case in point—I was at Cable Airport one day and I saw a pilot loading, loading and loading; four people, camping equipment and personal gear. The airplane was so heavily loaded and the load was so far aft the nose gear was almost off the concrete.

"I nosed around and found he was taking his mother and two other family members to the Colorado River. I didn't march up as an FAA inspector and berate him. I just sidled over and in a stage whisper said, 'If you love your mother, you'll leave her here and unload some of that gear.' He didn't react at once but I stuck around and soon he was unloading most of the baggage and repacking it in the car. Just maybe the FAA saved four lives that day."

Included in Sanell's typical schedule is weekend work—surveillance at the big, sport parachuting and gliding center at Lake Elsinore. This includes checking the "loft," the rigger's certificates and spot checking jumpers reserve chutes after the jump. Sanell points out that since reserve chutes are rarely

150

used they are not opened up, inspected and repacked as often as the main chutes. Concern about the booming interest in hang gliding convinced Al that sooner or later the FAA must get involved in regulating the sport, at least from a safety point of view. Al and a fellow inspector have taken a formal hang gliding course—at their own expense—and Al has made 15 flights. Sanell, by the way, holds a rating as balloon pilot and cheerfully admits to regularly taking a busman's holiday from his duties with the FAA to actively participate in the growing sport of free ballooning.

From the point of view of the maintenance inspector, what are the major problems found in aviation today? Sanell lists them like this:

"Unauthorized maintenance is a big one. Owners don't know what they are authorized to do themselves and what must be done by a certified mechanic. Also they take short cuts by allowing friends who 'know all about airplanes' to perform maintenance for them. Many of them look around for the cheapest job available and often find it in a shop where uncertified mechanics and even mechanic helpers are permitted to perform safety-critical work.

"Another area is simply understanding the why and wherefore of the maintenance requirements. They haven't been formulated just to make it difficult for the airplane owner. They can't understand why a lick here and a lick there to keep it running won't work on an airplane like it does on their automobile. Above all, they don't understand preventative maintenance and accept the fact that an annual inspection isn't enough. They don't even conduct an adequate pre-flight inspection."

On the question of pre-flight inspections, Sanell recommends something in addition to the recommended walk-around.

"Check all the items on the walk-around," he says, "and then just step off and look at the airplane from a distance. Often you'll spot something about the airplane that just isn't right, something you missed on the walk-around."

Sanell, who is the kind of gent who likes to get things done with a minimum of delay and red tape, likes his job in the field and exhibits an intensive pride in what he has accomplished.

"This is where it's at," he declares using the vernacular of today, "what we do here makes it all worthwhile!"

If you are about to ask, "How does he know so much, what about the top management levels where the real power rests?", don't. Al has the answer pat, he's been there. His long and varied experience with many types of aircraft and their maintenance problems earned him a jump up the golden ladder to FAA's Washington headshed and a slot in the General Aviation Maintenance Branch. In short, he didn't count his lucky stars but rather counted the days until he could once again get back into the field.

"That place has got to be the most frustrating experience in the world," he recalls, "especially if you really believe in the FAA and its responsibilities to the men and women who fly airplanes."

Sanell's place of business, the Ontario GADO, is one of 108 such facilities in the National Airways System. There are 68 GADOs, 16 FSDOs (a FSDO is established where the area has both general aviation and air carrier operating offices), and 24 Air Carrier District Offices (ACDO) situated geographically in the major air carrier operating centers. These offices are manned by some 1,160 inspectors—404 operations and 305 maintenance inspectors involved with general aviation and 329 operations and 122 inspectors involved with air carriers. In addition, 82 of the district offices—68 GADOs and 14 FSDOs—have accident prevention specialists.

These men and women who are especially trained to work directly with individual pilots, pilot groups, fixed base operators, flying schools and, in fact, all facets of the aviation community, are a recent addition to the district offices. Since more than 87 percent of all general aviation accidents involve some sort of pilot error, it became clear that the single most effective thing the FAA might do was to conduct an intensive program of flying safety education at the grass roots level. The accident prevention specialists today provide free of charge a wide variety of professionally-written safety literature, conduct regular seminars and flight safety clinics, offer "safety" flight checks to pilots who request them and give individual counseling as required. To assist in reaching the more than 800,000 licensed pilots across the country, they have developed a corps of accident prevention counselors, CFIs recruited as volunteers to actively bring flying safety right down to the local airport level.

It is unfortunate that FAA operations and maintenance inspectors are faced with the virtually impossible task of being charged with promoting aviation on the one hand and with enforcing the regulations that are necessary for flying safety on the other. As one inspector puts it:

"How do you gain the confidence of the pilot when one day you hold his hand as a friend and the next day have to rap him along side the head because he goofs?"

Since, in the final analysis the goal of the inspector is to make aviation as safe as possible, he often must walk a thin line and inject a whole lot of common sense and human psychology into achieving that goal.

That is the operating philosophy of today's inspector, but it wasn't always so and therein lies the cause of the major schism existing between the FAA and the flying public. Frank Allen, an aviation oldtimer if there ever was one and head of the Long Beach, Calif. FSDO, explains:

"When I learned to fly, the inspector was a little tin god. He could lift your license; ground your plane on the spot if he saw fit. I knew an inspector once who would not re-license your plane when you brought it around for an annual inspection if the safety belts hadn't been scrubbed clean. Inspectors were badge happy. We still are looked upon as part of the fuzz, yet only a small part of our job today is enforcement."

When it comes to recalling the yesteryear of aviation, particularly general aviation, Allen has an edge on a lot of us. He learned to fly in 1930 at the Hancock Foundation College of Aeronautics—a "live-in" school run on a military basis with a uniform and everything. The course was a 200-hour one leading to what was then known as the "Transport License." Instruction began in Fleets, moved into Great Lakes and finished in Stinsons and Ryan Broughams.

On graduation, Allen stayed with the school as an instrument instructor. The instrument course called for five hours of flight—the old needle, ball and airspeed kind—and graduation consisted of flying a triangular, 50-mile course navigating entirely by dead reckoning. One of Frank's students was the late Earl Ortman of National Air Race fame—Earl was known for his impressive record in the Keith Ryder Special.

"Well," Allen recalls, "Earl caught on to instrument flying right quick. He also quickly got bored with the routine. So we tried a little instrument aerobatics. That he liked. It got to where all he liked to do was to slow roll on instruments."

Allen's flying career also includes a stint at barnstorming which ended when he "smeared" his Barling MB-3 taking off from a West Virginia pasture after patching up the damage caused by hooking a fence getting into the same pasture. From there he had a crack at airline flying. As an American Air Lines first officer he took his training with America's current dean of aviation authors, Ernie Gann. In 1940, he joined the CAA and almost immediately found himself (certainly due to his long experience) in a top management job at the regional level.

"The early 40s," Allen explains, "were an interesting period for aviation. The war was over. Hundreds of military pilots, many of them with impressive numbers of multi-engine time, were looking for jobs. Also there were scores of surplus twin-engine and four-engine military transports available almost for a song.

"This was the beginning of today's fleet of supplemental air carriers, the original non-skeds like Flying Tigers, Slick and Los Angeles Airways. But it was a far cry from the highly professional, well-organized operation we have now. In those days, any pilot who could scare up a co-pilot and raise money for the minimum down payment on a surplus Curtiss Commando or Douglas Gooney Bird was in business—a one-man airline as it were. You wouldn't believe how scroungy some of those operations were. Many of them were little more than flying tramp steamers constantly moving from place to place looking for a cargo, living in the airplanes when they couldn't afford a cheap motel—and that was most of the time. I know of one crew that regularly used the back end of the cargo bay as their latrine because they didn't have a relief tube.

"Those were wild days. We had to move fast to keep up with them. There were a lot of unfortunate accidents before we got them properly regulated and even then it was tough. It was a new business with new regulations. Most of the pilots were military types who really didn't give a damn about civilian regulations anyway. But, we all learned and grew together. Today the supplemental air carriers are a major part of the aviation business."

Ask Allen how he sizes up the problems of the FAA inspector today and he thinks a minute. Then, choosing his words carefully, he replies:

"Well, I think one of the biggest problems is seeing that the new students get the right kind of training. The goal of most commercial pilots, it seems, is the air lines. That's where the big money is. As the airlines grow and hire, chief pilots and CFIs in the flight schools move on. There is a big turnover. Also there are hundreds of freelance CFIs who instruct just enough to keep their certificates valid or who moonlight instructing because they can't support a family with their full time job. We, the FAA that is, check fly all CFIs. We can certify them in terms of their knowledge and the quality of their technique. But the only way an instructor becomes a good instructor is to instruct. CFIs who are not working at it full time just aren't proficient enough. They know their business but they don't realize they aren't getting through to the student. One of the ways we have developed to combat this is the periodic flight instructor refresher clinics held under the sponsorship of local aviation organizations but conducted by a special team right out of the FAA Academy at Oak City."

CLEARED TO LAND!

Pilot flight checks are an important part of the general aviation inspector's job. Here an applicant for a commercial license gets the treatment. First, the inspector has him demonstrate that the aircraft is airworthy. Next comes an oral quiz on the cockpit instrumentation and the applicant's understanding of it. Finally, the inspector climbs into the rear seat for a check ride. Although most private, commercial and instrument applicants are checked by "designated examiners," many prefer to take their check ride with an FAA inspector.

THE INSPECTORS - I

What about today's general aviation pilots? Allen sees some correlation between the inadequate instruction some pilots receive and their subsequent accidents; a significant relationship between accidents and the currency of the pilot; and also a disturbing accident trend among the physician/lawyer/engineer/professional-man, high performance airplane owners.

"In terms of the student accidents," Allen feels, "a lot of these are the result of inadequate training. Flight instruction is expensive. Too many new students shop around for the cheapest rates. The cheap school usually isn't the best. Too often he elects to take his instruction from a friend-of-a-friend who is a CFI and who, more often than not, is one of those CFIs who instruct just enough to keep a valid certificate. Since the CFI himself isn't really sharp and current in terms of his effectiveness as an instructor, the quality of instruction suffers and ultimately the student. It is absolutely imperative that the student develop the right habits from the very outset. The instructor must get the job done during the training period. He never gets another chance."

The Long Beach FSDO chief doesn't have a ready answer to the correlation between pilot currency and the accident rate. He thinks the newly-acquired biennial flight review (BFR) is a step in the right direction but certainly still leaves a lot to be desired. The BFR, even if it is conducted correctly, can only bring to light—and then only every two years—a lack of pilot proficiency or lack of basic procedural understanding on the part of the airman that would tend to make an early accident a certainty. It cannot insure that the individual airman achieves and maintains the degree of currency (both in flight and in type) necessary if he is to react quickly and effectively in event of an in-flight emergency.

"That's where being current both in terms of recent experience and in the particular aircraft type you are flying pays the ultimate dividend," Allen declares.

"Almost any pilot," he says, "can get an airplane off the ground, navigate to the next airport and safely get it back on the ground as long as—and that's the big if—everything goes according to plan. But throw in something out of the ordinary, some minor mechanical or avionic malfunction, an unexpected change in the weather, a different approach made necessary by other traffic, a temporary physical impairment like a headache, nausea or blurred vision and things begin to go to pieces. That's where being current pays off. If the pilot doesn't have to work at flying and navigating the airplane he can cope with the extra mental and physical activity needed to meet the emergency."

Although there are no exact statistics, flying safety experts generally agree that in most situations recent experience is more important than total flying hours. In other words, the man who has only 200 hours but is flying currently at the rate of 10 hours a month turns out to be a lower accident risk than the pilot with 2,000 hours total time who flies a couple of hours a month. Along these lines there has been some discussion about establishing a mandatory flying time requirement, say on a monthly basis. Allen agrees with most other authorities on this question:

"Sure it would be desirable from a flying safety point of view but it would be entirely impossible to administer."

On the subject of professional people who own and fly their own airplanes, Allen agrees that the accident trend is alarming but he does not agree with a number of other authorities as to the causative factors.

CLEARED TO LAND!

Many CFIs, FAA inspectors and flying safety experts are of the opinion that the increasing number of accidents, many of them fatal, involving high performance aircraft and pilots who are professional men and women are the result of what they call "a professional arrogance" on the part of the pilots. They feel the pilots, because of the high level of professional training in their particular fields, tend to look down on the art of flying as something routine and largely mechanical, something that really doesn't merit a level of training and competency on par with that required in their profession. This does not elicit agreement from Allen.

"Certainly," he says, "entirely too many of these people are busting up their high performance airplanes. But, I don't really attribute it to any arrogance on their part. Rather, I think it is just a case of not making enough time in their schedule. These people have both the money and the requirement for fast air transportation. Speed unfortunately equates with complexity and sophistication. The fast four-place single engine and small multi-engine aircraft are just that. They represent a lot of airplane. Obviously, they require a much higher level of pilot expertise and proficiency—not to mention currency. But the men and women who can afford and operate them don't have the time to devote to developing and maintaining the necessary proficiency and currency. It's that simple, I think."

Allen's Long Beach FSDO is one of two in the nation with a continuing requirement for inspectors with a special qualification—a water rating. Both Frank and his principal operations inspector, Ed Perlis, are water rated. In fact, Allen's rating for float planes, flying boats and amphibians goes back a way.

While seaplanes operate in many parts of the country, only in Southern California and in the Miami, Fla., area have there been constant commercial seaplane activities over a prolonged period. Seaplanes have been operating between the Los Angeles/Long Beach area and Santa Catalina Island 22 miles off shore since just after World War I. The original carrier was Avalon Air Transport operating Douglas Dolphins. After World War II, one of the carriers acquired the big, four-engine flying boat (the Sikorski S-44) that took President Franklin Roosevelt to Casablanca. Today two carriers, Catalina Air Lines and Air Catalina, operate fleets of Grumman Goose aircraft on the route. Allen, who gave the original water ratings in the S-44, including that for the flight engineer, and Perlis are in great demand checking out the Goose crews. Recently Allen was called upon to give a water rating to Philipe Cousteau in his father's world-rambling Consolidated PBY.

Although most private, commercial and instrument check rides today are given by FAA "designated examiners"—CFIs especially trained, selected and authorized to act in behalf of the FAA in this respect—there still are a lot of rides that must be given by an FAA operations inspector.

"For instance," Allen says, "we fly all jet check rides (we have a number of general aviation jet operators in our area) and all CFI check rides. We can delegate airline transport rating rides but we tend to fly most of them around here. We give the water ratings and we fly six-month VFR and IFR (these are given separately) check rides to the pilots flying for air taxi operators. Obviously, we also try to honor requests for check rides from the general aviation public who drop in off the street. It is amazing how many pilots feel better just

156

getting a check from one of us every so often. Actually, we could spend all our time just flying check rides."

Ed Perlis hasn't been around aviation as long as his boss but during the 34 years he has been flying he has racked up an impressive 27,000 hours and can prove it. Unlike the majority of both old and new pilots today, Ed keeps his log book up to date (as the regulations require, by the way) and can show you what he flew, where he flew it and how long he flew yesterday or the day before or the day before that. He got his start as an aviation cadet in 1942 and graduated as a fighter pilot. Fate, in the form of his superiors who found in him the qualities they wanted for instructors, doomed him to spend most of the war teaching others how to fly the Vultee BT-13—the old "Vibrator," the North American T-6 and the doughty Boeing B-17. He finally broke loose from the Flying Training Command by volunteering for B-29s but even then things went awry. He ended up in Great Britain instead of the Pacific.

For nearly 10 years after the war, Perlis owned and operated his own flight instruction business at Long Beach, gravitating to the CAA and an assignment in Seattle, Wash., in 1958.

"It took me 14 years to get back home," he chuckles, "but I finally made it. I'll have to admit it was fun along the way—that is, except for the Seattle weather."

Perlis is one of many FAA inspectors who can't say enough for the quality and quantity of training the FAA provides for its people. Since joining the agency he has been jet qualified, helicopter rated, rated in lighter-than-aircraft and in gliders. These added to his airplane single and multi-engine land and sea ratings add up to a lot of capability and experience.

A hangar flying session with Perlis sooner or later must get around to his job and how he sees it today.

"I can't put my finger on any single major problem," he says, "I can't break it down. We have a lot to accomplish, flight tests, accident and incident investigations, counseling—they all take time and they all have their own little individual problems."

Not unlike other inspectors around the country, Ed Perlis is concerned with the quality of instruction new pilots are getting, but he points out that there is a check-and-balance-system. Even though a student might not get the very best instruction available, his deficiencies should be picked up when he takes his check flight with an FAA-designated pilot examiner.

How good is the examiner program?

"Like the instruction program," he replies, "as good as the man. But here we have a lot better chance to control it. We select the designees for pilot and instrument examiner. They don't select us. Sure, a qualified CFI can let us know he is available and would like to become designee but that doesn't necessarily cut any ice. When we need a designated examiner in a given geographical area we first look at people we know have an outstanding track record as instructors. Then we have to check further to see if they are, in fact, fully qualified. Once the designee is working in the system, we continue to monitor his effectiveness. We check some of his students, we check the examiner from time to time and, in larger aircraft, we ride shotgun and observe as he gives a check ride."

Perlis places great emphasis on the quality of the designated examiner because he says, when it comes to a "standard, uniform quality of instruction you are getting into a bag of worms."

"CFIs have it tough," he declares, "particularly if they are trying to earn a living and support a family on instructing alone. Unless the instructor is lucky to work for one of the big schools, he only gets paid when the prop is turning. Very few operators pay a salary or pay for ground work. Therefore the name of the game is to get the student into the blue and keep him there.

"Now, to do a really good job of training someone to fly and fly safely it takes at least an hour and a half on the ground for each hour in the air. If the instructor is trying to make ends meet for himself and his family he can't afford to give the student the ground time he needs. The student crams to pass the written examination. He retains little of what he has learned. He passes the flight test proving he can get the airplane off the ground, around the field and back on again with some degree of proficiency. Suddenly, he's a pilot."

Perlis and other inspectors deplore the fact that there are far too many of these kind of pilots flying today. As long as they stay with the aircraft in which they learned to fly; remain in an area with which they are familiar; avoid getting themselves and their airplane into any environment with which they are unsure; and, above all, fly only in blue-sky weather they'll be all right. Get them into marginal weather, over strange terrain or let them have a partial avionics failure, run into turbulence, experience icing or any one of a hundred other things that are part of the flying experience and they are in trouble.

The problems encountered today with establishing and maintaining a consistent high quality of flight instruction on a nationwide basis are what recently brought about new, tougher standards under FAR Part 141 which regulate the so-called "approved school." Allen, Perlis and their fellow inspectors agree that it costs a good bit of money to set up and operate an approved school and, therefore, flight instruction from that school comes dearer than most. But they feel, very strongly as a matter of fact, that like everything else in this world "you pay for what you get" and in the case of flight instruction, where the pilot's life and often the lives of others will depend on it, it doesn't pay to buy bargains.

Perlis also has one point he likes to make to every pilot that will listen. He feels it probably has kept a lot of his former students alive.

"It's just as important—maybe more important—to know what not to do when you fly an airplane as to know what to do!"

Still another perspective of exactly what the FAA operations inspector is and does comes from eavesdropping on a rap session between another old-timer, Cal Isselhardt of the Detroit FSDO, and a brand new inspector, diminutive Carol Rayburn, now on duty with the Salt Lake GADO.

Carol gravitated towards aviation when in the fifth grade. Her dad had flown in World War II and later became interested enough to buy a Champ and ultimately moved up to a Cessna 170. She began flying in high school, got her private license at 17, went on to a commercial license and began ferrying aircraft and dusting. While getting a degree in Political Science at South Dakota State University, she was offered a "good deal" on a flight instructor's rating and ended up as both a full time college student and full time flight instructor. Then, as she puts it, "I got my hands greasy" working as a charter pilot, flying for the Forest Service, instructing and a "little bit of everything." Actually it was her friends who pushed her into applying for an FAA inspector's position mainly because they felt she was the "kind of person the FAA needs."

Cal, on the other hand, remembers getting the bug watching blimps at the old Scott Field, Belleville, Ill., as a youngster. He enlisted in the Navy V-5 program as a seaman, went on through pre-flight and initial flight training in "Yellow Perils" at Corpus Christi, ending up as an instructor in OS-2U Kingfishers at New Orleans Naval Air Station. After the war, an old friend who "was crazy about airplanes" became the angel for an airport business back home in Belleville.

"He had the money and I had the experience," Cal grins, allowing as how "operating a local airport also requires getting involved in city politics." Cal became a CAA designated flight examiner and things were going well until, in 1951, "that big brown envelope came" telling Navy reservist Cal Isselhardt to report for active duty. When the Korean affair was over, Cal stayed in and finished 21 years, retiring to go directly into the FAA (he had applied during his final year on active duty).

Resting between training sessions at the FAA Academy, where Cal was getting his Jet Commander and Lear 25 ratings and Carol was completing her initial indoctrination, they swapped impressions of the FAA and their individual roles.

Carol—"Nobody had to brainwash me. I knew exactly what I was getting into before I signed up. Although I'm still pretty young in the business, I have been around a lot in the aviation industry. One of the first things I learned was that if you got to know your GADO and if you went to them, they could keep you out of a lot of trouble. I also found that FAA inspectors had gotten away from inspection with a badge and a club and had become education oriented. What I have learned at the Academy confirms that."

Cal—"That's right. You don't see the FAA hiding behind the hangar anymore watching to catch someone in an infraction. Today diplomacy plays a big part in getting our job done."

Carol—"Another thing, every inspector has to be able to put his money where his mouth is. You have to be able to do everything the other pilot can do but do it better."

Cal—"There is a whole new challenge for inspectors today. They must be much more literate. They must be more skilled in personal communications. They have to have a greater awareness of the need to maintain good public relations."

Isselhardt then added, grimacing, as Carol vigorously nodded in agreement:

"And you have to be more efficient in using your time. It's a real headache today with the new labor laws. We have to account for every hour of our time by category."

Notwithstanding this new look for FAA inspectors and the emphasis on education as opposed to enforcement, they still have all too much enforcement to do. It all gets back to people. People are just that and, to many of them, the very fact of imposing a regulation is like waving a red flag at a bull. Also, you can teach a man or woman to fly and fly proficiently, but you can't teach judgment.

Although all accidents do not involve the young pilot or student, many of them do. In 1973 the national ratio of fatal accidents to total accidents was one out of six but for students it was one out of three. Perhaps this case history underlines that critical area, an area enormously frustrating to all inspectors.

This happened in South Carolina . . . around 9:15 P.M.—late twilight—a woman heard an airplane flying low over her house. ("Low," she said, "like the airplanes that spray for mosquito control.") A few minutes later there was a crash, so loud that it woke her husband. He went out and looked around but found nothing. It was not until the next morning that the wreckage was located by a Civil Air Patrol search plane. The three occupants were dead. FAA and NTSB investigators moved in to find out what had caused the crash. As it turned out there were several causes.

One of the first facts they discovered was that the pilot was a student, who had neither the legal right nor the proven skill to pilot a plane carrying passengers. Another very pertinent fact was that the three men had been flying in a Cessna 150, which did not have a third seat. One of the passengers was apparently riding in the baggage area. This could certainly have changed the handling characteristics of the airplane, with serious consequences for an inexperienced pilot who was used to flying alone. Most light trainers are affected very noticeably by the addition of weight in the cockpit.

A second factor came to light with the toxicology test results. A high alcohol content was found in the blood of all three men and in the pilot and one passenger there was a drug of the type used for sleeping pills or "downers," which could cause a depressed state, impairment of judgment and decreased inhibitions. Either the alcohol or drug would have affected the ability to safely pilot an aircraft; in combination they could be—in this case were—fatal.

The flying history of the pilot was revealing, although incomplete. Records indicated he had applied for his second student certificate in January, 1973—about the time he bought the airplane. At that time he declared nine hours total time logged, with no flying in the previous six months. The instructor who had given him 4.4 hours of dual in January of 1972 and signed him off for solo in a Cherokee 140 also flew 1.2 hours with him in the 150 and signed him off to solo in that aircraft. Those 5.6 hours of instruction were all that the records showed.

Official findings of the probable causes of the accident listed continuing flight into conditions beyond his experience and ability; physical impairment with alcohol and drugs and unwarranted low flying. Although admittedly extreme, this case exhibits the many factors that may be present when student pilots carry passengers illegally, have minimal flying experience, are ignorant of the dangers of drugs and alcohol, and are unfamiliar with weight and balance problems.

A less extreme, but perhaps more common type of accident involved a pilot who had bought one-fourth of a Cessna 172 and, in realization of a longstanding dream, had begun his flight training. The night after he soloed he gathered with some friends to celebrate his achievement. Round after round of drinks were offered up to his success and toasts to "the greatest pilot in the world" became more believable with each round. When one of the girls in the group issued a challenge to "prove it," he headed merrily to the airport with the girl in hand.

Fortunately, he never managed to get the airplane off the ground. He lost control while taxiing, crashed into several airplanes parked on the ramp and virtually destroyed his own aircraft—but neither he nor his passenger were hurt.

What all this adds up to is the inescapable fact that the FAA inspectors——both operations and maintenance—will never be able to get away entirely from his enforcer image. Like the cop on the beat, they still must deal with the men and women who cannot or will not obey the regulations imposed for their safety and the safety of others. But, as Carol Rayburn sums it up:

"We're trying to wear our white hat a little more often!"

THE INSPECTORS - II 9

The next time you take a good look at the crew compartment of one of your local airliners notice the seats. The captain's and first officer's chairs seem almost throne-like; roomy, comfortably built with scientifically designed lumbar supports, three-way control, special cushions and other features. The flight engineer's chair is only a little less imposing, certain concessions having been made to that crew member's need to move quickly about the crew station.

Look closely, however, and you'll find another seat, sometimes two—in most aircraft just that—a seat, not a chair. This is the "jump seat" so-called because it usually is a folding seat, one which can be conveniently stored up against a stanchion or bulkhead when not in use. Its placement in the cabin usually is out-of-the-way, which simply means it is the least desirable place to spend a three-to-five-hour flight. In all respects, it represents a means to accommodate a person of little importance in the cockpit—someone whose presence can go literally unnoticed and who has no impact on normal cockpit routine.

Most of the time that is the case. In fact, most of the time the jump seat goes unoccupied. But sometimes a subtle yet powerful force seems to emanate from it. The captain, first officer and flight engineer become all too aware of that "presence." In fact, the "clank factor" has been known to come into play calling for an extra digestion tablet or two. It's check ride time and the man in the jump seat is Douglas Howard, Carl Whitman, Tom Fydell or any other of the 400-odd FAA Airman Certificate Inspectors and Operations Inspectors whose job it is to see that the nation's airlines and aircrews perform at peak efficiency in the interests of public safety.

For this ride let's suppose the man in the jump seat is Doug Howard. An Operations Inspector assigned to the Los Angeles Air Carrier District Office (ACDO), Howard has some 33 years of active aeronautical experience behind him. He learned to fly with the Army Air Corps in World War II and got a second crack at military aviation at the request of his government during the Korean conflict. Doug was head of Standardization and Evaluation for the 452nd Troop Carrier Wing and later did a tour flying Air Force Special Air Missions aircraft in Europe. Airline experience came as a line pilot with the Flying Tigers.

A stocky, greying man of medium height and a sober countenance, Howard is deadly serious about his job and the importance of professionalism in the airline cockpit. However, like most of his counterparts in other areas of the nation, Doug would much prefer to find good safety and operating procedures than to have to write up a pilot for unsafe operation or an infringement of regulations.

"Usually," Howard says, "we try not to spring a check ride as a surprise. In fact, we try to make an appointment. This isn't always possible since occasionally we have to get in a check ride as part of a 'positioning flight'—that's one where we have to meet an aircraft at another location and give a check ride on a 'demand' basis. Demand work usually is a ride required when a pilot is changing his certificate, for instance, upgrading the type of equipment he is certificated to operate. Demand work also can be generated by a request from another FAA region to give a check ride on a route segment in our area."

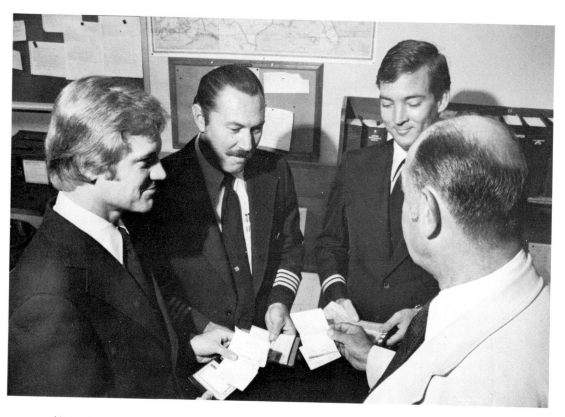

Air carrier inspectors are not just concerned with the quality of an airman's flying ability, they are concerned with every aspect of the flight—the proper paperwork, ground handling and loading, the aircraft, equipment and, of course, the crew. Typically, the first crew meeting with the inspector finds him checking their credentials (pilot certificates, medical certificates, etc.)

Doug admits that sometimes it just isn't possible to make an appointment and the first time the captain knows today is check ride day is when he reports to Flight Scheduling an hour before takeoff and the dispatcher points to Howard in the corner and says there is an ACM (additional crew member) on board. There are times when the captain may be an old friend. That makes for a more pleasant trip, but, Howard warns:

"It doesn't cut any ice when it comes to the check."

Whether the captain is an old friend or a complete stranger to Howard, there is a little formality that must be completed. Doug first shows the captain his FAA credentials and then asks that the captain reciprocate by showing his airman's certificate and medical certificate.

"It is important," Howard emphasizes, "that the inspector thoroughly brief the captain on the purpose of the check ride. For instance, it makes a difference whether the inspector is an ACI or an Operations Inspector and if he is not an ACI, whether or not he is qualified in the type of equipment in which the flight is to be made. An ACI always is qualified in the type of equip-

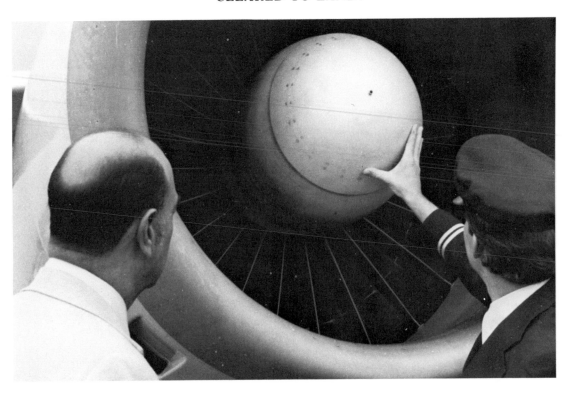

Like a shadow, he follows the second officer as he makes his all-important pre-flight walkaround inspection of the aircraft. The inspector eyeballs loading and stowage of bins on this cargo flight.

ment but an Operations Inspector may not be. If not, his inspection will be confined to procedures and adherence to regulations. If he is qualified in the equipment, he will also check all aspects of aircraft operation in the same manner as the ACI."

The check ride begins right there in Flight Scheduling when the inspector and the captain meet one another. As an ACM, the inspector follows through on every aspect of flight planning—weather briefing, NOTAMS (Notice To Airmen—special information put out by FAA whenever it is required detailing navigational aids which may be inoperative, runways which may not be used due to construction or damage, special hazards to flight in a particular area, etc.), takeoff weight and balance computation, fuel quantity on board and estimated consumption, the pilot's preflight inspection, the flight engineer's preflight inspection and the aircraft log book inspection.

"There are a lot of things to check on during the departure," Howard explains, "such as the starting procedure; the takeoff conditions including gross weight; the outside air temperature and the surface winds and runway conditions which dictate the takeoff roll and the safety margins; the runup; the captain's instructions to his crew on emergency procedures to be followed; the clearance record and readback and the various aspects of the takeoff and climb out itself. We are particularly concerned with altitude awareness during the climb out and adherence to the SID (standard instrument departure) instructions."

Enroute, Doug observes the crew noting compliance with minimum enroute altitudes (MEA), use of airborne radar and on-board navigation systems, adherence to the clearance, use of ground navigation facilities and, always—altitude awareness during the cruise, during the descent, during the approach. On the approach and landing phase, he also is concerned with the aircraft configuration (position and use of flaps, gear, spoilers, power settings, etc.), airspeed control, gross weight and the degree to which the approach is "stabilized."

Throughout the trip, Howard has been observing other areas of concern such as cockpit vigilance, crew coordination, judgment on the part of the captain, flight management, handling of emergencies if any, use of checklists, noise abatement procedures and the overall proficiency of the second in command and the flight engineer.

What about grey areas?

For instance, Howard explains, there is a fine line between when a pilot can make an approach. If the weather given prior to his reaching the Final Approach Fix (FAF) is below minimums he is obliged to abort the approach but if the ceiling and visibility change after he passes the FAF he can go down and "have a look see." If he has the runway threshold in sight at the Minimum Descent Altitude (MDA) or Decision Height (DH), depending on the kind of instrument approach he is making, he can go ahead and land. Sometimes it becomes a moot point just when the captain was informed of the existing ceiling and visibility.

Doug also mentions the question of altitude on circling approaches. This also becomes one of those fine-line questions. If the captain should find the ceiling exactly at the minimum altitude established for a circling approach, the captain will "bust" the minimum if he completes the approach. Essentially then, if the ceiling is, say 50 feet above the minimum, the pilot is okay for the approach. If it is at the minimum and he completes the approach, but doesn't have visual contact with the runway, he is in violation. Just where that ceiling was can be the subject of quite a discussion, particularly if it was a "measured ceiling" and the measurement was current.

"I don't know if every inspector would agree with me," Howard says, "but the way I look at it, you expect the pilot to do the best he can within the rules but if circumstances force him beyond the rules the measure must be good judgment."

What about the pilots of today as compared with those of yesteryear?

Tom Fydell, an inspector with 30 years in the business, admits he has asked himself the same question and has concluded:

"There is a difference but the change has been gradual. With few exceptions the day of the 'aviator' is gone. The aviator, by the way, was the Douglas Fairbanks-type of guy loaded with bravado and wearing a pencil-thin mustache, a white silk scarf wrapped about his neck, chasing every pretty girl he could find.

"Today airline pilots prove to be just everyday people with everyday problems like the car that needs a new transmission, the house that needs painting, the kids that need braces and the wife who gets tired of staying home alone—except for the kids, that is."

Contrary to general belief, inspectors are not super pilots—consummate practitioners of the art of flying whose skill and unerring judgment elevate them above all other airmen. Rather, they, like the men and women they must check, are human. They come in various sizes, colors, shapes, ages and degrees of individual pilot proficiency. When they pass judgment on the performance of an airline captain or crew member that judgment is not based on their personal or even professional opinion but rather on the degree with which that crew member or pilot has complied with established practices, procedures and regulations prescribed in FAA Regulations and in that particular airline's operations manual.

"That's where we must be the experts," Howard observes, "we have to know the FARs frontwards and backwards and we have to know the line's operations manual as well as the people who wrote it. Those regulations and manuals embody the safest practices and procedures yet devised. Our job is to insure that the crews comply with them."

Howard says that if an "unsafe" practice or procedure is observed, he must notify the crew member "right then!" Minor deviations are written up on the inspection report. Even then they first are discussed with the crew at the end of the flight.

"I get together with the crew," Doug explains, "and brief them on the deviations I have noticed and those I plan to write up. Where the problems can be resolved by discussion, we talk it out right there and any corrective actions are noted in the report. Rarely do I have to cite a captain or crew member for a violation and in less than one percent of the checks have I found practices or procedures which are unsafe."

What's a minor deviation?

Doug illustrates—during the preflight the captain fails to check the NOTAMS and on arrival at his destination finds the glide slope is inoperative and there is a displaced runway threshold; a flight engineer may cross-feed from the wrong tanks; the captain may make an unauthorized deviation from his flight plan.

How about a major discrepancy for which he might have to cite the captain?

"That's easy," he replies, "the captain busts minimums (goes below published ceiling and visibility minimums on his approach)."

"Most airline crews today are just all-American guys and a few gals. They are substantial citizens and competent technicians doing a competent job. They represent a high order of physical and mental health and they have a lot of respect for that little card (their airline transport rating) we provide them," Howard adds.

Tom Fydell feels that age group and seniority have little or nothing to do with the characteristics of the modern air crewman. Most of them are "good guys," he says, adding, "but like the old saying, 'There's one on every bus.' "

"However, it's not just the captain or the crew," he observes, "it is also a matter of our attitude. Rarely is there any resentment. We let them know we would rather find things that are right than things that are wrong. Even when there may be a lack of hospitality in the cockpit, if we take the right approach, we usually leave the airplane with a better feeling all around."

Fydell does make a point about writing in little black books during the flight.

"Sometime ago," he recalls, "I was on a flight through Wake Island and Hawaii to the mainland. We not only check on the aircraft and crew, we also take a look at ground facilities. While at Wake, I looked over the weather setup and made myself some notes later during the flight to Honolulu. When we arrived at Honolulu and I was leaving the flight, the first officer came up to me and asked how the trip had been.

" 'Fine,' I said, offhandedly. He apparently was worried about something and persisted in inquiring if I had found any discrepancies. When I responded in the negative he finally came right out and asked: 'Would you mind telling me what you were writing in your book, if you found nothing wrong?' Well, I quickly lied and told him I was writing a letter to my wife. I knew he would never believe the truth. But, this taught me a lesson. Now I warn the crews when I make notes and tell them whether or not it has anything to do with them. It takes away just a little of the clank factor."

One thing Fydell puts across with considerable emphasis. The average inspector, he says, has great respect for the crews with whom he flies "because they earn it!"

What does the average inspector think about his responsibility?

Carl Whitman—19 years an inspector, 39 years a pilot—makes no bones about how he feels. He looks you straight in the eye with a gaze so penetrating you can't help but get the message and be convinced of his absolute sincerity.

"My job," he says, "is like a religion. I represent the American public by insuring the best qualified people are flying those jet aircraft!"

Perhaps most inspectors would not phrase it exactly the way Carl does, but generally they feel just as strongly about the enormous responsibility that has been placed on their shoulders.

Whitman, who keeps an eye peeled for "bad habits that can get a pilot in trouble sooner or later," is quite frank about the fact that there is, on occasion, some resentment on the part of crew members.

"I don't find it very often," he says, "but there are times when you know it is there. It creates an element of tension in the crew compartment. When I feel that tension, I just sit back and quietly observe. On the other hand, there are captains who welcome you aboard like old friends. It is a pleasure to fly with them."

What about the job itself, the nature of airline flying over the years?

"There is no doubt there has been a change," Fydell responds, "in the early days it was seat-of-the-pants flying. Everything depended on the pilot's feel for the airplane and more operational decisions were made on the individual judgment of the captain.

"Now the decisions largely are made for you—it is strictly by-the-numbers. Nearly everything is pre-computed. The numbers tell you what to do and when to do it. Over the years there has been a complete transition."

This flying by the numbers and the fact that today's jet airliners normally fly high above the weather, in the clear above the clouds, the crews logging little actual instrument time, gives rise to concern in some FAA circles that something is lacking in the carriers' training programs.

These opinions certainly do not reflect any official FAA position on the subject and the inspectors themselves prefer not to be publicly identified as taking a stand not backed by agency policy. But, nevertheless, many of them share the belief that there exists a "difference of opinion about some procedures being flown by the airlines in company simulators and the real world requirements."

One veteran inspector who formerly flew with the airlines himself puts it this way:

"I call it the jet syndrome. The airline crews today always fly above the weather—they get little actual weather time. Also the name of the game is passenger comfort. Weather can be bumpy. When the airline pilot encounters weather he wants to get down out of it just as soon as he can.

"Another thing, he is used to flying above all the obstructions. Low altitudes, especially low altitudes close to the mountains and other obstructions, make him nervous—they are foreign to him. Again, here he wants to get down and out as soon as possible.

"This sets up the kind of situation that can lead to bad judgment. Say he has descended for an approach and is over a hilly area in considerable weather. Since he was an instrument student he has been taught to follow the approach plate. The plate tells him at what altitude to fly on each segment of the approach, when and where to begin his descent to the airport. Bumping along there in the weather he welcomes the words of the approach controller, 'You're cleared for the approach,' and immediately—without regard for the approach plate and without a thought to checking his actual position at the time, relying entirely on the controller to monitor his position with regard to obstructions, he cranks in nosedown trim, eases back the power and starts down. The next thing could be big trouble."

Some veteran inspectors think this is the kind of situation that set up the Dulles disaster in 1974 where the airliner crashed into the brow of a hill while approaching for a landing at the Washington, D.C. airport. The accident resulted in a flurry of accusations and counter accusations between FAA officials and senior airline captains invited to testify as expert witnesses—the air traffic control people blaming the captain and the airline pilots blaming the air traffic control systems, the controller handling this flight in particular. The disagreement finally was resolved by the FAA issuing a clarification to procedures—stating in new language what most airmen had understood all along: that it is the responsibility of the pilot to make the final decision as to when it is safe to begin an approach based on his precise knowledge of his position with relation to the terrain and obstructions.

This is a step in the right direction, another inspector says, but it isn't the answer. The real problem is too much flying entirely by the numbers, too much reliance on today's sophisticated air and ground systems, too little opportunity in the training and proficiency programs for the pilots to test their own judgment and too little actual experience flying in the soup instead of above it. Obviously, with the high cost of aircraft operation and the salary structure in today's air carrier operations it isn't practicable to send pilots out in DC-10s and Boeing 747s poking holes in the sky getting weather time. But, they point out, the simulation programs could be made more demanding. They could include more time grinding around at lower altitudes, in mountainous terrain, shooting some of the more difficult instrument approaches in the nation. In other words, get away from routine—routine that can be the breeding ground for bad habits—and throw in some surprises to keep the trainees on their toes.

The inspectors who advocate these changes frankly don't feel they will ever come about, but they do feel such changes might avoid another Dulles disaster.

In the aggregate, FAA air carrier inspectors are quite satisfied with the quality of today's airline crews.

"They are all pretty professional," Doug Howard observes, "and with the prime carriers, all personnel are very well qualified."

He does admit he would like to see a little higher level of overall proficiency from the smaller lines. One beneficial thing that has occurred with the increased sophistication of the aircraft is the fact that "they are all doing it the same way now." There was a day, he recalls, when airline pilots sort of lived by a double standard. They did it one way for the FAA and another way for themselves.

"Those days are gone," Howard says, "because the complexity of equipment and the air traffic control system eliminated the option the captain used to have. He can't fly by a double standard today. Now the guys fly by the book simply because that's the easiest way to fly the airplane. Even the old-timers have recognized this."

Although airman certificate and operations inspectors are in the majority—there are 402 of them nationally—they aren't the only men and women responsible for keeping an eye on air carriers. In addition, there are some 156 maintenance inspectors and 63 electronics inspectors manning ACDOs across the country. Even so, the work load is significant. Take the Los Angeles ACDO, for instance. Not including Wayne Garrison, the chief whose forte is operations, and his deputy, Charlie Zenith, who has been maintaining airplanes "practically forever," the office has 28 ACI and operations inspectors, eight maintenance inspectors and four avionics inspectors. They are supported by some seven clerical specialists.

On the surface, this seems adequate, perhaps more than adequate. Guess again! The Los Angeles ACDO is responsible for air carrier activities on five airfields—Los Angeles, Ontario, Burbank, Palm Springs and Santa Barbara.

This man may be a veteran captain but even with his experience he must prove to the air carrier inspector he thoroughly understands the systems on a new aircraft being added to his long list of ratings. Such oral examinations precede the actual flight check in the simulator and in the actual aircraft operating on the line. From his perch on the jump seat, the inspector observes all the crew members in action and evaluates their performance.

THE INSPECTORS - II

This means the 40 inspectors monitor the activities of 19 domestic airlines and 16 foreign flag carriers operating on one or more of these fields.

The office "holds the certificate" (meaning it is directly responsible for four carriers)—Continental Airlines, Western Air Lines, Flying Tigers and Air Cardinal. These carriers have 1,600 pilots-in-command (PIC) domiciled in the Los Angeles area, 2,700 crew members—second-in-command (SIC) and flight engineers, 300 other air carrier airmen—navigators, company check pilots, dispatchers (they also are certified by the FAA) and three airline training facilities. In addition there are three schools in the area giving flight engineer training that must be monitored.

In the maintenance area, the office maintains surveillance over 168 air carrier jets, 3,800 maintenance airmen, three maintenance schools, three repair stations, three maintenance bases, two sub-maintenance bases and 28 carrier line stations.

How does the job get done?

Garrison, who began his 16-year career with the agency after a long stint as a Navy pilot, shrugs his shoulders and says:

"We get pretty pushed sometimes, but we manage somehow."

Getting it done includes adhering to Garrison's personal policy of "flying" at least once every year with each of the 1,600 captains domiciled in the Los Angeles area.

"There are certain flight checks we must do as part of FAA regulations," he points out, "we must fly annually with every carrier check airman, we must fly with every pilot when he concludes his 25-hour initial operating experience (IOE) period with the airline (the pilot has flown that 25 hours under the watchful eye of a company check airman) and in certain other instances. Regulations permit most of the annual checks to be made by check airmen assigned to the carrier. But my personal policy is that someone from this office flies with every one of those 1,600 captains once a year, either in the simulator or on a route check. We spot check the ground schools on a regular basis. We observe the seconds-in-command and flight engineers in the simulator to evaluate the effectiveness of the carrier training program. In the simulator, we can peg marginal types (captains included) and schedule them for an enroute check."

So much for the operations job at the Los Angeles ACDO, the maintenance work load goes without saying, right?

Charlie Zenith nods in agreement mumbling, "Boy does it!"

Air carrier operations, maintenance and avionics inspectors, general aviation operations and maintenance inspectors—they are a more visible part of the FAA iceberg. But what about the airplanes? Not only do the men and women who fly have to meet stringent requirements designed to enhance the safety of flight, but steps must also be taken to insure that the aircraft they operate are designed and constructed in accordance with standards that, if anything, are even more stringent. This insurance is the responsibility of still another group of FAA specialists—the Engineering and Manufacturing Inspectors—backed by a staff of professional engineers, experts in airframes and structures; hydraulic, electrical and mechanical systems and equipment; propulsion—jet, turbo-prop and reciprocating engines; and a hardy group of test pilots.

Some 145 Engineering and Manufacturing Inspectors do business from

CLEARED TO LAND!

Engineering and Manufacturing District Offices (EMDO) strategically situated around the country. EMDOs function under the Region Flight Standards Division except in the Western Region where aircraft engineering is a separate division. This is a holdover from the days when the region consisted of the 11 western states where the original big four air carrier manufacturers—Boeing, Convair, Douglas, Lockheed—were situated. Although Boeing now is in another region and Convair is out of the transport business, Lockheed and McDonnell-Douglas still are very much in the air carrier picture. In the Western Region, Engineering and Manufacturing District Offices are known by a different name—Aircraft Engineering District Offices (AEDO). But the work and responsibility of the Van Nuys AEDO, for instance, isn't materially different from that of EMDOs in other parts of the nation.

Al Hoover who heads the Van Nuys AEDO is typical of the expertise represented by engineering and manufacturing inspectors throughout the agency. A former Marine Corps dive bomber pilot and later a helicopter pilot, Hoover exudes an aura of quiet competence. His broad military experience is combined with a stint as a helicopter test pilot—on the Brantley B-2—and a number of years as the plant manager for Brantley at Frederick, Okla. In other words, he knows the business from both ends—the operational and the manufacturing.

Currently, the office's geographical area of responsibility extends from a line roughly bisecting the Los Angeles megalopolis, north to the Oregon border and east to a line extending north from San Diego. It is easy to see why Al Hoover and his seven inspectors spend a good deal of their time on the road since the area has some 150 manufacturers of aircraft, aircraft systems and equipment. A partial list of "prime" manufacturers includes Lockheed; Weatherly Aviation of Hollister, Calif., producing agricultural aircraft; Ted Smith of Santa Maria, Calif., manufacturers of the Aerostar, a high performance business/executive aircraft; Hiller of Porterville, Calif., manufacturing helicopters and Fahlin Propellers of Sunnyvale, Calif.

The office exercises surveillance over some 27 major manufacturers of systems and equipment. Suppliers designated by the FAA for surveillance, Hoover points out, include those whose products "have a critical effect on airworthiness." Among them are manufacturers of hydraulic components, bonded structures, assemblies that subsequently are closed up when they arrive at the prime manufacturers and thus cannot be inspected at that juncture and "low-time-life" items.

Then there are the manufacturers of items of equipment covered by Technical Standards Orders (TSO) granted by the FAA. The Van Nuys AEDO has some 34 of these companies to check.

Finally, there are the firms holding FAA Parts Manufacturing Approvals (PMA). These mostly are modified or replacement parts manufactured under license from the original parts manufacturers from the original FAA-approved designs. For instance, this might include all new replacement parts being manufactured for the Pratt & Whitney 985 and other popular radial engines no longer in production but still in wide use.

"Beyond this," Hoover smiles, "it can include everything from soup to nuts—from exhaust gas temperature gauges for general aviation aircraft to complete entertainment systems for transport aircraft."

Engineering and manufacturing inspectors follow up on a report of the Quality Assurance Systems Analysis review team to insure that recommendations and corrections noted by the QASAR team are implemented in the manufacturing facility.

CLEARED TO LAND!

"We are the eyes of engineering," he explains, pointing out that the engineers at the regional level usually get involved in establishing the initial relationship with a manufacturer—either a new one or an existing manufacturer preparing to introduce a new model aircraft—and work with the company to develop the design and manufacturing data stage.

"We get into the act when the company begins cutting metal," he says, "that's when we go out to the plant and check to insure that the prototype is being built precisely in accordance with the specifications called out in the data our engineers have approved. From that moment on, we sort of live with the manufacturer through the time when he has an Approved Type Certificate (ATC) for the aircraft, has in being a documented quality assurance program that conforms to the ATC, has established an Approved Inspection System (APIS) and has been granted an FAA Production Certificate (PA)."

Once the FAA is satisfied the manufacturer has in being the systems to insure quality and perform the required inspections—and the facilities, equipment and personnel to implement these systems—the responsibility of the Engineering and Manufacturing Inspectors is reduced to one of monitoring except when it is necessary to trouble shoot a problem or conduct a special investigation as the result of an accident, critical failure of an aircraft or part in operation or because of a service difficulty.

"The EMDO," Hoover points out, "continues to have the management responsibility for all PA holders in its area. For instance, we go in and perform a detailed audit when the need arises such as in the case of a company management change or a major system change."

Formerly the district offices were responsible for periodic surveillance. Fund cuts and manpower cuts within the agency forced the FAA to look for a more effective method of insuring that a manufacturer complies with all the provisions of his PA. A modern, management system called QASAR for Quality Assurance Systems Analysis Review was set up with QASAR branches established at the regional level. The QASAR team—a blue ribbon group of experts—determines if the manufacturer is meeting the standards required in the FARs. However, it remains the responsibility of the EMDO to monitor QASAR findings and see that corrections are made where needed.

The Engineering and Manufacturing District Offices also are involved in the business of granting Supplemental Type Certificates (STC)—certificates which cover modifications to an aircraft already holding an ATC. STCs can range from simple things like substituting a different model of propeller for that called out in the original ATC to completely reworking an aircraft as in the case of converting surplus military aircraft like the Grumman S2 and TEM into fire bombers. They also may involve "radical" modifications. Here again the major work load falls on the engineering staffs at the regional level and the responsibility of the EMDO is one of insuring that the actual work conforms with the engineering data included in the STC application.

"This business of STCs is a complicated one," advises Al Strickfaden, a former industry flight test engineer and general aviation pilot with virtually all the ratings. Now an FAA aeronautical engineer, Strickfaden primarily is concerned with STCs.

"Frankly," he says, "the amount of paperwork required scares the hell out of the average individual but it is necessary if we are to insure the airworthiness of the final configuration. People, primarily general aviation air-

Among the many new aircraft certificated in recent years is this modern version of the Ford Tri-motor called by its manufacturer the Bushmaster. Even though the general configuration and many of its features come from the original Ford airplane, this essentially is a completely new aircraft and was certificated from scratch with the help of the local EMDO.

craft owners, try to shortcut the system and really get bogged down. It isn't just the general aviation people, however, often people who know better try to run around left end and we have to pull them up short. It's all a question of safety. More often than not the work is largely a fait accompli when the owner applies for the STC and in many instances the owner ends up really hurting in terms of time and money."

This problem could be avoided, Strickfaden says, if the individual would start with the FAA. Often the STC can be granted on a "field approval" by an EMDO or a Maintenance Inspector at the local GADO. "If the modification does not involve structures, flight characteristics or performance," Strickfaden points out, "and if the GADO or EMDO has enough data on hand they may sign off the FAA Form 337 "Major Repair or Alteration." The applicant goes happily on his way. If not, the application is forwarded to the region where our people will then work with the owner or his mechanic advising him on what data is required, determining what tests may be necessary and, in certain areas, performing those tests. We even have certain types of test equipment not ordinarily available outside a manufacturer which we will place on loan to the applicant to facilitate his own tests. Granted all this takes some time and the applicant may feel there is a lot of red tape involved, but he will be better off in the long run. He'll probably spend a lot less money doing it right from the beginning and the real payoff comes in a safer aircraft."

What does the FAA look for and what tests will the agency perform?

For instance, Strickfaden says, the FAA will run the fuel flow check on an engine modification; FAA engineers will help with and witness static tests; the Aircraft Modification Branch performs flight tests that do not require "-

qualitative" testing such as cooling, performance, airspeed calibration and carbon monoxide checks; an FAA engineering test pilot will run tests for stability, controllability, trim, flutter and vibration. Obviously, the FAA will check closely to insure that the modification complies with the regulations and that it conforms with the data provided in terms of form, fit, finish and material.

Al also offers this word of advice—check through the FAA and the manufacturer of the basic airplane to see what previous STCs have been granted. The modification may already have been approved; it may even be available in kit form.

"But as a general rule," he concludes, "don't expect a lot of help from manufacturers either with parts or data. They are very reluctant to provide this help and the newer the airplane is the more reluctant they are. Once an airplane is considered obsolete—in other words, it is out of production—they are more willing to provide drawings."

Al, by the way, knows whereof he speaks. He recently turned the tables on himself and became the applicant modifying a Piper Tri Pacer back to the original Pacer tail-dragger configuration and adding a 180-horsepower engine with a constant-speed propeller. His project dragged way behind the average STC application as it moved through the FAA because, as he puts it:

"I had to be tail-end-Charlie. I couldn't be put into the position of becoming involved in a conflict of interest. I had to put everyone's application ahead of my own."

Al Hoover and his EMDO counterparts across the nation also are the people to see for a TSO (this involves both a design approval and a production approval). An Engineering and Manufacturing Inspector must approve the applicant's quality control program before the region will issue the TSO.

Still another responsibility of the EMDO people is airworthiness certificates for agricultural aircraft; certificates for aircraft that have never had an FAA certificate (for instance, an aircraft manufactured here but immediately put into foreign registration and now being returned for operation in the U.S. or used aircraft that went into foreign registration and now are being returned for use in this country); all Experimental certificates and all Restricted certificates.

Experimental certificates include those for aircraft being used in research and development; those being used by a manufacturer to show compliance with the FARs; those being used by the applicant for crew training and those being used for aerial exhibitions. In the Restricted category fall aircraft being used for forestry patrol, seeding, etc.; aerial photography or mapping; powerline patrol; agriculture, weather control and aerial advertising. To a large extent these also are surplus military aircraft converted to civilian use.

There is yet another type of inspector with the FAA. This one isn't concerned with the proficiency of pilots, the adequacy of aircraft maintenance or the manufacturing, modification or licensing of airplanes. This inspector isn't even called an inspector. The average air carrier or general aviation pilot isn't even aware he is there as long as he does his job. But let him fall down on the job and his absence will immediately be felt by the men and women plying the nation's air routes.

The people are men like Hartley Graham, Lee Beldin, Ken Rogers, Jack Kelly, Dick Corbutt, Joe Sarrano and Paul Butler.

The job—to spend the greater part of their lives in airplanes constantly moving across the country checking to see that each of the nation's nearly 3,-000 electronic navigation aids is working as it should; flying hour after hour at high altitudes navigating their aircraft with such precision as to place it at a particular spot in three-dimensional space with an accuracy of a few hundred feet in all three dimensions; shooting landing, after landing, after landing

Over the years the FAA, and the CAA before it, employed a variety of aircraft in the flight inspection system. Typical are the Waco Cabin and the Cessna Bobcat (better known as the Bamboo Bomber) used in 1941.

checking instrument landing systems and precision radar systems to insure that they are operating within the stringent tolerances required for safe aircraft operation; exercising the doppler direction finding capabilities of the FSS and providing precise targeting information against which the long range radars can be calibrated.

CLEARED TO LAND!

It's a boring job for the pilots who fly the flight check aircraft and for the Flight Inspection Technicians and the Flight Procedures Specialists who man the sophisticated electronic monitoring gear aboard and interpret the results of these checks. It's 10-to-12-hour flights, day in, day out in the Convairs assigned to the SAFI (semi-automated flight inspection) and hundreds of landings in the reliable, old Douglas Gooney Birds (DC-3/C-47) performing instrument landing system checks. The Gooney Birds, by the way, will be out of service by 1977, replaced by Sabreliners and Jet Commanders carrying a new generation of automatic equipment that will permit the checks to be made more effectively, with greater accuracy, and with significantly greater speed. Also the use of the executive jets will result in a major economy. Notwithstan-

The venerable Douglas DC-3 or Gooneybird now being phased out by the jet age.

ding their infinitely greater acquisition cost, a group of 15 Sabreliners and five Jet Commanders will replace some 44 DC-3s and three T-29s on the flight check routes. Modernization of the fleet also has reduced the total manpower assigned to Flight Inspection by 30 positions, or a total of 505, and the closing of 10 field offices.

In recent times FAA flight inspection pilots, technicians and specialists have logged an average of 8,000,000 miles each year meeting the requirement that every one of the navigation aids is flight checked once each 90 days. The faster jet aircraft will reduce the total annual flying time by a considerable margin. New techniques made possible by fully automated equipment aboard also will reduce the work load. For instance, with the DC-3s and current

One of the FAA's remaining Gooneybirds sits side by side with the agency's new Rockwell Sabreliner, which is replacing not only the DC-3s used for local flight check work but also the Convair 540s employed on the SAFI routes.

methods, it is necessary to land and place a technician and equipment on the ground to flight check an ILS. Then the technician on the ground uses a theodolite to precisely determine the position of the aircraft with regard to centerline and glide-slope as a second technician on board the aircraft notes the position as represented by the aircraft ILS instruments and a second set of carefully calibrated test instruments. With the Sabreliners and Jet Commanders the entire job can be performed in the air.

Use of the jets in this area will be a major improvement since inspections of ILSs, which require extremely close tolerances, are conducted with greater frequency than other navigation aids. Also more time is planned for and used on an ILS facility than any other type of facility.

A flight inspection technician familiarizes himself with the highly automated console in one of the new Sabreliners.

In addition to periodic flight checks of the nation's air navigation system, the flight inspection crews play an important part in locating and commissioning new facilities. To a great degree, the flyability of a facility affects its location as well as the type of antenna installation selected for use.

Also whenever an accident occurs involving the possibility that a navigation aid might have been a causative factor, flight inspection crews immediately swing into action going to the area and flight checking all the navigation and landing aids which may have been used by the aircraft involved.

Largely unheralded, working quietly and almost invisibly behind the scenes, these flying inspectors make what may well be the single most important contribution to FAA's overall national effort to insure aviation safety.

FACILITIES 10

Lake Pontchartrain, La., is a unique body of water. Forty-one miles long and 25 miles across at its widest point, its average depth runs only 12 to 14 feet. Just north of New Orleans, the lake connects with the Mississippi River and the Gulf of Mexico through other smaller lakes and channels.

Where any one of the frequent tropical squalls typical to this humid, wet part of the nation may whip up two-to-three-foot waves in the open sea, the very size and the shallowness of the Pontchartrain doubles their size. And in really bad weather—not even necessarily hurricane weather—the winds create waves from 15 to 30 feet high.

It is in this environment that the men of the Lakefront Sector Field Office, New Orleans Airway Facilities Sector, work to keep New Orleans VORTAC (MSY), a critical navigational aid along the Gulf Coast, in service.

The primary responsibility falls on Bob Payne and his back-up man Charles Nezat, but when a trip to the VORTAC—located in the lake—is necessary they seek out Tab Walker. Tab has one of those unusual jobs in the FAA. He is a boat operator, a very special operator of a very special boat—a 38-foot, twin-diesel, high-sided craft built just for the unique water conditions found on Pontchartrain. Even with the boat designed to accommodate the unique wave action, crews do not venture onto the lake if the seas are running higher than five feet unless Air Traffic has studied the aircraft movement at any given time and determined that the impact of MSY being down will justify sending Payne, Nezat and Walker into Pontchartrain's furious maw.

"It's a hell of a decision to make, every time it must be made," says Jim Eaves, New Orleans Airway Facilities Sector manager, "and we don't like to make it. When the waves are over five feet, they just don't go unless it is absolutely necessary. MSY is a critical VORTAC, however, and any outage has a high impact on traffic flow all along the Gulf."

Emergency maintenance isn't the only problem associated with MSY. Its very location makes for unusual difficulties in terms of normal surveillance and preventative maintenance. Even keeping the diesel generators that provide emergency power fueled is a hassle. The fuel must be delivered by boat and the drums manhandled by the maintenance team. The cable traveling underground beneath the lake floor is subject to frequent breaks and hardware life is significantly curtailed by salt air corrosion.

"Corrosion is a problem all through this area," according to Eaves who says that air conditioning equipment purchased off-the-shelf by FAA for use on a national scale normally has a useful life of five to seven years but "is eaten up in two years down here."

MSY isn't the only trouble spot in Eaves' bailiwick. On Grand Island, Leeville VORTAC (LEV), situated at the southern tip of Louisiana—the tip of the toe at the end of the Mississippi Delta—presents its own unique problems. At low tide the "island" is 12 to 18 inches above the water. At high tide, particularly with a southerly wind blowing, it is under water. During a severe Gulf storm or hurricane, "forget it!" Winds in the area have been clocked in excess of 100 miles an hour—FAA records stop there because anemometers usually blow away even before that velocity is reached.

CLEARED TO LAND!

"I'll give you an idea just how powerful those winds can be," Eaves says, "in one hurricane the VORTAC antenna was picked up and carried more than 100 feet into the swamp. That antenna is a rigid structure and it weighs a quarter of a ton. Now that doesn't blow away easily!"

George Ford, a retired Coast Guard technician employed by the FAA to maintain the Grand Island facility, can attest to the hurricane winds. He's already had one house trailer blown out from under him. To guard against a recurrence, he anchored his new trailer between telephone poles sunk into the ground.

"It's been flooded but it hasn't blown away," he reports.

There is no question but what the New Orleans Sector has more than its share of unusual circumstances—capricious Lake Pontchartrain, hurricanes and, to top them off, cottonmouths.

"It's got to be the only place where technicians ride bicycles to keep from getting bitten by the water moccasins," Eaves declares, explaining, "the middle marker for runway One Zero at New Orleans International is 3,000 feet from dry land and is reached by a catwalk built from the levee into the swamp bordering the lake. Normally the catwalk is three to four feet above the surface of the water. During periods of high winds the cottonmouths climb on the catwalk to escape the pounding water. In the old days, the technicians had to make their way carefully along the catwalk using a long stick to knock the snakes into the water. That was not only slow, it was hairy. Now they use a three-wheeled bike. This enables them to make good time and still keep their feet and legs out of the danger area."

Since hurricanes are a regular threat along the Gulf Coast, Eaves and his people must have a comprehensive disaster plan worked out to react immediately when and if navigational/communications facilities are knocked out. A feature of that plan is an extensive high-frequency, single sideband, radio network covering the area that is checked out weekly.

"We're pretty well organized," he says, "in fact we'd be doing a pretty lousy job if we weren't under the circumstances. We're set up to react quickly and effectively."

He admits, however, there is one potential problem—one he hasn't had to meet yet and one that probably doesn't have any real solution anyway.

"We've got a long range radar at Slidel," he says, "and it consists of a 40-foot antenna in a 60-foot radome. So far, according to our records, it has withstood winds up to 90 knots (103.5 miles an hour) but it wasn't built for that. Frankly, every time we have another hurricane we wonder if this is the time."

In all, the FAA is responsible for maintaining more than 12,000 individual primary air traffic control, navigational and communications facilities across the country. There are 20 highly complex air traffic control centers, 97 surveillance radars, 505 remote air/ground communications sites, 917 VOR/VORTAC facilities, 217 NDBs, 407 towers, 319 Flight Service Stations, 158 airport surveillance radars, 546 instrument landing systems, 152 doppler direction finding facilities and many other remote communications facilities serving the 133,000 miles of jet airways and 177,000 miles of low-altitude airways in Alaska, Hawaii and the 48 contiguous states.

Keeping the air transportation system of the United States moving means keeping these facilities on the air and functioning as they are designed to func-

FACILITIES

The many and varied faces of FAA navigation and landing aids are a photographer's dream, but this multiplicity of design and engineering differences as well as the wide diversity of climate and terrain in which they function, taxes the capabilities of the men and women who must install and maintain them to the limit. A typical VOR antenna (above). A simple complex of approach lights (below).

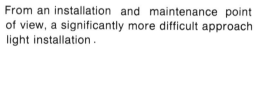

From an installation and maintenance point of view, a significantly more difficult approach light installation.

An airport surveillance radar installation.

tion. It's a formidable job and one that, by and large, goes unrecognized by the very people whose lives depend on them. As one technician puts it:

"We don't mind the controllers getting the glory just as long as a few people know that without us there wouldn't be any controllers or any glory!"

The men and women—and there are women, too—who keep the nation's airways functioning are an independent, hardy lot. They have to be. While their job doesn't have the psychological pressure felt by the controller, it has its own pressures and, above all, it requires a high level of physical stamina along with technical expertise.

The 25-year veteran who manages the Las Vegas Airway Facilities Sector is typical of the breed. Standing well over six feet and weighing in at over 200, Roy Pickett moves in the sprightly fashion of a lightweight. Pickett also is another of the hundreds of FAAers who worked his way up the career ladder, all the way to the Washington headquarters, and then beat a hasty retreat.

"I must have the satisfaction of being able to see results of what I'm doing—hard accomplishments to make it all worthwhile," he says, "and you sure as hell don't see that in Washington. I went to Washington and, thank God, managed to bail out in six months. I wanted out so bad I took the first job available. I didn't even ask where, I said I'd go anywhere. It turned out to be Guam.

"Obviously, someone has to man the headquarters. That work has to be done, but, it isn't for me. You get buried in the red tape. It is just too frustrating. At least in facilities, managing a sector like I am doing now is about the highest you can go and still have the satisfaction of seeing things accomplished."

Pickett, who started at the bottom of the technician ladder in Alaska, and the men and women under him have the responsibility for 183,000 square miles of some of the roughest, toughest country in America. The sector embraces much of three states and serves traffic controlled by the Oakland, Los Angeles, Salt Lake City and Albuquerque centers. Individual facilities number between 80 and 90 (some are slated to be decommissioned, others are planned to be commissioned). Terrain ranges from 14,000-foot peaks covered much of the year by snow to Death Valley where temperatures soar to 130-plus degrees.

"We seem to have practically every kind of terrain and climate from barren, desert land to huge lakes—Powell and Mead," Pickett points out.

While all the facilities in the Las Vegas Sector aren't unique or present special problems, like Eaves in New Orleans, Pickett has more than his share. From a technical point of view, Tonopah, Nev., is unusual. It is the nation's single "beacon only" site. Usually the antenna used to communicate with airborne transponders is co-located with a radar antenna. Tonopah, however, has only the beacon antenna. Situated at the intersection of three center areas—Los Angeles, Oakland and Salt Lake—the facility tracks the transponder beacons of aircraft traversing the huge expanse lying east of the High Sierras and west of the Great Salt Lake and transmits its information to computers at the three air traffic control centers. The area is heavily populated with military test activity and the beacon facility helps maintain separation between the high performance military craft and civilian carriers serving the busy Las Vegas-Reno-Los Angeles triangle.

Unlike Tonopah, which presents no particular maintenance problem,

CLEARED TO LAND!

Wilson Creek VORTAC (ILC), 185 miles north, northeast of Las Vegas, is one of the toughest facilities in the nation to keep on the air. The facility is situated on 10,000-foot Mount Wilson and during the winter months it takes a combination of several people and several different vehicles to reach the station. Maintenance technicians who keep a watchful eye on Wilson Creek are permanently based at the Pioche Field Office, a mile high and only 29 miles from the station.

"Sometimes that 29 miles can be the longest 29 miles in the world," Pickett says.

A typical winter trip on a bad day goes something like this: Bundled up in layers of foul-weather gear, the crew and equipment are loaded into four-wheel-drive vehicles and move out to the bottom of the mountain. There the vehicles form up behind a powerful road grader and the battle against the drifting snow begins. Usually—but not all the time—the grader can make it up the mountain to a point some six miles from the site where a snowcat is kept. Here the crew transfers to the ungainly tracked vehicle.

Gingerly the cat begins the final climb, moving cautiously, the operator straining his eyes to see the long, narrow stakes protruding from the snow that mark the road. One mistake can be the last. Finally, topping the last rise, the cat moves onto level ground where engineers have lopped off the mountain peak to make room for the antenna, equipment buildings and emergency quarters. Those quarters are a comforting sight—even though stocked with a supply of less-than-gourmet fare (military C rations)—because frequently the weather closes in trapping the crew for several days at a time.

"About the third day," Pickett grins, "even C rations taste good."

Already half the work day is gone. The trip took six hours—six hours to go just 29 miles, most of it the last six. There's a lot of work to be done. Even though the facility is functioning normally, the equipment must be checked. Daily checks must be made of certain items. The only times they aren't made is when the crew can't get there. Then there are certain more detailed checks which must be made weekly while others are performed on a monthly schedule. These are preventative maintenance steps, steps designed to prevent the facility from going off the air. If it is off the air, it means troubleshooting to find the problem, corrective action and then the required preventative maintenance.

There are only about 14 days a year when crews from the Pioche Field Office do not visit the Wilson Creek facility. If the station is off the air the men will attempt to ride the grader to the snowcat area. There are times, however, when even the grader and the cat can't make it. And when the snows are gone, heavy rains often threaten to wipe out the road. In these periods, the crew continues all the way to the top in the four-wheel-drive vehicles but with the assistance of a huge, D-7 Caterpillar tractor. Sometimes the crew has to dynamite massive snow overhangs, avalanches waiting to be triggered, before they can continue. Even in the best weather, the trip cannot be considered routine.

How fast could the facilities people react if the station were wiped out?

Pickett smiles at the question. He has the answer; he knows, because in 1974 he and his people faced just such a problem.

For whatever reason—some kind of demonstration against the establishment, a grievance against the FAA or aviation in general, or just plain

186

mindless vandalism—the mountaintop structures were demolished by a fire. At that time, the emergency quarters consisted of a trailer connected to the equipment building. The arsonists gained entry through the trailer and, from a reconstruction of events, apparently first ripped off all the cabinet doors, carried them outside and built a bonfire. When this didn't seem to inflict sufficient damage, they re-entered the buildings, doused the interior with a flammable liquid and ignited it.

"With the high winds whipping around the peak," Pickett says, "the flames were so intense they melted the equipment—constructed primarily of aluminum—in the steel racks. It was a total loss. The antenna, however, were not damaged."

Portable radar antenna installation that can be airlifted to a critical site when the existing antenna is damaged beyond rapair.

Wilson Creek VORTAC was again on the air in six days. A portable VOR was airlifted in from San Francisco and a TACAN was delivered by air from the FAA Aeronautical Center at Oklahoma City. The equipment and shelters were dragged up the mountain by the D-7 and crews worked day and night to restore operation.

"We wouldn't want to have to do this often," Pickett says, "but it did prove what we can do when we have to!"

Jack Neely has good reason to remember Wilson Creek. He has had two narrow escapes on that treacherous mountain. The first left him with permanent injuries. Neely was driving a truck loaded with fuel for the emergency generating plants on the mountain. Suddenly, on a blind curve halfway up the mountain, he met another truck coming the opposite way. Neely slammed on the brakes. His load shifted forward with the deceleration forces, crushing the cab with him in it. Doctors say he was lucky to survive.

Neely's second brush with the mountain was during a period of heavy snow. Often the frozen stuff is packed six to eight feet deep on the road. He was operating the D-7 when the snow and road beneath it gave way. The huge cat plunged down the mountainside. Fortunately the heavy blade kept the cat oriented straight ahead. Neely rode the vehicle like a bucking bronco the length of a football field down the mountain before it came to a stop. This time he didn't get a scratch.

Harold Henry is another FAAer who tangled with a mountain and lives to tell about it. Henry was descending from a trip to the Angel Peak radar, a 9000-foot mountain west of Las Vegas near Parumph Intersection on Victor Airway 105. Angel Peak is a facility that, if anything, has more snow than Wilson Creek. Snow plows always are required to reach the station in the winter and permanent-type emergency quarters with "plenty of C-rations" are provided. Henry credits use of a seat belt with saving his life when his vehicle slid on the icy roadway plunging over a 150-foot cliff. The vehicle was demolished but Henry escaped, bruised, shaken up and with a new respect for the mountain.

Deep snow, gale-force winds, avalanches and mountain roads aren't the only problems with which Las Vegas Sector men and women have to reckon. Goffs VORTAC (GFS), a critical navigation aid on the busy approach to the Los Angeles Area from Las Vegas, is, as Pickett puts it, "in the middle of nowhere." Geographically, it is situated in a never-never land in the high desert between the Los Angeles Basin and Peach Springs, Ariz. Summer temperatures range in the 120s and it is at least 25 miles from the nearest habitation. For some 15 years the Sector had been trying to get commercial power for the facility since it took one mechanic full time just keeping the two diesel generator units going. Today it has commercial power but the lack of it nearly cost Omer Owens, the mechanic, his life.

It was just another day for Owens. As usual, he made the 100-mile round trip across the desolate span of rock and sand from Needles on the Colorado River. One of the cantankerous diesels was down and Owens spent most of the morning working on the unit. The generator was mounted close to the ground, on four-inch legs, and to complete his work Owens needed to get beneath it for a final adjustment. Laying his jacket on the ground, he extended his arm under the unit. He heard the ominous warning rattle just as the sidewinder's fangs sank into the flesh of his forearm.

In most cases, the panic of knowing you are at least an hour's drive from help would set up a flurry of physical action that pumps the deadly poison directly into the nervous system. Death would then come in a matter of minutes. Owens, however, is built of sterner stuff, in fact, the sternest. Calmly, he gave himself first aid—cutting open the wound and sucking out the venom. He telephoned the Flight Service Station at Needles and with a makeshift tourniquet above the punctures, he put his tools away, got in the truck and headed for medical assistance.

Simultaneously, a sheriff's deputy summoned by the FSS, departed Needles for the VORTAC site. At about midway point, some 25 miles from the site, the deputy met Owens and stopped him to check out the situation. As his truck came to a halt, Owens opened the door and promptly passed out. He had apparently been going on nerve alone. The deputy manhandled him into the radio car and, siren screaming and red lights flashing, headed for Needles and the hospital.

Here, again, Lady Luck took a hand. Unbeknownst to anyone except Owens' wife (who was a nurse at the hospital) he was allergic to anti-venom.

FACILITIES

Under ordinary circumstances, anti-venom would have been the first step in treatment and if it had been administered his own calm deportment and the deputy's wild drive would have been for naught. As it was, his wife was on duty. Apprised of the situation, she was able to warn the doctor. Alternate treatment was prescribed. Owens is alive to tell the story.

Like the water moccasin problem along the Gulf Coast, the snake—deadly desert rattlers—is a major concern with facilities in the western deserts. Snakes crawl into doorways and access shelters where the sun-heated concrete provides warmth during the cold desert nights. Doorways are lighted so that technicians can see danger lurking in the corners. The rule of thumb is "look before you leap."

A good part of Pickett's job is planning to meet current and future demands with respect to facilities. Money, the lack of it, that is, always is an obstacle but it is even more frustrating when the funds are available and still you can't reach the objective. Political pressure—from the local politicians, the Congress and the administration— always has and probably always will play a significant role when it comes to establishing facilities or relocating those which no longer meet the requirements.

Take the Angel Peak radar, for instance. Situated where it is, the Mount Charleston Range "blacks out" this electronic eye to the west and north. A series of studies has demonstrated that better coverage in these directions (as well as a better look at the Mexican border area south of Blythe, Calif.) could be achieved by moving the radar to Crossman Peak near Lake Havasu, Ariz.

You might say, "Well, what's the difference, one peak is the same as another, move it." You also might be wrong. For months the environmentalists have stymied the FAA at every turn.

It seems that a species of billy goat lives on the slopes of Mt. Crossman. It is their "natural habitat" and the environmentalists claim that the radar station would destroy their home. Testimony of naturalists and wild life experts to the contrary, those opposing the move will not be budged. Even some who admit that in all probability the goats would not be disturbed strongly object to a "scar" the road to the station would make. Greater safety offered to the crews and passengers of military and civil aircraft traversing a now blacked-out stretch of rugged peaks appears to be of less concern than the esthetics involved with the road. Such are the new problems that face FAA facilities people in the mid 1970s.

Still today's problems, political and operational, seem pale somehow when compared with those faced by the facilities men who actually built America's airways. Dale Heister, a long-time veteran of the CAA/FAA, now spending his retirement in Santa Barbara, Calif., chronicling the saga of the airways pioneers, writes of those early facilities and the herculean efforts it took to establish and operate them. One in particular, he describes this way:

"The facility at Donner Summit, at an altitude of over 7,000 feet, was installed under conditions similar to the ones encountered by the early railroad and highway builders. Heavy snows, high winds, extreme cold weather and construction problems plagued the installers. Dog teams were pressed into service upon one occasion.

"The two buildings, the Airway Radio Station and the radio range, were completed during favorable weather, but before the range masts had been placed, heavy snows arrived and made it necessary to haul the five heavy steel

The long-range air route surveillance radar antenna at Horicon, Wisc.

More "architecture" of today's airways system. Approach lights to Minneapolis.

A direction finder antenna at South Bend, Ind.

The airport surveillance radar antenna at O'Hare.

The localizer antenna at Des Plaines, Ill.

poles in sections for two and a half miles by dog teams from the highway up the mountain. Wooden masts generally were used for the loop range masts, but in this case it was impossible to obtain properly-seasoned poles because of the presence of wood-boring termites in the locality. The poles became unfit for use if left unprotected in the open long enough to become seasoned.

"Because of the solid rock surface it was necessary to blast postholes for the masts. It also was necessary to build up the foundations of the houses on top of the rock surface. Excavations for foundations was impossible. The buildings were anchored with wire cables as protection against the winds which at times attained a velocity of 70 miles per hour or more.

"The houses were built eight feet above the surface as a protection against the heavy snows, at times as much as 700 inches in depth lasting as long as seven months out of the year.

"The station was about three miles from the railroad tracks crossing the mountain pass and a considerable distance from the transcontinental highway. It overlooked beautiful Donner Lake. Altitude of the pass was over 7,000 feet. Surrounding peaks rose 3,000 feet higher, with deep gorges and mountain lakes between. The southern branch of the Yuba river flowed through the area and the headwaters of the American River were visible to the south another 2,-000 feet below. Farther on, at Emigrant Gap, the old trail road from the east descended the mountains from a height of over 5,200 feet to the valley of the Sacramento River.

"Installation of stations at Pleasant Valley, Nev., and Strevell, Ida., was difficult. The former was approximately 60 miles from the nearest settlements—Winnemucca and Beowawe. The location, about 5,000 feet in elevation, was the only point that could be utilized on the cut-off between Beowawe and Fernley and was the most suitable place for a weather reporting facility.

"One of the chief problems encountered in establishment of the station was that of hauling material by truck from Winnemucca over dirt roads. After snow began to fall the location of the road was difficult to discern and made the possibility of losing the way a serious problem particularly in the absence of suitable landmarks. Heavy snows and occasional thaws made the roads impassable a large part of the time during winter months. The presence of rattlesnakes was a problem not to be ignored during good weather. Even after the station was completed they were found at times in the station quarters.

"The station at Strevell was located in the Minidoka National Forest on the pass overlooking Great Salt Lake and was considered the most strategic point from which to observe the weather through the passes between Burley and Salt Lake City. It was 70 miles by mountain roads from the railroad at Burley, Ida. The country was rugged and the airway normally went around a mountain 9,000 feet high. However, in favorable weather, the pass between Burley and Strevell could be used. The radio operators were provided dwellings for their use, since they were there year around. These two stations were among the first established under the Air Commerce Act of 1926."

Today's airway facilities are vastly different from those of the early days—-long range radar, transponder beacon receivers, VORTACs, DME. Modern electronic navigation aids coupled with today's aircraft capable of operating at altitudes above the mountains move traffic clear of the nation's geological obstructions to flight. Not so in the beginning days of the national airway system. Reciprocating engines without superchargers labored in the rarified atmosphere at higher altitudes while lack of inflight oxygen placed similar restrictions on pilots and passengers. Thus the earliest airways sought valleys, canyons and passes through the Alleghenies, the Rockies, the Sierras, the Cascades and scores of lesser ranges.

For instance, the Columbia River, winding through the Cascade Mountains where it forms the boundary line between Oregon and Washington, provided the most practicable route for a difficult flying region between Portland, Ore., and Pasco, Wash., by cutting a huge gorge through the mountains.

"The timber of the Columbia National Forest and the rough peaks of the Cascades," Heister says, "would have presented baffling problems to engineers planning an aerial route in any other location. But the gorge served admirably as its bed was level and much lower than the adjacent mountain region. Moreover, the gorge itself—because it is swept by winds is almost invariably free from fog although the surrounding region is often blanketed. The ceiling above the gorge might be low but an airman flying the route could be reasonably sure that the fog would not close him in entirely. The Portland-Pasco section of the Portland-Spokane airway followed the Columbia River as far east as Umatilla, Ore., where it branched off to Pasco and on to Spokane. At Pasco it connected with the Salt Lake City-Pasco airway.

"The gorge, about 50 miles long, was marked for the use of airmen flying the route at night by installation of colored lights which outlined the safe flying region. Peculiar climatic conditions produced dense fogs in the upper part of the gorge frequently resulting in 250-foot ceilings. When these fogs formed the regular long-range rotating beacons, located for the most part at higher altitudes, were blotted out; thus the system of low-altitude lights installed at prominent points on the walls of the gorge. These lights kept an airlane free from obstructions between Cape Horn, 25 miles east of Portland, and Lyle, Wash., 50 miles farther east. These low-altitude lights were known as 'side lights,' and were designated by their mileage from the western terminus of the Portland-Spokane airway. Twelve sites were located on the Washington side of the gorge and eleven on the Oregon side. Nineteen of these twenty-three sites were established between Beacon Rock and Hood River, a distance of approximately 30 miles, which included the narrowest and most dangerous portion of the gorge. To provide for instant orientation by the pilots, the Washington lights were equipped with green shades while those on the Oregon side were red. Two 300-millimeter airways code beacons were installed at each site, one as primary and the other functioning as a reserve unit put into operation automatically on failure of the beacon in service.

"Installation of the side lights presented many problems not ordinarily encountered. The steep, often perpendicular, gorge walls made construction difficult. At the 55-Mile Station on the Washington site, the site could be reached only by a way of a lumber flume built for floating logs down the side of a mountain from the timber cuttings to the mill at river level. It was necessary for the engineers to construct a sled which would fit the sides of the flume and slide the tower, beacons, control cabinet and other accessories more than half a mile to the site from the nearest point accessible by truck. The flume, supported by a trestle, was, in places, 250 feet above the mountain side and was paralleled by an unguarded 12-inch catwalk used by the men in guiding the sled.

CLEARED TO LAND!

"At two other sites on the Washington side it was necessary to transport materials three-quarters of a mile by boat from the nearest point accessible to trucks. At one of these sites an abandoned windlass was found near the site which, after repairs had been made, was utilized for hauling materials 300 feet up the cliff from the river bank.

"Other sites were located on rubble-covered slopes so steep rock slides were a constant threat. Very little soil was encountered at the side light sites. Practically all excavations for tower legs were made in solid rock by the use of dynamite. Some of the sites were obscured by tall trees which had to be removed in order to provide visibility for the pilots from light-to-light. Many of the trees were first-growth Douglas firs, 60 to 70 feet in height."

The airway beacons, side lights, the low frequency radio range stations, the Federally-operated emergency fields—they all are gone now just as the Douglas M-2, the DeHavilland DH-4, the Pitcairn Mailwing, the Boeing Monomail are relegated to aviation history books and museums. But, just as a special breed of pilot flew these aircraft and pioneered today's far-flung air transportation system, so did a special breed of men and women install and maintain the early airways facilities setting the standards for generations to come.

Today's facilities engineers and electronics technicians, even though equipped with the best modern technology can provide, still face challenges often as great as their predecessors.

Take building the Boulder City, Nev., VORTAC (BLD), for instance. Operations and engineering studies established a preferential location for the facility—the top of a solid rock peak. Now, the nature of radio—the management of electromagnetic energy—is such that an antenna requires two sides, a driven element and a ground side. In the case of vertically oriented antenna, such as VORTAC, where propagation in all directions is desired, the earth itself usually provides the ground side or "ground plane" as it is called. Ordinarily where a VORTAC is installed on a mountain top, the peak simply is bulldozed off and a flat area sufficiently large to provide an adequate ground plane is created. Not so with the Boulder site. No way could the solid granite peak be leveled. A solution was found in providing a man-made ground plane (or counterpoise as it also is called). Some level ground was available at the site so it was possible to locate the buildings and a portion of the antenna (the vertical element) on solid rock. The remainder of the ground plane was constructed of structural steel—extending out into space above the sheer rock wall.

"A measure of the human effort needed to construct the counterpoise," Pickett says, "can be seen in the size of the job. The counterpoise is 200 feet in diameter—two-thirds the length of a football field—and the longest of the steel legs extending down to solid rock at the bottom of the cliff is more than 100 feet long. Twenty million pounds—10,000 tons—of steel went into the structure and that's a bunch."

Construction of the Boulder counterpoise certainly wasn't the only unusual engineering task involved in establishing today's network of airways facilities and it won't be the last. Traffic requirements, terrain, the propagation characteristics of electromagnetic radiations and now environmental considerations dictate the location.

For instance, the location of the Lake Tahoe VORTAC (LTA) on 8,849-

194

Facilities technicians who maintain Squaw Peak have to be accomplished outdoorsmen adept in the use of snow shoes and skis. In fact, ski training is part of the job for the technicians assigned to the Reno Airways Facilities Sector.

foot Squaw Mountain west of Reno and north of the famous resort community poses some interesting maintenance problems. Construction of the site was no more difficult than a number of other mountain top facilities although the buildings had to be anchored down to bed rock by steel cables strung over them.

"Normal" winds run 20 to 30 miles per hour and peak winds of 100—the equipment could not record the estimated 125-mile velocity—are not uncommon.

"The winds on that peak can flatten you," according to Bob Rhodes, chief of the Nav-Comm Unit of the Reno Airway Facilities Sector, "they will knock you down and roll you off the edge if you aren't careful. It they get you, the only resort is to spread-eagle and hang on."

"The winds," Rhodes adds, "are so powerful they will pick up rocks, as large as six inches in diameter, and hurl them through the walls of the buildings."

When it is snowing, access to Squaw Peak calls upon the crew to be expert skiers. They travel by four-wheel vehicle to the lower ski lift, transfer to the upper lift and they strike out on the boards. (The FAA pays for ski lessons for the crew.) Final approach to the facility is through a tunnel constructed of galvanized iron for some 800 feet and then cut through solid rock for another 800 feet. The tunnel ascends some 400 feet in its 1,600-foot length—a rise of one foot for every four feet traveled.

Obviously, in winter it isn't possible to climb to the station every day. Since this is a critical VORTAC, to insure preventative maintenance and inspections are carried out on a regular basis, crews stay at the top for periods of three or four days at a time—if they are lucky. Crews have found themselves trapped on the peak for as long as three weeks.

With the combination of freakish winds, travel by ski lift and skis and difficult roads, crews maintaining Tahoe VORTAC have been lucky. There is only a single death on record. One crewman was injured so seriously in a fall he later died as the result of the injury. And there have been some close calls.

Rhodes remembers vividly being trapped on the ski lift. Rescue crews had to shoot a line to him and three others and then lower them in a rescue chair. Not only was there considerable danger involved, but he recalls,

"It was cold as hell up there in the wind."

Tahoe VORTAC presents one of the few engineering problems the FAA hasn't yet been able to lick. Due to the wind effect, the antenna ice up to the point where operation degrades significantly at times.

"We've licked the mountain," Rhodes declares, "but we haven't found a way to beat the ice yet."

Another facility in the Reno Sector which gives the men a fit is Battle Mountain VOR, east and south of Lovelock, Nev. The facility is at the 9,688-foot level and the mountain rises some 4,800 feet from the mile-high valley below. From approximately October 15 through May 15 each year, it takes a two-man crew full time just to keep the roads clear.

Larry Alexander, chief of the Reno Technical Support Unit, knows Battle Mountain well and has reason to.

"It's a rough one," he says, "and I've seen it drift to 14 feet from a no-snow condition in just three hours. I remember one trip when it took me five hours to go the final 150 yards to the facility.

FACILITIES

"That road is something else. In places, it is bounded by sheer cliffs dropping a thousand feet straight down. One of our guys, Beryl Dewey, is lucky to be alive. He went off the road during a snow storm. Fortunately, he didn't go off one of the cliffs but plunged down a steep bank. A boulder stopped his snowcat after about 200 feet. He wasn't injured but he had to stay there the night wrapped up in the emergency clothing we keep in the cats. We sent up a man to spend the night with him to be sure he didn't go into shock. The next morning we got 'em out. Dewey sure was shook up and I can't blame him."

From a purely technical point of view, maintenance of FAA's far-flung navigation and communications facilities isn't as difficult as it was in the old days, or even just a few short years ago. The men and women don't have to build, operate and maintain the equipment like those pioneers who many times designed their own transmitters, put them together, handled the key mike and then had to keep them on the air. The advent of solid state technology has brought about a significant increase in reliability over the vacuum tube technology of the 50s and 60s.

However, in the opinion of veteran FAA electronics engineer Dave Earley, more attention could be paid by the designer and manufacturer to "maintainability."

"In just the past few years," he says, "there has been a 10-fold improvement. Today, how easily a piece of equipment can be maintained has become as important as how well it operates and its mean-time-to-failure rate. We still could use more attention in this area. Too many times maintainability still is an after-thought. But there is more emphasis now and I see the situation continually getting better."

Earley also sees an unusual side effect to the increased reliability of today's solid state devices.

"The extreme reliability we enjoy now," he says, "is having an adverse effect on the efficiency of the technician. When malfunctions were more frequent he became more proficient in trouble shooting and making repairs. Now, when a piece of equipment goes for several months without trouble, he tends to lose his sharp edge. This is analogous to a pilot maintaining his flying proficiency and being current in a particular aircraft type.

"To combat this we are putting a lot of effort into improving the training devices he can use on the job. We're introducing video tape demonstrations and are requiring that the technicians take constant refreshers.

"Another problem exists with sophisticated new equipment like ARTS III. It is a 'single-thread' system. We don't have in-place spares available for the technician to practice on. With older VORTAC equipment and the like, we had plenty of redundancy and equipment for training was no problem."

What about the quality of new technicians coming into FAA facilities maintenance?

Earley thinks they are "great." One good trend he sees is the increase in trained technicians coming from the military services and choosing the FAA as a career.

What words of wisdom would Earley pass on to young men and women still in school about preparing for an FAA career in facilities work?

"Get sharp on the fundamentals of math and physics.

"Develop the ability to deal with people.

"Learn to read, write and speak—learn to express themselves effectively."

CLEARED TO LAND!

Would he recommend this as a career for young people?

"You're darned right," he declares, "and I think most FAA men and women in this line of work would agree with me. But you had better have a strong constitution!"

THE ACADEMY 11

A Holiday Inn, gasoline station and an 8-Days Motel mark the southeast corner of the intersection of Interstate 40 and Meridian some seven miles as the crow flies from where Oklahoma City's Liberty Bank Building towers over the city.

Grouped around the intersection are a half dozen other motels—Hilton, Ramada, Crosswinds among them. Huge tractor-trailer rigs inundate the area with a perpetual roar that increases in volume as dawn begins to break over the plains.

Each weekday morning beginning at six o'clock a variegated group of specie homo sapiens—men and women representing a wide range of age, color, dress and ethnic background begin assembling just east of the Holiday waiting, some quietly, others with obvious impatience, for the first of several large motor coaches showing the colors of the "Jordan Bus Lines." One by one the men and women, most of them carrying notebooks and briefcases, board the coaches. Promptly at half past seven the driver of the last bus guns his engine as a signal for final stragglers to make a dash or get left.

The coaches move out South Meridian about three miles to the boundary of Will Rogers Field, then zig to the right and zag to the left along MacArthur, passing through the gates of one of the nation's genuinely unique institutions of learning—the FAA Academy.

As the coaches stop at designated points, students—young men and women in their early twenties and old-timers with snow on the roof; sharp dressers in business suits, tie and pocket handkerchief, and the "in" crowd casually garbed in jeans, flares, sweaters and brightly colored T-shirts—disembark at Air Traffic, Airways Facilities, Flight Standards.

This "campus" occupies a major portion of a 253-acre reserve which is the FAA Aeronautical Center at "Oke City" (as it is generally called). Co-located with the Academy are the FAA Depot responsible for the management of the agency's central materiel inventories and distribution system; the Procurement Division which provides agency-wide contracting and procurement support; the Civil Aeromedical Institute (CAMI) responsible for a continuing program of aeromedical research as well as the medical certification of the nation's three quarters of a million active airmen; the Aircraft Services Base which manages and maintains the FAA's fleet of more than 90 aircraft; the Flight Inspection National Field Office (FINFO); the Data Services Division; and the Flight Standards Technical Division which includes all phases of operational safety for U.S. aviation from the development of airworthiness standards and preparation of the many FAA examinations for pilots, mechanics and parachute riggers to certification of airmen and registration of all U.S. civil aircraft.

At any given time, the FAA Academy is home to some 1,160 students involved in courses ranging in length from a few days to as many as 42 weeks. During a year's time some 16,000 controller trainees, flight service specialists, electronics maintenance technicians, general aviation and air carrier inspectors and other specialists arrive, learn and leave the Academy better prepared to perform their jobs in the field.

CLEARED TO LAND!

Approximately 25 percent of the student body are controller trainees while some 60 percent are airways facilities technicians. Some 7 percent of the approximately 10,000 electronics maintenance technicians in the FAA are almost always in attendance keeping up with today's rapid developments in technology. Until recently, all controller trainees did not attend the Academy since parallel training at operational facilities (using materials and methods developed by the Academy) was available. About 10 percent of the enrollment is general aviation and air carrier inspectors in for initial indoctrination or for retraining. Air carrier inspectors must get up-dated at the Academy or by contract twice each year, while general aviation inspectors are brought up to date and qualify in new aircraft types every two years—unless they are involved with complex jet aircraft, then they attend more often.

Permanent party at the Academy runs about 800 with the bulk, averaging 575, assigned as instructors. Instructors all are professionals from the field on temporary assignment to the Academy for tours of two to six years. Instructors rotate at the rate of from 150 to 200 yearly. In addition, the Academy has some 40-plus professional educators who are responsible primarily for development of instructors and training materials. For its 385 available courses, the Academy has some 618 texts representing 184,000 pages—all researched, developed and written by the Academy staff. No texts are procured from outside the FAA.

The task of operating the FAA's seat of higher learning on a $20 million an-

The Aeronautical Center at Oklahoma City is the home of the FAA Academy and a half dozen other major activities such as the Civil Aeromedical Institute, the Flight Inspection National Field Office, the Data Services Division and the Flight Standards Technical Division.

nual budget rests not too lightly on the shoulders of a tall, well proportioned, articulate, FAA careerist who became an "educator" only after spending more than 25 years learning about the real world of aviation from the bottom up.

Leon C. Daugherty, who has been superintendent since 1974, began his career as an electronic technician with the CAA in 1947. After nine years in the field, Daugherty was selected to instruct at the Academy for a three-year tour, moving from there in 1959 to the Office of Personnel and Training in Washington where he became Training Program Manager. Other assignments which give Daugherty his practical as opposed to theoretical point of view vis-a-vis current Academy philosophy include Frequency Management Engineer, Regional Appraisal Officer, Navigation Aids Program Manager, Evaluation Officer (systems maintenance) and assistant chief, Maintenance Engineering Division, at FAA Headquarters.

FAA trainees at the Academy get "hand-on" experience with every piece of equipment in use throughout the national airways system. As the faculty puts it; "We've got one of everything." Working with this air route surveillance radar antenna installation on the roof of the laboratory building, trainees become familiar with the real thing before they move into the field.

CLEARED TO LAND!

While Daugherty evidences the utmost respect for the academic community and, in fact, points out that the Academy could not function effectively without the services of a number of professional educators, he also makes it abundantly clear that he believes the student must "get his hands dirty and work up a sweat at the same time he is absorbing theory."

"If we are going to accomplish our objectives in training controllers, flight service specialists, inspectors and electronics maintenance technicians capable of functioning in the real world," Daugherty declares, "we have to see they get the opportunity to work here at the Academy with the same equipment they will use in the field."

That's the way it works at Oke City. Inspectors check out and maintain their currency on contemporary air carrier aircraft like the McDonnell-Douglas DC-9, the Boeing 707 and 727 and, for prop jet pilots, the Convair 580. General aviation inspectors work with today's general aviation aircraft from the little, single-engine, two-place Cessna 150 up through the Beech Baron and 99A to the Jet Commander and Learjet. In the Airways Facilities classrooms and laboratories, you find one each of the newest equipment in service with the National Airspace System—including an ARTS-III which operates on input from an operational airport surveillance radar and ATC beacon system. The Academy even has an IBM 9020 computer complex identical to those used in the field for radar data processing. Air carrier and general aviation inspectors and electronic/computer maintenance technicians get maximum "hands on" training along with the theoretical.

In one area, however—possibly the most important, depending on how you look at it—the training given at the FAA Academy has been significantly deficient and Daugherty makes no bones about it.

"There had been a day," he explains, "when the capability of this institution to train air traffic controllers was second to none in the world. We had the latest and the best. In addition to our own, we trained air traffic controllers for at least 120 foreign nations. This, by the way, had a powerful impact on the U.S. balance of trade. It was natural for controllers and supervisory personnel trained on U.S. state-of-the-art equipment to exert a significant influence on the procurement of equipment for their systems. Hundreds of millions of dollars in U.S. electronic equipment went into foreign air traffic control facilities as the result.

"In recent years we hadn't enjoyed this advantage and more important our controllers were not getting the quality of training we should have been giving."

Where was this training deficiency and how did it come about?

That's a long story, a story tainted with bureaucratic procurement procedures, intra-agency political maneuvering and plain, old fashioned short-sightedness.

Today, in the field, the controller is using automated radar systems so advanced they can be said to be "on the cutting edge of technology." Obviously, a couple of hundred aircraft can't be used on a daily basis to provide input to an ARTS III for training at the Academy. Current methodology with other agencies is computer simulation. Case in point—the Navy at San Diego has a computer simulation system which can create a real-time "radar, electronic warfare and electronic warfare countermeasure environment" involving up to 11 ships and carriers and dozens of aircraft (enemy and friendly). In each of

Although much of the total national airways system is automated today and traffic control primarily is exercised with radar, there still are some areas of the country where the tried and proven manual system is in use. Controller trainees at the Academy learn manual as well as radar control techniques.

the training rooms (each one the exact duplicate of the combat information center—CIC—aboard ship) the men and officers might as well be in the midst of a raging battle. It's that real. At the same facility Navy air controllers are taught to provide radar approach to carriers—all through simulation. This level of computer simulation sophistication is duplicated many times throughout the Department of Defense and it has been available for some time.

Not so at the FAA Academy, much to the chagrin and dismay of Daugherty and many of his top aides. As long as Daugherty has been superintendent (and according to other top Academy personnel, for some time before) they had tried to bring the air traffic control training program up to speed with modern computer simulation. As they saw it, new controllers should be brought to the Academy, learn the principles, methods and techniques of air traffic control and then put that knowledge to the test in practical situations provided through simulation. With a thorough grounding in the basics and sufficient "hands on" experience with the same equipment they would use in the field, the controllers then would only have to familiarize themselves with the peculiar traffic environment at their duty station and develop further proficiency.

Unfortunately, the air traffic simulation capability of the Academy was limited to a level commensurate with radar target generators which were a "gift" of the Navy 20 years ago—circa Korean War devices that one instructor refers to as "junk, junk that took half our time keeping it in commission."

One of the reasons the FAA had dragged its feet in giving the Academy a computer simulation capability equal to those in the Department of Defense was the basic disagreement between the Academy and the individual FAA regional directors over centralized training versus on-the-job training for controllers. Many regional directors (who, by the way, enjoy an unusual degree of autonomy) believed that on-the-job training augmented with a little academic indoctrination at the Academy was the way to go. Thus, they traditionally failed to endorse Academy requests for a simulation capability which could support centralized training for controllers. Until recently, FAA headquarters did not take a positive stand on this question and when a procurement finally was authorized in the early 1970s the effort got blown out of the water when the electronics company placed under contract could not deliver the goods. The contract—and the program—was cancelled. Now a new procurement is under way with equipment delivery scheduled for mid 1977.

All this is not to say that controllers attending the FAA Academy have not been properly trained. They have. Curriculum, methods and techniques were developed to take into consideration the lack of in-house simulation capability and to strongly reinforce the practical, on-the-job training made available to the controller in the field.

"It's just that it was a hell of a lot harder that way," declares Lowell Lunn who heads the Air Traffic Branch at the Academy.

Walt Ericson, another training supervisor, puts it into perspective this way:

"The FAA had never really settled the question whether or not to standardize on centralized training. Further, the training dollar—insofar as travel funds are concerned—was left up to the discretion of the regional director. If he wanted to spend the money to send controllers to the Academy, he did. If he wanted to train them on the job, he did."

Not only do the men and women who operate the Academy believe the agency should insist on centralized training for its controllers, they also feel that centralized hiring should be the rule.

"If we had used both centralized hiring and training for controllers," Ericson says, "we would not have had as high a washout rate in the latter stages of training and in the field. Only four out of 11 regions regularly sent their controllers to the Academy. Washington did not exercise enough clout to enforce a real national training program. Thus the agency suffered and the controllers suffered."

Although, almost without exception, Academy staff members are in favor of current programs to hire qualified minority personnel, they also are in general agreement that the effort as it is being implemented "discriminates against the majority—the white, Anglo, male." This is, they say, having an "adverse psychological effect."

What are the advantages of centralized training with, of course, modern computer simulation capability?

"Plenty," Ericson emphasizes, "we already give the trainee a solid grasp of the concept of air traffic control, the procedures and the techniques. With computer simulation we can show him what the real world of radar traffic control looks and feels like—develop what I call the skills of the moving target. For instance, what is the profile of an aircraft on radar going 240 knots and making a 20 degree turn? We can acclimate him to the third dimension—altitude—and familiarize him with descent rates, speed adjustment and spacing relationship.

THE ACADEMY

"We can do all these things without involving an operational facility. When the controller gets to his duty station he already can be thoroughly familiar with the real world environment long before becoming involved with separating real, live airplanes."

"As it has been," Ericson adds, "with the capability currently available at Oke City, we couldn't prepare the controller well enough before he got into the real thing. Controllers did get the necessary operational training at their duty stations and we do not question the quality of that training. But we felt that it would be a lot better if that phase of training were completed before the controller was immersed in the high pressure environment of actual traffic control."

It takes only two or three days of eyeball-to-eyeball discussion with instructors and students at the Academy to come to the conclusion that overall the training is of the highest quality, the staff is highly motivated and thoroughly competent and in all the areas other than air traffic control the training aids and systems are of the highest caliber and represent the state-of-the-art. In general it appears that controllers eventually are well trained (including their on-the-job training at the duty station). But, it is clearly evident that controller training would be significantly more effective and could be achieved at less cost in the aggregate if the agency would adopt a policy of centralized training for controllers with periodic short courses for updating as new, more sophisticated equipment comes into use—in the same manner as the Flight Standards Branch.

General aviation and air carrier inspectors at the Academy for initial indoctrination or periodic re-check are fortunate to receive hands-on training in the

Like the controllers and technicians, general aviation and air carrier inspectors attending the FAA Academy get "hands on" training in the latest equipment. Instructor here conducts a session for two air carrier inspectors in the Boeing 720 simulator.

The Academy either maintains in its own fleet or leases as necessary a wide variety of aircraft in which to train inspectors. They range from single-engine lightplanes to this Boeing 727 trijet transport undergoing a periodic inspection in the Academy shops.

latest and most sophisticated equipment available. As mentioned earlier, the FAA has available its own Boeing 727 and 720 aircraft and a McDonnell-Douglas DC-9. Where the DC-8, Super DC-8 or new family of jumbos—the Lockheed L-1011, Boeing 747, McDonnell-Douglas DC-10—are required, the agency contracts out for the aircraft on an as-needed basis. In the business jet area, the Academy contracts out for Sabreliners, Jet Commanders and Lear-jets for its Executive Aircraft Unit. For inspectors working with the air taxi community, the Academy offers the Beech 99 and 90 turbo-prop aircraft. Even tail draggers are on the Academy flight line, among them a sharp Cessna 180.

A typical, brand new, FAA General Aviation Inspector has been hired by the region and arrives at the Academy for initial indoctrination after spending about six months at his duty station familiarizing himself (and this is the editorial "him" since there are a growing number of women inspectors, controllers and flight service specialists with the FAA). He first gets a five-week overview of the total duties of an inspector including standardized flight inspection procedures. Aircraft familiarization—actually thorough checkouts—in everything from single-engine trainers to light twins follows the indoctrination. Now the inspector returns to his GADO (General Aviation District Office) for additional on-the-job training and full duty as an inspector. In from one to two years, he returns to the Academy for a refresher course and/or upgrading in new or more sophisticated aircraft. On this second tour the inspector also usually gets a light twin instrument and performance refresher and bones up on any new methods for pilot flight testing or instrument flight testing (usually one or the other). Exceptions to the one-to-one year recycle through the Academy are the jet specialists. They return for refreshers and currency checks every six months. If they are working with air taxi operators they take a companion course—Air Taxi Certification—which covers in depth Federal Air Regulations Part 135 and portions of FAR 121.

Inspectors working with helicopters take three special courses. In the initial qualification they become commercial helicopter pilots with certificates as instructors in rotorcraft. A job function course equips them to thoroughly understand the operational problems of rooftop and other specialized rotary wing activity. Critical here is the problem of external loads. At least every two years they are expected back at Oke City for a refresher.

Prior to the advent of the small, executive type jet aircraft, FAA operations inspectors—except for air carrier inspectors—had little or no opportunity or requirement to become involved with jets. However, as Learjets, Jet Commanders, Sabreliners, Citations and a family of foreign imports began to proliferate, it became necessary to get FAA operations inspectors at Flight Standards and General Aviation District offices up to speed—jet speed, in fact. Today most district offices which have in their area of responsibility executive and/or air taxi jet operations has jet-qualified inspectors. Keeping pace with this development, the Academy conducts both initial jet qualification and jet refresher courses for inspectors. It maintains a leased Lear 25 and Jet Commander and its own Sabreliner for this purpose and, as necessary, rents/leases other executive jets. Inspectors recommended for jet training can plan to spend four weeks at the Academy involving 10 to 15 hours of flying for initial qualification and the rest of the time spent in the check pilot's seat with the instructor playing the part of a student. Jet rated inspectors then can expect to return to the Academy twice a year for five-day periods devoted to refresher training.

It's one thing to check a man out in an executive jet and yet another to equip him to check others. In that half of the program the Academy really wrings them out.

In recent years, the FAA had noticed an apparent wide discrepancy region-to-region in terms of compliance and enforcement actions—a general lack of standardization. Thus an airman or mechanic cited for an infraction in one region would be treated in an entirely different manner than one in the very next region.

"We've taken steps to cure this situation," say Academy instructors, "with an intensive compliance/enforcement course for operations, maintenance, security, legal, engineering and manufacturing inspection. The emphasis is, of course, on standardization."

Also changing is the manner in which operations inspectors flight check certified flight instructors. Traditionally, notwithstanding the existence of specific guidelines in the Federal Air Regulations, inspectors have tended to insist that CFIs absolutely pattern their instructing techniques after that of the inspector. In other words, "do it exactly my way" was the name of the game.

No two pilots fly exactly the same although both may be equally proficient and equally capable. This also is true of instructors. Today operations inspectors—both in their initial tour at the Academy and in subsequent refresher tours—are being taught to place less stress on absolutely duplicating instructional techniques and more stress on the practical aspects of flight instruction.

CLEARED TO LAND!

This philosophy also is getting disseminated directly to the CFIs through the medium of the Flight Instructors Refresher Clinics held each year at various locations throughout the country. A special team from the Academy conducts these courses which are sponsored by local aviation organizations such as the Civil Air Patrol, Ninety Nines, etc., thus insuring that "the word" being given in each part of the nation is the same.

In addition to working with the inspectors, the Academy also assumed the responsibility for conducting the initial check-out and subsequent recurrency training of the flight crews assigned to the Flight Inspection National Field Office. These crews whose job it is to flight check the nation's navigational aids, VOR, ILS, TACAN, DME, NDB and associated facilities, receive their initial indoctrination and yearly refreshers at the Academy. This applies not only to the crews assigned to the domestic flight inspection mission but also those assigned to the European, Alaskan, Hawaiian and Far Eastern (Tokyo) offices.

If there is any one characteristic that represents a common denominator among the instructors at the FAA's Oklahoma City "campus" it is experience and then some. While a handful of academicians are on board to insure that modern teaching techniques are employed and that the curriculum reflects state-of-the-art methodology and educational philosophy, the men and women who come eyeball-to-eyeball with the student body are chosen from the ranks of the best the field has to offer.

Walt Quitter, who is in charge of Airways Facilities training, is a case in point. Walt has been in the business for some 28 years. He had proved himself as a field technician before first being selected to instruct at the Academy—he instructed in ILS maintenance during his first Academy tour in the 1950s. He now has been back for three years running the store. He also is a rated pilot although he admits it took him some 25 years before he decided he had better learn "how the other half lives."

Look for a typical instructor and you may as well pick Ed Kauble of Denora, Pa. Ed got into the field as an apprentice electrician with the Navy. His "good grades" earned him a shot at becoming an electronics technician and he ended his Navy career as a journeyman electronics mechanic at the Long Beach, Calif. Naval Shipyard. He joined the FAA at Des Moines, Iowa, in 1971 as a developmental technician and came to the Academy for special training in radar—particularly ARTS III. Ed returned to the Academy in 1974 as instructor in computer up-date equipment (input/output devices associated with the Automated National Airspace System.

This particular class, although extremely specialized, is representative of most of those conducted in Airways Facilities. Sixteen students spend six weeks alternating between lectures and laboratory problem work under the guidance of three instructors—one gives the lecture, one supervises the problem work and one supervises the lab. Instructors generally rotate between the lecture, problem work and lab assignments.

"We have to give them the fundamentals," Kauble points out, "but we also give them as much 'hands on' trouble shooting experience as possible. The important thing is that when they go out in the field they not only understand the theory but they have a solid grasp of the practical problems they will face and how to go about minimizing equipment down time."

Classroom/laboratory hours are from 7 A.M. to 3:30 P.M. with breaks for

Typical classroom at the Academy. Most classrooms are equipped with electronic teaching aids which permit the instructor to selectively sample the learning curve of individual students. Each trainee position is equipped with a trio of buttons connected to a monitoring panel at the instructor's position. Students thus can answer questions quickly and privately and the instructor can assess the individual's progress without embarrassing him.

With the computer playing an ever increasing role in managing the nation's airway system, the Academy places heavy emphasis on providing the best in computer training. Typical of the facilities is this complete IBM 920 installation identical to those employed in the field. Computer programmers learn on the real thing, computer maintenance technicians learn to maintain the real thing.

lunch and morning and afternoon coffee. Although the subject matter, hours and curriculum are identical class-to-class, Kauble observes that "each class has its own distinct personality."

"One class, for instance, may be super punctual," he says, "while another may lean toward outstanding laboratory work. What it boils down to is that each class develops a class leader, one individual whose personality tends to dominate those of the other students. As each new class reports to the Academy and begins its work, the personality of the emerging class leader determines the personality of that class."

Sometimes this can pose trouble if the class leader isn't with the program. One such area, Kauble points out, is when the dominant class personality is an old-timer in electronics and computer technology. That person often either knows it all or has become set in his ways. Such a situation can impede the otherwise smooth progress of the class.

One change Kauble is beginning to notice is the increasing number of women reporting for training in the technical fields. Most of them, he says, are quick to learn, sharp and strongly motivated, particularly in the sense that they are pleased to have an opportunity to work in an interesting and often challenging field, one quite different from the secretarial/administrative work which has been women's lot for so many years.

"Often the presence of a sharp girl picks up the performance of the men in a class," Kauble chuckles.

What about the quality of new employees entering the ranks of the FAA facilities technicians? They're bright and eager, but, according to William Wortham—otherwise known by his middle moniker "Gordon"—they don't seem to have the background in electronics new hires used to have. Gordon, by the way, has been around a few years. "An Oklahoma hometown farm boy" as he describes himself, he got into electronics by way of the amateur ranks longer ago than he really wants to remember. Enough to say he was one of the early amateurs and later became an instructor of the National Radio Institute.

Gordon joined the CAA in 1960 as an electronics technician at Will Rogers Field; flew as a pilot in World War II instructing in B-25s and B-24s and for 14 years has been an instructor at the Academy. For an old vacuum-tube technology type, you might expect him to be a bit standoffish about solid state devices, but "no way!" As he puts it:

"I made the transition to solid state technology very early and immediately felt at home with it."

Looking back over his 14 years at the Academy, Gordon Wortham observes:

"Some years ago the overall experience level was higher and it appears that the initial electronic training of new men and women has been in greater depth. The young ones are good. I don't mean to give them short shrift, but they need more training at our level in many of the basics. They used to have more background when they came to the FAA."

On the other hand, Walt Quitter observes, hiring old-timers also isn't the answer. Most of the technicians who came along with the vacuum technology find it is a "real transition" for them. College grads also aren't the answer.

"Would you believe?" he asks. "We get college graduates who don't know what a vacuum tube is."

THE ACADEMY

Today's FAA electronics technician needs, above all, specific knowledge of the specific system he is charged with maintaining and must be able to trouble shoot quickly and efficiently. Little of their work— only five to 10 percent—- is in installation. The bulk of their activities is keeping the systems on the line. Inherent in the requirement to keep systems in operation is one for preventative maintenance. Detect the incipient failure before it happens and prevent it from putting a critical system out of commission, perhaps just when it may be most needed.

Life of the technician in the field is anything but dreary. In fact, as Quitter puts it, "It can get downright unusual."

Sitting back in the comfort of his chair, Quitter recalls incidents like:

° the day the technician shot a hole in his boat crossing New Orleans' Lake Ponchatrain trying to kill a water moccasin that wanted to share the ride.

° how you have to kill the cottonmouths lying in the sun along a quarter mile of wooden catwalk leading to the ILS marker.

° the helicopter "rescue" of a technician from a remote communications site not because he was in danger but because if he was left there he would "go on extensive overtime trying to get back to civilization."

° the constant threat of the high voltage power systems sometimes within knuckle-bumping distance when working in a live system.

° the "you-only-get-one-chance-at-it" pressures trying to get an ILS system back on the air in a real time/emergency situation.

Field technicians keeping the airways system operating seldom have an opportunity to take the easy, change-out-the-black-box approach. Field maintenance, Quitter says, frequently is down to the component level—even circuit board repair.

One thing that bugs Quitter and many of the technicians is the fact, he says, that "facilities men go unrecognized."

"To the controller," he grumbles, "that VOR out there is just a nav check point, nothing else. To the pilot, he never thinks about it unless it's out of commission. Then hear him holler. Everyone takes the nav aids and landing systems for granted and it never occurs to them that there are a hell of a lot of men and women out there working their butts off under all kinds of circumstances, all hours of the day and night, in all kinds of weather keeping that stuff on the air. It gets mighty frustrating after awhile."

Like the flight operations and facilities maintenance instructors, the men and women who teach air traffic control also represent the cream of the crop from the field. All instructors at the Academy, by the way, get there because they have attracted the attention of their supervisors in the field and have been recommended by them for Academy duty. Even then many of those recommended don't make the grade when they are screened at Oke City.

Journeyman controller Dan Widdowfield of Batavia, N.Y., instructs in tower procedures. A long stint as an Air Force air traffic controller and 11 years in the busy Washington National Airport tower as both a radar and a manual controller preceded his assignment to the Academy.

"One thing we try to instill in the controller," Widdowfield declares, "is pride. We hammer home the thought that pride equates with capability. This is what keeps the man or woman going as well as the organization."

Joyce Spires of Jamestown, N.Y., another military-turned-FAA controller, agrees. Joyce is married to a former controller and has two children. When

211

her husband retired in the mid 60's, she tried something else—they bought a cocktail lounge and Joyce became the "bar maid" in Florida. But when they moved Joyce went back to the FAA. She is an air traffic control center instructor at the Academy now and loves her work.

Carrying on a dialogue with Joyce and Dan Widdowfield reveals not only a further insight into the training philosophy at the FAA Academy but also provides a penetrating look at what the duty controller now finds in the real world.

Joyce: "There was a day when we tried to give a trainee everything we had. Now we concentrate on the 'need-to-know'."

Dan: "We carefully study each trainee and depending on how he is progressing and his ability to retain the massive amount of need-to-know material, we add the nice-to-know."

Joyce: "Too many controllers have no empathy for the guy up there. They rattle off a clearance, for instance, without taking into consideration the experience level of the guy on the other end."

Dan: "That's right. With more general aviation activity today, more pilots with high performance aircraft loaded with communications and navigation equipment but with limited experience, it's a different ball game. We're not just working the pros now, we have to remember that. We also have to instill in the controller a sense of judgment. There are times when he must bend a little depending upon the situation. For instance, even if the standard procedure calls for a frequency change at a particular place or time, if you have the guy involved in low altitude maneuvering that's not the time to give him a change. That only leads to pilot disorientation and possible disaster."

Both Dan and Joyce agree that the quality of controllers has declined in recent years. They say it appears to be attributable largely to management requirements imposed by the agency. The so-called mobility concept—either up or out—and a lack of strong, centralized training are contributing factors. They also agree with the position voiced by Daugherty and other top Academy officials that controllers should first get a thorough grounding in the fundamentals at the Academy and then become involved in the program of practical, on-the-job training in the field, not the other way around. They believe the new controller needs a broader view of the air traffic system. Joyce especially feels the Canadian system is better, wherein a controller actually begins his career in a flight service capacity and then moves on to first a VFR tower, radar tower, etc.

"The Canadian system," she says, "has another advantage. There if you don't cut it you can go back. Or, if you like the work where you are, you have the option to stay. You are not forced up or out like you are by our mobility concept."

Joyce's position is widely supported by controllers at all levels throughout the ATC system. While they all agree that a controller cannot be permitted to become stagnant, they also insist that controllers—who like their geographical location, who are thoroughly familiar with their particular area and its traffic and who, in the opinion of their supervisors, are doing a good job—should have the prerogative of remaining in that position if they so choose.

Dan and Joyce decry—along with many instructors and students interviewed at the Academy—the attitude of a number of top supervisors in the field.

THE ACADEMY

"Many young students," Joyce points out, "are hired into a facility and are there just long enough for their supervisor to tell them, 'Yes, you can go to the Academy. Then when you come back we'll make a controller out of you.' They come in with the feeling that the trip isn't really worthwhile. I think it speaks well of our approach and the caliber of our teaching staff that within a week they usually change their minds, but that is a week wasted."

Along with many other instructors, they also deplore the fact that the "pass/fail" system no longer is in effect at the Academy. Agency personnel practices, many of them dictated by employees unions and associations and others by ethnic and racial pressure groups, eliminated this traditional carrot-and-stick approach. A record of performance as a student goes back to the facility, but ultimately the evaluation is made at the facility and more often than not on grounds other than performance.

Obviously, new people must be attracted into the FAA in each geographical area just as recruits for military flight training are brought aboard at the local level. But the military recruits get standardized training at central locations and during their training period are subjected to intensive evaluation. If they fail to pass muster during this period they are returned to civilian life. It would appear that in today's demanding aviation environment controllers as well as many other FAA specialists need to be trained and screened just as exhaustively as the pilots they must support.

It usually is the case in a bureaucracy that the men and women involved in getting the job done become aware of deficiencies long before the policy makers. Often this is due to the ingenuity and inventiveness of the folks in the field. Faced with making the system work, they develop ways of coping with those deficiencies, blunting their effect. That is what the men and women of the FAA Academy have been doing. They have been getting the job done despite the deficiencies thrust upon them.

Fortunately, the word finally filtered up the ladder.

The new procurement aimed at equipping the Academy with state-of-the-art, computer-directed simulation for air traffic controller training is under way. And, as important, FAA management bit the bullet and made a decision to "fundamentally change" the way in which it hires and trains controllers. The new approach calls for hiring controllers in groups of 204, putting them through extensive training at the Academy (about 15 weeks) and returning those who pass the Academy course to the field for the remainder of the developmental period (which will include training on operational equipment in a simulated environment).

And the washout problem is being attacked—in two ways. First the FAA has added screening at "key" points in the new Academy program in an attempt "to identify the potential to effectively perform controller's functions" and, second, it is working on a series of studies designed to improve its ability "to identify controller potential more effectively" at the time individuals are being considered for employment. The first group of new-program controller trainees reported to the Academy and began their training in January 1976. The second class reported in March of that year.

FAA has given this new approach "top priority" and is working to maintain an even flow of new trainees into the field. Hard evidence that the agency really means it is the fact that funds for the operation are located in a central pool and therefore are not subject to diversion by field officials.

COMBAT ZONE 12

"What is a nice, peaceful FAA type like me doing in a place like this?"

The thought kept repeating itself in Jack Hardy's mind as he nursed the ancient Volkswagen along the road, threading it among the motorcycles, pedicabs, military vehicles, bicycles and swelling clumps of terror-stricken refugees.

To the rear—the Cholon district of Saigon where Hardy was billeted—the crump of mortar shells and rocket bursts punctuated the stuttering exclamations of US-made M-16s and Russian AK-47s. It was Tuesday, January 30, 1968 and the beginning of the three-day Vietnamese Tet celebration marking the beginning of a new lunar year—a celebration traditionally marked in typical oriental style with fireworks. Only this year the fireworks weren't just for show; they were meant to kill, maim and strike fear in the hearts of the celebrants.

Ahead—Saigon's huge Tan Son Nhut airbase—Viet Cong, reinforced by North Vietnamese regulars infiltrated into the south, were making a determined effort to knock out the nerve center of U.S. airlift support to the armed forces of the Republic of Vietnam (ARVN). Since Tan Son Nhut was the FAA-man's destination, this morning's trip was an exercise in "out of the frying pan and into the fire."

The answer to Hardy's question represents an untold and heretofore unequalled chapter in the story of the men and women of the Federal Aviation Administration. Certainly, since the inception of the nation's aviation regulatory agency, they had been involved in wartime activity. Although ill-prepared and literally unequipped, they had met the challenge of World War II and the Korean conflict growing in stature and capability with the effort. But, that had been accomplished in the security of their homeland. Now, for the first time, they found themselves—200 of them—doing their thing in a combat zone, living with the constant thought that around the corner ahead might lie oblivion in the form of a blob of plastique explosive planted by a North Vietnamese saboteur or a bullet fired by a VC sniper.

The reason Jack Hardy, Ed Jensen, Irv Kitley, John Jones, Clyde Trusch, Jim Buecheler, Dick Turnbull, Ray Walthers, Bert Pickett and dozens of others found themselves dodging bullets and rockets is another untold story itself, the story of the most massive airlift in the history of aviation.

Even to the uninitiated the words Berlin airlift and Korean airlift paint the picture of scores of heavy transports dotting the skies. The Vietnam airlift, however, eclipsed them both and then some. It represented the greatest mass movement of people and cargo ever undertaken by air. During the five-year period from 1965 through 1969, civil air carriers—not the military transport arm, but civilian pilots and crews in civilian planes—transported 5,265,536 passengers and more than 1.5 billion pounds of cargo to Southeast Asia in direct support of the war effort.

In December 1966, for instance, civil carriers airlifted 99,980 passengers and 37.4 tons of cargo to Vietnam. This exceeded the total airlifted to Korea during the entire year of 1951. In 1968, civil carriers averaged 130,700 passengers a month to and from Vietnam as compared with only 7,600 to

Korea each month.

The key word was civil. These were civilian airlines—some 20 of them with 15 to 16 operating at any one time—and it was mandatory that they fly in accordance with the Federal Air Regulations governing civilian operation. Further, for the most part, they were equipped to function safely in the civilian electronics/communications environment, not the military's. Thus it fell to the FAA to establish and supervise the operation of air traffic control centers, control towers, navigation aids and communications circuits commensurate with FAA requirements for crew and passenger safety. One of the many FAA specialists who volunteered to accomplish this was Jack Hardy, an FAA controller since 1953 and an Air Force controller before that.

The first rocket attacks hit Saigon at 0300 that morning and by the time Hardy set off for Tan Son Nhut small arms fire could already be heard just blocks away from the apartment he shared with several other civilians assigned variously to the USAF, the Central Intelligence Agency and British Intelligence. As the Operations officer for the Civil Aviation Aid Group (CAAG), Hardy was involved in a variety of supervisory and training activities. One of those areas of concern was the Saigon Air Traffic Control Center at Tan Son Nhut. That is where he was heading now as a brassy sun accented the black, roiling smoke marking a city now beginning to feel the full fury of the attack.

The normally 30-minute drive dragged on and on, congestion on the road increasing by the minute. Finally, Hardy arrived at the Tan Son Nhut main gate only to be told he could not enter. The military police informed him the base now was under full attack with North Vietnamese regulars already advancing across the golf course on the opposite side. Across the field he could see the blue-grey pall of smoke from small arms and the ugly black puffs as mortar shells exploded.

"No amount of arguing would move the guards," Hardy recalls, "so I backtracked about a mile and a half to an apartment building where most of the maintenance and controller personnel were billeted. Under pressure, people tend to look toward management for leadership or at least to share the problem at hand. I figured I could do some good."

Hardy remembers it as a "sweaty time" with concentrations of VC along a canal only 300 feet from the building and the constant roar of Huey helicopter gunships and their thudding 50-caliber machine guns keeping them at bay.

"Now I knew it was for real," he says, "we had been receiving intelligence reports for months that the VC would bring the war to us but there had been so many false alarms we had come to disbelieve it. We saw the coffins being shipped stateside every day but still remained removed from the reality of combat. We tended to assume a 'it-can't-happen-here' attitude. But I knew better with the dead bodies right there out the window."

Although, in the distance, Hardy could see Cholon burning, it seemed at the time a good idea to get back to his billet and check out things there. With a final word of encouragement to the FAA people in the apartment, he headed the VW back along the road to Saigon. MPs told him he could go home if he could get by the road blocks but warned him that if he made it all the way he might not be able to get out again.

The return trip proved uneventful. By nightfall, he and seven other civilians made it back. Although fire fights were underway close by, Hardy and his mates felt relatively secure since the apartment employed mercenary guards—tough Cambodians. The sense of security was shortlived, however, when it was learned shortly that all but two of them had taken off for parts unknown.

"That's when we broke out the weapons," he recalls, admitting it was "a bit scary. Fortunately, we were well armed. Or I should say the CIA men were well armed. They had enough to go around."

Hardy and the others were trapped in the building for the next four days as fire fights continued in the streets about them.

"It was weird," he says, "listening to pop music on AFRS (Armed Forces Radio Service) with machine gun fire and mortar shells exploding in the background."

Hardy taped the incident and early in 1976 dug out the tapes, playing them for his wife and daughter.

"It scared the hell out of them!" he said.

The more than 200 FAA personnel who served in Vietnam during the Southeast Asia conflict were singularly fortunate when it came to being killed or wounded, but it wasn't because they were not exposed to the reality of all-out war. These Air Force security police are repelling one of several Viet Cong attacks on Saigon's Tan Son Nhut Air Base, attacks that brought the sound, the smell, the ugliness of war right to their doorstep.

Aside from the fact the FAA men and women were working in the middle of a hot war, there were other unique aspects to the assignment. For one thing, Hardy remembers, it was like "going backwards in time when we walked into Saigon Center."

"Working in that center," he says, "was like working in a U.S. center in 1944. The whole system was 20 years behind the times. It was really bad. There was no radar. Point-to-point communications were archaic. Air-ground communications were almost unusable. Phones were even worse. The center had only a high frequency, single sideband link with Hong Kong."

One communications link was most unusual. It was a direct CW (continuous wave or, in other words, an old-fashioned radio telegraph link) with

The barbed wire enclosure separating this civilian aircrewman on a turnaround rest period from the cameraman is silent testimony to the environment in which air carrier crews and FAA men and women got the job done.

the North Vietnamese. The circuit was necessary to coordinate flights of the UN International Control Commission aircraft to prevent them from being shot down by mistake.

This wasn't Hardy's first encounter with the Vietnamese. As a training supervisor at the FAA Academy in Oklahoma City, he had trained some 20 Vietnamese controllers to take over the ATC function in their homeland. Both during that period and later in Vietnam, Hardy found he liked the people and was impressed by their determination.

"As a people," he says, "the Vietnamese are clean, courteous and most determined. When they make up their mind to do something they stick to it. Also, I was impressed with their ability to absorb technical training. I think most Americans, particularly the military, lacked patience with them. The language barrier was a difficult hurdle but once you were able to communicate with them it was a different story."

As early as 1956 a handful of personnel from the CAA, predecessor to today's FAA, became involved in a project sponsored by what then was the International Cooperation Agency (later the Agency for International Development or AID) to help the Vietnamese build an air traffic system that would meet international standards. However, the system—to include aeronautical ground facilities, air traffic control and a communications system—was intended to handle aircraft of the DC-3 type and a low traffic density. Fortunately, this objective had been reached by the mid-1960s providing a foundation for the state-of-the-art system needed when the U.S. build-up and massive civil airlift began.

From 1956 through 1962 it was possible for AID to concentrate on development of South Vietnamese civil aviation without much concern for military influence. From 1963 until the last FAA representative left Vietnam in 1974, the effort was heavily influenced by the accelerated military activity and the presence of an enormous amount of military aviation. So great was the demand for further development that funding (through AID) was assumed by the Department of Defense.

AID's Civil Aviation Assistance Group consisted of only three to five specialists from the CAA in the early days but as the airlift grew CAAG numbers increased proportionally. At its peak, the group had some 65 FAA personnel assigned including controllers, electronics engineers and technicians, facility and airport engineers and operations specialists. By 1973 that number was down to five and in 1974 the last FAA representative left the country just ahead of the victorious Viet Cong and North Vietnamese who inherited an air traffic control system as good as anything in the world and alone worth some $14 million.

FAA personnel also provided direct support to U.S. military aviation activities during the latter part of the conflict. Four different projects between 1965 and 1973 saw the installation and activation of 24 transportable control tower systems, 10 tower control consoles and 15 mobile towers for the Army; four towers for the Air Force. The systems were designed, built, installed and supported by FAA during this period.

It was these programs that brought people like Clyde Trusch, Irv Kitley, Jim Buecheler and Dick Turnbull to "Nam."

A native of Buffalo, N.Y., with a civil engineering degree from the University of Arkansas, Buecheler had gone directly into the CAA in 1957. He arrived in Vietnam with wide experience in the design and installation of modern air traffic control facilities and plunged immediately into a project to equip Air Force bases at Phan Rang and Cam Ranh Bay, Vietnam, and U-Tapao and Nakhon Phanom, Thailand, with towers capable of handling high density traffic.

Obviously there were a number of options available to the government in filling the Air Force requirement. But in terms of time and money it appeared prudent to bring in the single agency with the most expertise. The FAA had the design, the trained personnel, the materials and the know-how—in the aggregate the capability to handle the job from the "hole-in-the-ground" stage to installation of the sophisticated electronics. In practice, the Army was to supervise site preparation and completion of the foundations. U.S. and Vietnamese contractors would perform the actual construction work. The FAA men were there to coordinate the various efforts and supervise the overall project. At least that's the way the effort appeared on paper. That wasn't the way it worked.

Take Cam Ranh Bay for instance. The site was to have been prepared and the foundation was to be completed. Arriving at the air field, the FAA team was met by its military hosts and after the necessary introductions were over asked to see the site.

"It's across the field," the guides said and proceeded to load up the jeeps and strike out via a rutted sand trail alongside the runway. Fifteen minutes later the officer signaled a halt, climbed from the lead jeep and pointed beyond the cleared area to a spot in the dense jungle.

"There it is!" he said proudly.

One of the major contributions of FAA personnel to the Vietnam war was the rehabilitation of existing control towers and the construction of new ones—all in record time. Rehabilitation of the Da Nang tower underway.

The Tan Son Nhut tower after rehab work was completed.

The new tower at Cam Ranh Bay. Even rehabilitation of existing towers was a major task since the antiquated radio equipment had to be replaced with state-of-the-art electronics and radar.

CLEARED TO LAND!

"Despite the initial delays," Buecheler recalls, "the program was completed in record time. Here in the states it takes from one to two years to get a single tower going under the best working conditions. In Nam we got four done in 18 months primarily due to the industry and diligence of the local people and the fantastic logistic support received from stateside—particularly the FAA Depot, FAA Pacific and Western Regions and our Washington head-quarters."

The facilities team had some definite advantages when it came to getting things done. There were no labor unions, no eight-hour days, no holidays and no coffee breaks. The work went on from sunup to sundown and then some. Once construction was started it kept on until the job was done.

"We took pride in those towers," Buecheler says, "they never leaked. Those we build here at home with our own people always seem to have a leak or two."

The major problem, as he recalls it, was the language barrier. This was, however, considerably alleviated by the attitude of the Vietnamese who, he says, "were eager to understand and to please" although getting across to them did take a "lot of arm-waving."

"If you couldn't talk and explain things with your hands you would have been lost over there," he says, "we got a lot of exercise with all that arm-waving."

Like most of the FAA people who served in Vietnam, Buecheler tends to play down the danger and the fact that he was in the middle of a war zone. Perhaps like most of us, he prefers to remember the good things, and it takes a bit of thinking to recall the others. Jim does remember a convoy from Cam Ranh Bay to Phang Rang and the unusual restraints under which the U.S. military was forced to conduct the war.

"Clyde Trusch and I went along with 15 trucks of equipment," he relates, "in a jeep driven by Gordon Hubbard, an Air Force civilian. We had a Military Police escort but the orders were 'don't shoot back.' The concern apparently was civilian casualties and most of the time it was impossible to distinguish the VC from the friendlies. It was a very sensitive proposition.

"Well, we started out on the 40-mile drive. Generally, there were open fields on either side of the road. At one point there was a long stretch where the edge of a rubber plantation extended parallel to the road about 100 yards away.

"Gordon always carried an M-16 with him laid out across his lap under the wheel. Suddenly, shots rang out from the direction of the rubber trees—only a few shots but enough to send Clyde and me burrowing into the floor of the jeep. Gordon just continued to drive with one hand while he shouldered the M-16 and banged off a few rounds at the trees. That's all that happened. We weren't hurt. No one was hit. But the amazing thing was that the MPs came back and chewed the hell out of Gordon for shooting back. Some war!"

Strangely enough, Buecheler says, enemy action had little or no effect on the tower building effort. The action was close enough to be visible and audible, he recalls, but it wasn't a daily thing and although the tall towers represented perfect targets they were not attacked by mortar or rocket fire.

"It was as if the VC and North Vietnamese deliberately left them alone so they could use them after they won the war," he observes.

Buecheler's co-worker during much of his Vietnam tour was a University of Idaho graduate from Sagle, Idaho, who volunteered for the program on

COMBAT ZONE

Thanksgiving 1965. Dick Turnbull left the states in mid-January 1966 arriving in Saigon after a two-week stay in Hawaii where he got to know the Air Force and Navy people at CINCPAC (Commander-in-Chief, Pacific) for whom the FAA was performing the Southeast Asia construction effort.

"We had a PanAm flight to Saigon," Turnbull recalls, "and, as we expected, the people who were to meet us at Tan Son Nhut weren't anywhere around. My first experience with the Vietnamese convinced me that they were industrious to say the least. I got the job of watching our baggage—all 20 pieces of it—while the others tried to find transportation and instructions for housing. There were some Vietnamese there whose job it was to move baggage and that they did. They scampered around like little mice doing their job—moving baggage. I had a hell of a time keeping track of ours."

To Turnbull, the immediacy of the war was quickly evident.

"One of the first things that made me realize we were in a war zone was the fact that everyone went around armed. Even in Saigon you always could hear the sounds of rockets and mortar shells. You soon became aware that this was unlike former wars where a civilian might work behind the lines. Here there were no lines—literally any street could suddenly become a combat zone. Except for the White Mice (white helmeted Vietnamese police) and allied military personnel you didn't know if the people with whom you were rubbing shoulders were Cong or not. Any one of the bicycles passing you on the street could be carrying saddlebag bombs.

"One day right outside SCOMO (Saigon Commissioned Officers Mess) the ARVN (Army of the Republic of Vietnam) caught a busload of VC. When the fire fight was over bodies were strewn all over the place."

Much of Turnbull's work took him up and down the long, narrow finger of Vietnam under control of the South and over into Thailand. There he ran into one of the major obstacles to getting on with the job—transportation.

"All transportation was via military air," he remembers, "and although we had a top priority it rarely did us any good. When you had a trip, you went to the terminal with your orders in your hand and then waited—sometimes sweating it out for 24 to 36 hours. If you missed a seat when your name came up you moved to the end of the line. If you wanted to get out at all you just slept and ate right there."

Turnbull also recalls a "minor" problem on the sites—cobras:

"You always had to keep your eyes peeled for cobras, especially in the areas where there wasn't a lot of activity or first thing in the morning when you came on the job."

Close calls? There were a few. Thanks to being in the wrong place at the right time, he's around to tell about one.

"I joined a convoy from Phan Rang to the bay just 15 minutes away. I was riding at the head of the convoy with the colonel. At the last minute he got a call. The convoy pulled out and we joined up at the rear. Half way to the bay the lead vehicle hit a land mine. Luck was with the colonel and me that day."

One thing that impressed Turnbull was the number of people available to do a job. To say the least, there was no shortage of labor, he says, adding:

"You wouldn't believe the number of people they (the Vietnamese contractors) would make available for a job. In the states we might have 20 workers. In Vietnam I saw days when we had 100 to do the same amount of work. Take a simple task like sawing a piece of pipe with a hack saw—three or four just to

CLEARED TO LAND!

The civil airlift to Vietnam and Southeast Asia was by many times
the largest ever attempted in the annals of aviation. In a single day, for instance, civil air
carriers airlifted more passengers and cargo into Vietnam than the total airlifted to
Korea during all of 1951. Supporting the military buildup, civil carriers accounted for 5.2
million passengers and 1.5 billion pounds of cargo in a five-year period. Typical scenes:
a braniff 707 at Da Nang; a contract carrier at Bein Hoa.

hold the pipe?

"Another thing, you would not believe some of the materials we used—priceless, priceless here in the United States—solid teak for form lumber!"

Turnbull is one of those people who enjoy life wherever and whatever they are doing and he enjoyed his tour in Vietnam and Thailand—especially the latter.

"Those Thai people were wonderful," he recalls with a smile, "so friendly and warm. And Thailand is a beautiful country. You know—I could go back there."

Ray Walthers who served as a supervisory engineer to CAAG is another FAAer who has warm feelings for the people of Southeast Asia and would return again if need be.

"The outcome of the Vietnam War," Ray says, "leaves many of us frustrated. The Vietnamese people were a wonderful people and we let them down. The GIs that went in, went there to fight a war. For the most part they didn't get the chance to know the people like we did so they didn't think much of them."

Walthers particularly recalls how his Vietnamese counterparts looked out for him and protected him from harm.

"They knew things we didn't," he says, "and when I had to go someplace and there would be real danger, they would warn me. If they knew I planned a trip, say to Da Nang, I would get a call. 'Mister Walthers, you go Da Nang tomorrow?' When I answered in the affirmative, my friend would say: 'Mister Walthers, you no go Da Nang tomorrow, VC out!' Even the peasants were concerned about us. The people who took care of our living quarters would stop me when I was going into town. 'Watch your pocketbook, watch your pocketbook, Mister Walthers,' they would say.

"Those people, the Vietnamese, are family oriented. There is a lot of love in their hearts. I'm sorry we let them down."

Walthers tells a humorous story of Thanksgiving in Vietnam when he and those sharing the quarters bought a huge frozen turkey at the military commissary and then invited their Vietnamese caretakers to share the dinner.

"They would not eat a bite of that bird," he recalls, "because they never had seen a 'chicken' that big before. If you've seen a Vietnamese chicken hanging in a local market, small and scrawny, mostly skin and bones, I guess you'd understand how they felt about that big, fat U.S. turkey."

Ray's job in Vietnam was to translate into technical improvements the requirements outlined by Jack Hardy who was concerned with operational capabilities to support the massive airlift. It proved to be a herculean task.

"When I got there," Walthers reports, "it was like the dark ages in airways communications and traffic control. The teletype was always broken down. Their only radar was short range, about 30 miles. Radio communications, when they were operating, were bad. Most NDBs were not functioning.

"Every day was a hassle. Each of the services had requirements, each one wanted something different. One of the major requirements was a system for long range VHF communications. Ultimately, a system of high-gain, directional antenna oriented along the airways was designed and installed. The antenna supported a VHF/UHF repeater relay system which linked Da Nang with Hong Kong, a distance of 620 miles.

"We built it based on theory," Walthers says, "and when I left I didn't even

Pan Am 707s on the ramp at Cam Ranh Bay.

know if it would work. I sure hoped it would because they needed it badly. One day I got a call from Jack Hardy in Vietnam. 'Ray, it works, it works!' he told me. That was great news."

Ask Ray Walthers about his Vietnam tour and inquire if he would do it again. The reply is immediate, loud and clear:

"You're darned right, I would do it again!"

The unprecedented participation of FAA personnel in a hot war environment was the direct result of the unprecedented participation of civil air carriers in an airlift which saw them looking directly down the muzzles of guns held by "bad guys."

The rapid expansion of the airlift in 1966 and the lack of preparation for operation of airline aircraft in a tactical environment was shot with problems. FAA guidelines for the surveillance and monitoring of such an operation were nonexistent, though augmentation of the Department of Defense airlift requirements by civil aviation had long been a part of advanced DOD planning. Contingency procedures were set forth in the "Civil Reserve Air Fleet" (CRAF) program in 1952 to provide for incorporating civil aircraft in the Military Airlift Command (MAC) operation but these CRAF procedures, even though updated, had been designed for designated national emergencies and contemplated a more traditional war situation with front lines and zones free of combat behind them. They didn't fit the Southeast Asia situation. First, no national emergency was ever declared. Secondly, there were no front lines, the war was everywhere.

As U.S. commitments in Southeast Asia intensified in the 1960's, the amount of "airlift" purchased by MAC from U.S. air carriers increased steadily. As the civil airlift grew, the number of operational irregularities, maintenance discrepancies and, on occasion, failures to comply with the Federal Aviation Regulations also grew. It was apparent that more surveillance was required by the FAA since DOD as well as the FAA was determined there was to be "no double standard," notwithstanding the battlefield environment which sometimes surrounded the "civil" operations.

No specific plan existed for the overall surveillance of an airlift of the magnitude developing nor were there any organizational guidelines suggesting how widespread elements of the FAA could collectively monitor activities of carriers over such an enormous area and in such numbers. It became evident that the responsibility for surveillance of these global operations should be assigned to one FAA office. Therefore, the Pacific Region prepared a report to the administrator on April 16, 1966, which gave the status of the airlift and proposed a series of actions.

In June 1966, the administrator, General W. F. "Bozo" McKee, assigned to the Pacific Region the responsibility for monitoring the unusual conditions and problems affecting the civil airlift and establishing such rules and procedures as were necessary.

To accomplish this, the region created three technical positions and assigned specific duties to each. The positions included that of the Airlift Coordinator at the region headquarters in Hawaii to monitor all aspects of the airlift and recommend actions to be taken by air carrier companies and Washington headquarters.

A second position established an FAA representative at Tan Son Nhut airport in Saigon where he could monitor the environment of the destination area and furnish on-the-scene decisions for operations into what was, periodically, a combat zone.

The third position was that of an FAA Air Carrier Maintenance Inspector at the primary embarkation point, Travis Air Force Base, Calif., to monitor the condition of aircraft prior to departure for and upon return from Southeast Asia. He also served as advisor to the Air Force on air carrier maintenance procedures and other matters as necessary.

Procedures were established so that a daily flow of information from the FAA representative in Saigon would reach the regional office in Honolulu where it could be reviewed and correlated with intelligence reports and other data. Decisions necessary to maintain an adequate level of safety were then made with the benefit of the latest and most comprehensive information available. Additional provisions were made to provide a fast means of advising the carriers of actions required. Briefing facilities were prepared at Pacific Region headquarters so that a comprehensive status of the airlift could be presented both to agency and air carrier management.

The type of equipment being used in the airlift and the change to turbine as opposed to reciprocating-engine aircraft also had an effect on the overall situation.

Introduction of the turbine fleet saw many changes in the route structure across the Pacific. For the first time the longer range turbojets made it possible to overfly Wake Island while enroute from Honolulu to Southeast Asia and flights that stopped at Guam could now proceed directly to Southeast Asia with no stop at Clark Air Base in the Philippines. On return trips, many of which were empty ferry flights, the jets could make one relatively short hop to Yokota Air Base, Japan or Kadena Air Base, Okinawa and from there fly nonstop all the way back to the continental U.S.

Operation across the North Pacific became commonplace. Many flights were now able to operate nonstop from Travis to Japan and others could easily operate via Anchorage to Japan along the Great Circle Route. Utilization of these routes placed increased requirements on Yokota, and facilities had to be expanded to care for this civil turbine fleet. Partly as a result of the Yokota expansion, civil airlift operations into Tachikawa Air Base, Japan became a thing of the past.

In addition to a trend toward the use of the route structure across the North Pacific and the increased use of Yokota and Kadena, the turbojets made it possible to airlift a larger percentage of men and supplies destined for Southeast Asia from U.S. bases other than Travis. Many flights could now be dispatched from Air Force bases throughout the nation such as McChord near Seattle, Wash., and Norton near San Bernardino, Calif., as well as Kelly AFB, Texas, and McGuire AFB, New Jersey. Occasionally, flights also originated at Dover, Del., and Charleston, S.C.

The FAA policy during the 1950s and early 1960s was for air carrier certificate-holders to request necessary surveillance from Air Carrier District Offices (ACDO) or International Field Offices (IFO) that held geographical responsibility for the areas in which the carriers proposed to operate. Some air carrier principal inspectors made a practice of familiarizing themselves with a carrier's entire route structure by taking extended surveillance trips on their carrier's entire route system, while others found it difficult to get away from their other duties for such long periods.

At locations such as Tokyo, where the East Asian International Field Office is located at the U.S. Embassy some 30 miles from Tachikawa and Yokota, local surveillance of carriers was extremely difficult. Due to the irregular nature of their operations, it was not at all easy to justify the necessary travel time (two or more hours each way in almost unbelievable Tokyo traffic over terrible roads) to Yokota, to conduct a ramp check on an airplane which might show up hours late or perhaps not at all.

In the Philippines, travel from the Southeast Asian IFO in Manila to Clark was more arduous since Clark is 60 miles from Manila. Train service was primitive and almost nonexistent. Highway travel was even worse and required three hours one way.

The closest domiciled air carrier inspector to South Vietnam air bases during this time was at the Southeast Asia IFO in Manila—two hours distant by air via infrequently scheduled flights or a combination of five hours by way of Clark AB.

On the U.S. west coast, air carrier surveillance at Travis was far easier, but since the San Francisco IFO is 50 miles from Travis, travel was still time-consuming.

As a result, air carriers were operating through some of these bases with little or no surveillance.

Expansion of the airlift brought an increase in reports of navigational discrepancies, maintenance difficulties, Air Defense Identification Zone (ADIZ) violations and general user complaints which made it increasingly apparent that closer surveillance was needed. In addition to drawing attention to this situation the April 1966 report by the Pacific Region outlined the status of such things as security at Tan Son Nhut, air traffic in the Saigon terminal system, and airports in use in South Vietnam. Recommendations were made as follows:

1. That scheduled passenger service on U.S. flag carriers into Tan Son Nhut be permitted to continue.

2. That the FAA delegate authority to each regional director to authorize deviations from the operations specifications of pertinent FAR's to air carriers under contract to DOD. The reason for this recommendation was to enable the agency to grant necessary waivers on a timely basis. Ordinarily a carrier requested a waiver and DOD certified to the FAA that it was essential to the national defense before the agency would act on the waiver itself, all of which was a time consuming process.

3. That MAG make it a contractual requirement that carrier aircraft be equipped with ultra-high frequency (UHF) radio and air traffic control (ATC) transponder equipment—UHF radios because UHF was the primary communications equipment at military bases and transponders to enable ground radar units to quickly identify and monitor progress of civil aircraft.

Bozo McKee accepted the Pacific Region report and its recommendations in June 1966 launching the FAA on the necessary paperwork which ultimately caused the big, bluff chief of the Chicago Air Carrier District Office, Ed Jensen, to shake the dust of the Midwest from his boots and plant them in Vietnam.

Jensen, a former Navy PBY pilot, like the other FAA personnel assigned to Vietnam, was a volunteer.

"There were some 50 applications for the job," he recalls, "so I considered

The Flying Tiger Line was a major participant in the unprecedented civilian airlift to Vietnam. A Tiger Super DC-8 arrives at Tan Son Nhut. Another discharges cargo. Strangely enough, a number of civilian transports suffered damage but none were destroyed by enemy fire.

it an honor that I was accepted. It also turned out to be a hell of an interesting period in my career. I got there in 1966 and stayed until 1973. Then I was sent back on temporary duty and didn't leave until four days after the last civil carrier took out the last GI passenger on March 29, 1974."

Jensen, who now looks back on the Vietnam tour as a high point in his life, wasn't so sure he had made the right choice when he landed in Saigon about 11 P.M., on a hot, humid Southeast Asian night.

"My first impression was that it was miserable," he recalls, "not only the weather, but the whole situation. I looked about the ramp at Tan Son Nhut and it seemed like the most disorganized airfield in the world—cargo stacked all over the place. I almost got back on the flight that brought me there and went home."

By the time Ed left Vietnam for the last time seven years later, he had changed his mind.

"I got to understand the people," he says, "and found I liked their simple way of life. Sure there were some hairy times, but nothing we couldn't handle. I guess the closest the war got to me was when we had enemy tanks at the end of the runway at Tan Son Nhut and had to blow up our own ammo dump to keep the VC from getting it. And one night we took rocket hits in five buildings around our quarters. But they missed us."

Jensen was not part of CAAG (FAA personnel assigned to that organization came under the Department of State during their tour) but reported directly to Pacific Region. His responsibility was to assess the total situation on a day-to-day basis taking certain local actions and recommending others to Honolulu and Washington that would enable the civil air carriers to do their job—operate under combat conditions and still remain within the scope of FAA regulations maximizing passenger safety.

He sums his job up this way:

"How to keep the carrier legal and still permit him to operate in a hostile zone."

As he points out, this had never been done before. Even in Korea the civil carriers did not operate in the war zone. They flew their cargo and passengers to Japan where the military transport fleet took over. Included in Jensen's bailiwick was security of the civil aircraft and their passengers. Although the physical problem of security was the responsibility of the military, it was Ed's job to constantly oversee it as it pertained to the civilian planes, crews and passengers involved. Based on just how hot the war was in a particular area, Jensen could close or open airfields to inbound civil traffic or keep aircraft on the ground.

How did the airline crews take to all this?

"Frankly," he says, "a lot of them didn't like it at all. They just weren't that happy about taking the chance of getting shot at. The pay was good, however, and the job had to be done. We also had the kind that just didn't give a damn—the kind that were frustrated combat pilots. From the standpoint of the risk we had both the over-cautious and the under-cautious."

The FAA's report, "The Vietnam Civil Airlift," almost two inches thick, provides an additional insight into just what it was like both for the civilian crews operating into the area and the FAA personnel who helped make it possible. While damage to civil air carriers was slight and virtually all FAA personnel completed their tours relatively unscathed (Joe Zaremba was wounded in a rocket attack), the weekly reports made to Pacific Region (begun in June 1966) underlined the ever-present danger both in the air and on the ground. Entries, though concise and sparse in detail, are nevertheless graphic:

...''Saigon RAPCON VHF transmissions which were noisy last week, continued to deteriorate. The problem is leaky control/audio cables and wet weather. After flying several RAPCON approaches, our inspector was seriously concerned that the VHF transmissions had deteriorated to the point requiring immediate corrective action or restriction of IFR operations at Tan Son Nhut. Significant improvement in RAPCON transmissions was reported June 17, apparently the result of removing some nonessential control circuits from the cable pending the installation of the new cable reported to be completed by June 21. All regions have been requested to advise their MAC carriers of the possibility of communications problems with the RAPCON until the new cable is completed.''

...''Tan Son Nhut Attack. The terrorist activity that took place on December 5, 1966, was carried out by a special cadre of 50 well-trained members of the Viet Cong, starting about 1:00 A.M.

''The newly erected, double-perimeter fence—separated by a mine field—apparently was effective and acted as a deterrent to penetration since the VC were forced to gain access to the base in an area where the old single fence has yet to be replaced. Also, this area has not yet been seeded with the new mines.

''The VC were able to assemble a 16-mm mortar on the base and fire a few rounds before they were dispersed by security forces. They escaped with the mortar 'chute' but abandoned the heavy base plate. It was reported that the swift reaction by canine patrols and armed, flare-dropping helicopters was very effective in dispersing the attacking force and rendering it ineffective as far as causing further damage to the airfield or airplanes.

''The airport was closed for approximately seven hours as a result of the attack. There was no damage to U.S. civil aircraft and no casualty to civilian personnel. Two Flying Tiger aircraft diverted to their alternate of Bien Hoa while Tan Son Nhut was closed.''

...''Security at Tan Son Nhut Airport has improved greatly since the December attack by the Viet Cong. All of that section of the airport known as the northwest side now has at least eight fences and two mine fields. On the northeast side of the field, there are triple to quadruple fences with one heavy mine field. All the vegetation on the airport and inside the fences has been removed and the area is now cleared. Two 75,000 candlepower lights are installed along the northwest side and light up the entire fence area. On both the northwest and northeast sides, lights on poles approximately 100 feet apart have been installed. The installation of electrical conduit for this lighting is underway at the present time.''

...''On March 8, 1967, while being radar vectored to Tan Son Nhut Airport, Pan American World Airways' MAC Flight 3873 observed and encountered artillery explosions at approximately 8,000 feet altitude which were close enough to feel the concussion to the aircraft. The incident occurred just southeast of Bien Hoa, although there were no reports of artillery firing. An investigation is being conducted by U.S. Air Force and Army officials to determine the actual origin of the firing.''

...''Bien Hoa was attacked on May 12, 1967, by Viet Cong. Approximately

125-140 hits by various type mortar were received on the air base. There were six fatalities and more than 30 persons wounded. First reports indicated they were Americans. No damage to U.S. civil air carriers. Useable runway reduced to 5,000 feet due to shell holes. Continental Airlines flight took off immediately prior to attack. No known damage to this flight."

..."On September 23 a PAA B-707 sustained a small caliber arms hit, presumably near Da Nang. After departing Da Nang, the flight landed at Kadena and refueled the center wing tank. A stream of fuel revealed the bullet hole near the drip stick position in the left-hand glove area of the center wing tank. This brings the total hits since September 1963 to five, three of which have been at Da Nang since January of this year."

..."On October 15 at 1223 local a Pan American World Airways DC-6 was struck by one bullet while approaching to land at Da Nang. The hit occurred approximately nine miles from the airport at 3,000 feet. It penetrated the heater compartment door and expended itself in passenger luggage. By means of a Vietnam Operational Message, all carriers have been reminded of the 5,000-foot restriction until within 10 miles of airports in Vietnam. The same message reminded them of the availability of the 4.5-degree glide slope and that these procedures were incorporated to minimize danger from ground fire hits."

..."Recent increases in unfriendly anti-aircraft artillery activity in the vicinity of Amber 8 between Da Nang and Ubon has necessitated raising the minimum enroute altitude to 20,000 feet. Certificate holding offices have been informed."

..."Despite explosive enemy action which erupted throughout South Vietnam early Tuesday morning, January 30, 1968, an almost normal airlift operating status into Vietnam has been restored as of this morning.

"The initial results of enemy activity throughout South Vietnam restricted or closed all air bases to civil airlift movements with the exception of daylight operations into Da Nang and Cam Ranh Bay.

"During this initial hostile action, one U.S. civil aircraft sustained damage. A Seaboard World DC-8 was hit seven times by small arms fire while taking off from Tan Son Nhut at 0300 hours local time on January 30. This was a ferry flight and the crew was unaware they had been hit until after landing at Yokota. The aircraft sustained four hits in the right wing, one in the left wing, one in the vertical stabilizer and one in the fuselage.

"The Saigon Center was affected and could no longer guarantee positive control. An advisory service on a limited basis was offered and secondary radar service was provided within radar ranges of 150 NM in Saigon.

"The airlift quickly adapted to the restrictions placed on South Vietnamese bases by terminating at Clark, Kadena, Guam or other points short of South Vietnam. Continued dispatching of these flights was operationally controlled from these downline stations based on the changing conditions and operational environment existing at that moment.

"This morning the Saigon Air Command Post advised us that all FAA personnel in Saigon are safe but still confined to their quarters by a 24-hour curfew and sporadic enemy activity in the city. Our last contact with our FAA representative, Ed Jensen, was at 2300 on January 30. At that time, he advised he had attempted to gain access to Tan Son Nhut but was forced back to the relative security of his quarters because of the heavy street fighting in the vicinity of the airport. Subsequently, all civilians were confined to quarters except for high priority movements which were permitted only under armed escort. Ralph Thomas of the Manila IFO and Rudy Schaefer from the Miami ACDO were barricaded with Jensen in his quarters. Subsequent attempts to contact them at this location have been unsuccessful due to inoperative telephone circuitry.''

...''Since the initial Tet attacks which began January 30, there has been a total of 44 separate launchings of rockets/mortars against the bases in use by civil air carriers; however, only 17 of these attacks consisted of 10 or more rockets. The remaining 27 attacks have been harassment launchings of one to four rockets launched at infrequent intervals.

"Of the 17 heavier attacks, three were on Tan Son Nhut. Nearby Bien Hoa has had five of the heavier attacks launched against the base. Da Nang was the first base to come under attack in the Tet offensive launched and was hit again for a total of four of the heavier attacks. Cam Ranh Bay was attacked for the first time on March 4 with a total of 12 rockets/mortars striking the base. Phu Cat was hit once on February 20 with ten mortars which is reported to be the first time Phu Cat has been hit even though the city and area around the base were under attack on January 30. Pleiku sustained attacks of 10 or more rockets/mortars on January 30 and again on March 5 and 9. The only civil carrier using this base is World Airways, Inc.''

...''The second round of VC/NVN attacks was launched May 5, 1968. There were 14 rocket attacks between early Sunday morning and Friday noon and all airlift bases except Cam Ranh Bay were hit. The attacks involved 2 to 25 rockets. Tan Son Nhut was most frequently hit having been subjected to six of the 14 attacks. The Tan Son Nhut Vietnamese Base Commander was killed during the attack on May 6. Damage to all bases was generally light with operational damage restricted to runway hits which were repaired within a few hours.

"The eighth ground fire strike on civil aircraft occurred at 0630 local time on May 5. A Pan American Boeing 707 crew observed tracers at 700 feet when one mile out on final to runway 25L at Tan Son Nhut. Inspection after landing revealed one 12.7 mm bullet hole in #1 tank, two feet inboard of #1 outboard drip stick.''

Not all FAA personnel who got a taste of Vietnam during the conflict were ''in-country'' residents for extended periods. Frequently, engineers, technicians and inspectors from stateside were sent to Southeast Asia on temporary duty. One of those was Rudy Schaefer, then principal avionics inspector assigned to Eastern Air Lines in Miami, Fla. Schaefer's trip report read like this:

"I arrived at Tan Son Nhut approximately 1:30 P.M. Tuesday, January 30 and visited facilities at the airport with Ed Jensen, the FAA representative. At the end of the day we drove back to the city where I was quartered for the night.

"The following morning, Wednesday, I was scheduled for a 5:30 departure on a MAC charter flight to return to Clark where I would catch an EAL MAC flight which would be returning from Bangkok enroute to the U.S. At 3 A.M. the attack on the city was launched by Viet Cong/National Liberation Forces. From our roof we could see three areas of concentrated military action. Helicopters were launching rockets at all three positions, and C-47

'Dragon Ships' were being used against the two more distant ones. Small arms fire could be heard at a distance, but nothing was heard in the immediate vicinity. We had no indication at this time as to the extent of the fighting, so Jensen backed the jeep out and we started for the airport in order to better assess the effects of the action on air operations. Not far down the street, we were stopped by Vietnamese military forces who refused to let us go any further in that direction. We turned back and went down another street to circle the roadblock but a few blocks further on we were hailed by armed Vietnamese not in uniform. We tried to ignore their shouts and continue but when they brought their weapons to bear on us we stopped and backed up. I noticed the face of one of them and was convinced by his nervous actions that he was ready to pull the trigger. When we stopped, I could see a sandbag emplacement which we hadn't noticed before because of the darkness. At this point, they recognized us as Americans and their smiles relieved our trepidation. They told us that we could not continue toward the airport because of reported Viet Cong between us and the base and further advised us to return to our quarters for safety. We had some difficulty in getting back to the quarters because by this time forces had moved in behind us who did not want to let us through. We had parked the jeep and walked out into the intersection to find out from two jeeploads of American GI's what was happening. As we walked up to the jeep, I was vaguely aware that the machine gun mounted on the vehicle nearest us was tilted upward, but apparently the others failed to notice this. While we were talking, one of the GI's touched off a burst from this gun and Ed Jensen proved his youthfulness when he beat several of the young GI's to the deck. When the momentary confusion calmed down, the two jeeploads of GI's moved further down the road and the FAA inspectors beat a prompt retreat to their quarters.

"We tuned in the Armed Forces Radio and heard the announcement (which was to continue through that day, Thursday, and Friday) that all military and civilian personnel not on base should remain in their quarters and off the streets until further notice. A short time later Wednesday morning, President Thieu declared martial law in South Vietnam and the entire area was under a red alert. We had telephone service on Wednesday, but lost it early Thursday and from then on had only the radio for outside contact. Electric power was lost about the same time.

"On Thursday we remained in quarters—on the roof most of the time to watch the activity. We could hear the firing. Friendly armed forces continued to work on the three pockets of activity mentioned earlier. On Thursday evening, as we were watching, we heard small arms fire in our neighborhood and could see tracers. We heard a bullet go over our heads with only a few feet to spare. We retreated to a safer location downstairs.

"On Friday two of the helicopter gunships (Bell Cobras) fired six rockets from almost directly over our heads into an area in the center of the adjacent block. Through all these days there were helicopter gunships overhead and tanks, weapons carriers and other military vehicles passing our street intersection frequently, so we did not feel abandoned.

"I ran out of clean clothes and took over the duties of laundress, hanging clothes on the roof. One of the 'friendly' forces' helicopters spotted me and came down to take a close look to be sure I was not a Viet Cong on the rooftop. After hovering quite close, he decided I was okay and left me to my chores.

"Large numbers of helicopters were seen, some apparently bringing in troops and others flying gunnery missions. On Saturday afternoon the MAC officers who share the quarters returned and advised that we could now get through to the airport.

"On Saturday night (I had moved on to Da Nang) I was given temporary quarters at the airport since the curfew would have made it impossible to return to catch the flight in time the next morning. I remained overnight at Da Nang and took advantage of this time to visit with my son, a Marine officer, stationed not far from Da Nang Airport. I spent part of the visit with my son standing guard along with the Marines and then trying to sleep on a 'soft bed' of sandbags in flak vest and hard helmet. We had contact with the Command Post and had a doctor and chaplain in the foxhole with us, so I felt more secure than I had in Saigon."

Schaefer ended his report with the calm note he had experienced "enough excitement for the present" and was eager to get back to "peace and quiet in Miami."

As is the case with wars, most Americans have begun to forget Vietnam and perhaps rightly so. But, since it would appear that the Southeast Asian conflict may well be the pattern of wars to come—and since history tends to dictate that wars are virtually inevitable—the lessons learned there are topics of current concern among FAA planners today.

While the capability and dedication of the agency's men and women enabled it to cope with that challenge, coming from way behind the power curve to do so, it is imperative that the FAA be ready when it again is called upon to function in a combat zone.

SECURITY SERVICE 13

"Southern Airways Flight Forty-nine is now ready for departure."

The feminine voice through the public address system at Birmingham, Ala., Airport was pleasantly slurred with the soft accents of the Deep South. Notwithstanding the languid delivery, the voice caused a handful of dawdling passengers to hurry out the gate and climb aboard the DC-9 jet transport.

His passengers all snug in their seat belts, Captain Bill Haas smoothly taxied the aircraft to the end of the runway. Checklist completed, he told the tower:

"Birmingham, this is Southern Forty-nine ready to roll."

Forty-nine, you're cleared for takeoff," came the reply.

Haas rolled the jet onto the runway, pushed the throttles forward, took a last look at the engine instruments and nodded to his first officer who placed his hand on the throttle quadrant ready to back up the captain during the takeoff. Brakes released, the twin-jet began to roll. So began a 29-hour ordeal which saw the aircraft, originally bound for the Alabama capital, Montgomery, a short flight away, travel to Cleveland, Ohio; Toronto, Canada; Lexington, Ky.; Chattanooga, Tenn.; Havana, Cuba; Key West, Fla.; Orlando, Fla.; and finally back to Havana.

Within minutes after departing Birmingham, the aircraft was under the control of three desperate men—all refugees from criminal prosecution and armed with a variety of weapons including pistols, a rifle and hand grenades.

During the terrifying 29 hours the gunmen, who originally demanded $10 million dollars, food, beer, a guarantee of amnesty and safe passage to Cuba, ordered Haas to crash the aircraft into the Oak Ridge, Tenn., atomic plant; rescinded the mass suicide/murder order; and shot Haas' first officer in retaliation for efforts by lawmen to ground the aircraft by shooting its tires during the Orlando stop.

In the Orlando departure, made at gunpoint over Haas' objections, the crew and passengers, along with the hijackers, came near death. With flat tires and without the help of his first officer, Haas was ordered to get the aircraft off the ground. Using every bit of runway available and narrowly avoiding what could have been a disaster, the captain got the crippled airliner into the air and later landed it successfully in Havana.

Later Haas told newsmen:

"They told me (to take off) or they were going to start killing people. So I went ahead and pushed the power up. I didn't think (we) would get off the ground."

For U.S. commercial aviation, the Southern Airways hijacking was the turning point in the long battle to bring Federal agencies and the airlines together in a joint program which could stem the tide of airline piracy which had begun with a vengeance eleven years earlier—May 1, 1961, quickly followed by further hijackings on July 24, August 3 and August 9. In fact, hijackings or "sky-jackings," as they were tagged by the press, probably made more headlines during the 1960's than any other single type of news event.

From the very beginning, there had been no question that the place to stop skyjackers was before they could board an aircraft. But the hang-up was: who should pay for this protection? The government? The airlines? Airport operators? Passengers?

For the last five years, Federal agencies and industry groups had been trying to work something out. But while they talked: hijackers attempted to commandeer 134 U.S. airliners—about one out of every 17 planes in the fleet; the nature of these crimes escalated from "random" and politically motivated acts to include well-planned crimes, often involving extortion, brutality, narcotics-induced hysteria and even murder; and sky criminals found ways to slip through experimental "screening" systems (introduced in 1969) at key airports.

Even the presence of some 1,200 Federal "sky marshals" aboard selected flights (started in 1970) had failed to provide an effective deterrent.

In frustration, a one-day walkout was called by the world's airline pilots on June 19, 1972, to call attention to the problem. At least now Congress gave a top priority to the preparation of "omnibus" anti-hijack legislation.

The United Nations' aviation arm, the International Civil Aviation Organization (ICAO) had drafted a treaty aimed at putting enforcement machinery into three earlier anti-hijack pacts. For after a number of meetings, ICAO found itself hopelessly stalemated by the conflicting politics of its 130 member nations and was unable to produce a satisfactory treaty.

Congress also ran into problems in trying to resolve the differences between an anti-hijack bill passed by the Senate, and one adopted by the House. Lacking a compromise, the legislation "died" with the close of the 92nd Congress—less than two weeks before the Southern hijacking.

The threat of air piracy (a more accurate term for what we call hijacking or skyjacking) isn't new. As early as 1920, author G. Holt Thomas in his book "Aerial Transport" devoted a chapter to "flying pirates." He postulated a situation where a criminal operating from a remote island would prey on commercial aircraft once routes were established. Thomas, however, didn't think the scheme held out much promise, observing:

"He would then find that aerial law has a phenomenally long arm and that a net of observations and detection would speedily enmesh him."

FAA researcher Dr. John T. Dailey (who has performed outstanding work for the agency in the area of developing a behavioral profile for air pirates) amassed considerable historical information on the subject. Dailey says:

"One of the earliest airlines facing active aerial piracy was the French Lignes Latécoére during the years 1923-26 when it was establishing air carrier service across the Spanish Sahara. The desert was infested by pillards (pillagers) who lay in wait for any airplane in distress. They would seize the aircraft and crew and would torture and murder the crew or hold them for ransom. The tribesmen would also shoot at the planes as they flew over the desert. There was once a mutiny of the pilots at Casablanca who refused to fly the dangerous stretch of desert.

"In 1926, pilots Gourp and Erable and mechanic, Pintado, were attacked by the tribesmen after a forced landing in the desert. Because of the threat of pillards, the airplanes always flew in pairs so one could rescue the other. Erable landed to rescue Gourp and Pintado. Erable and Pintado were killed outright in the attack. Gourp was wounded and carried off by the attackers. In captivity he attempted suicide by drinking iodine. He was rescued after payment of the 'usual ransom' but died later.

SECURITY SERVICE

"During 1930 and 1931 a number of revolutions swept through South America breaking out in Bolivia, Peru, Argentina, Brazil and finally Chile. Pilot Tom Jardine of Madison, Wisc., was seized at Arequipa and forced to ferry an armed band of revolutionists to Taena, Peru. Upon landing he managed to escape on foot to Chile. Pilot Byron Rickards of Oak Park, Illinois, was ordered at gun point to fly revolutionists from Pisco to Lima, Peru. He refused to do so and somehow managed to avoid being killed.

"In 1931 a Pan American Sikorsky was 'kidnaped' by a mechanic and taken to a revolutionary group who two days later flew it into a mountain.

"Another area subject to the threat of violent attacks on commercial aircraft was China in the early 1930's when Pan American was beginning its penetration of that area. An early Pan American survey flight there narrowly escaped capture by Chinese pirates. It was concluded that 'any plane forced down along the China Coast would be in grave danger unless armed with a machine gun'."

One airline in post World War II Alaska used to "frisk" the passengers on some flights and take away all their guns, knives and booze. When some passengers objected to being frisked the pilot had a five-cell flashlight filled with shot ready to 'conk' any uncooperative passengers. (He never had to use it.) The pilots carried guns as part of their regular flight equipment and locked the cabin door. When the passengers were heard to be fighting the pilot just "pulled back on the stick and smacked the passengers back into their seats." To quiet unruly drunks they would put on their oxygen masks and go up until the drunks passed out.

"Airlines from the very earliest days," Dailey points out, "have had to face the threat of violent attacks on their aircraft. The nature of these attacks has changed with the years, but there seems to have been a fairly regular and continuous evolution in the nature and modus operandi of individuals or groups attacking and seizing control of commercial aircraft for various purposes. Modern hijacking did not spring suddenly out of the blue but has a long line of antecedents as do most social phenomena. It is interesting that seizure of aircraft for ransom is one of the very oldest and also most recent types of armed attack on commercial aircraft."

Former Air Force General Benjamin O. Davis, Jr. put it this way while he was Assistant Secretary of Transportation in 1974:

"In the course of one decade—the 1960's—the world reached a state where anyone, anywhere could fall victim to murderous acts performed in the name of nationalism and self-determination. Invariably, the perpetrators of such acts made use of the world's commercial aviation system; it became to the terrorist his conveyance, his escape mechanism and his means of extortion. The age of international terrorism parallels what we call the jet age.

"Even a casual reader of history knows that anarchy and political violence have been vented on innocent people down through the centuries. But until the decade just past, gunmen and bombers could not travel at 600 miles an hour, arriving at a destination thousands of miles away in a few hours. They could not flee in the course of an afternoon to another country that would shelter them. The contemporary terrorist travels by jet plane with his weapons packed in expensive luggage; his modus operandi has the efficient, unwitting support of full flight schedules and passenger booking. Today, he is the world's problem."

CLEARED TO LAND!

Security specialists in a regional FAA office man a commandpost during one of a series of regular exercises designed to develop and perfect techniques and procedures to handle incidents of air piracy when they occur. Smooth, fast coordination between all agencies, the airline and crew involved is essential if the pirates are to be foiled without loss of life.

"Political motivation may have been the initial cause for incidents of air piracy," Davis continued, "but worldwide publicity had begun to lure stranger fish. People who were mad at the world, frustrated and demented people, loners seeking notoriety, turned to skyjacking as their outlet. Because of instant communications, one high-altitude drama almost always inspired another."

The FAA began its security efforts with limited pilot programs that used a "profile" screening system; it was hoped to eliminate the inspection of each boarding passenger by singling out certain individuals, a move expected to be palatable to the airline industry and to the public. The screening system to the entire industry on a voluntary basis was recommended.

Augmenting the profile, the FAA encouraged the development of the metal detector, the magnetomer, and provided Federal funding for its deployment at the boarding gates. Then the agency formed a contingent of "sky marshals," armed security men assigned to selective flights and promoted the concept of armed law enforcement officers on ground stations.

The whole program was voluntary. The FAA asked the air carriers to try it and most of them complied. When the system was conscientiously employed, it was both effective and economically attractive. When it broke down, there was a hijacking.

From 1969 to 1972, government and industry engaged in a deadly game of check and checkmate with air pirates. The Federal action did show results.

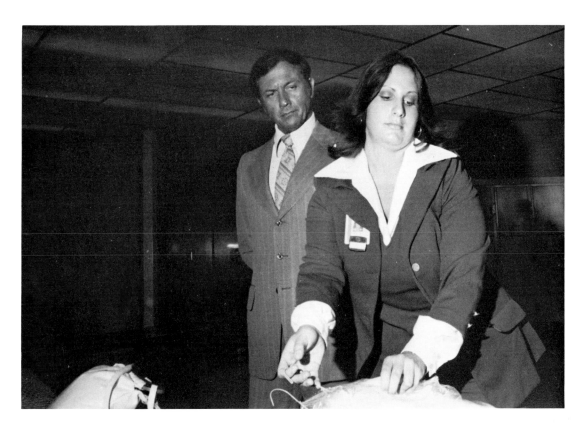

Surveillance, surveillance and still more surveillance is the day-to-day lot of the security specialist. This inspector scrutinizes an airline employee as she checks passenger baggage. Touching base with the local law enforcement officers assigned to airport duty. Checking the electronic screening devices installed at the passenger boarding gate to insure they are operating properly.

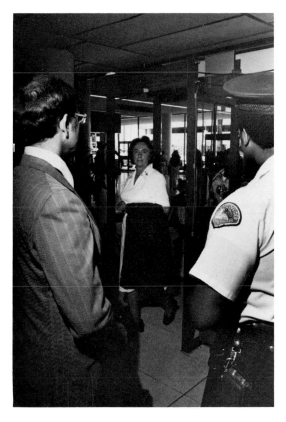

CLEARED TO LAND!

The pivotal year was 1972 and the Southern incident brought things to a head. The tempo of violent acts involving aircraft and air facilities stepped up, both at home and abroad. The FAA responded by ordering a regulatory program into effect. Determined to stop the hijacker on the ground, to intercept him before boarding; that concept called for tougher regulations, more metal detectors, more guards, and tighter ground security. Most of the sky marshals were taken off the airliners and reassigned to the boarding gates.

The government then dealt a final card—100 percent electronic screening or physical inspection of all passengers and their hand baggage and the positioning of armed law enforcement personnel at each screening point. The rule applied to all passengers and their luggage, on all scheduled flights, all of the time.

Most people said it couldn't be done—they said the job was just too big. Half a million people fly commercially in the United States every day; they pass through 2,800 boarding gates at over 500 airports and they are carrying millions of articles and pieces of carry-on baggage. With the cooperation of the airlines and airport operators, it began to work.

In 1973, a total of 3,439 passengers were denied boarding and 3,156 passengers and others were arrested. The weapons confiscated included a total of 2,162 guns, 3,459 explosives, and 23,290 knives. The "successful" hijack rate in the U.S. dropped to zero that year.

In its third semi-annual report to Congress on the effectiveness of the civil aviation security program published in April 1976 and covering the last six months of Calendar Year 1975, the FAA said:

"The detection of an increased number of weapons and other dangerous items at screening stations and the absence of successful hijackings indicate that procedures in use remain effective. However, documented instances of one unsuccessful U.S. air carrier hijacking and 15 possible hijackings prevented during the reporting period highlight the fact that the threat of aircraft hijacking remains with us and is, in fact, comparable to the peak periods of hijackings in the country (1969—1972). During those four years, there were respectively, 40, 25, 25 and 27 hijackings of U.S. air carrier aircraft.

"Sabotage and threats of sabotage constitute the other basic element of the threat against civil aviation. Since 1972, 132 people have been killed as a result of 17 explosions aboard U.S. aircraft or at U.S. airports. Of the total 26 actual devices and explosions during that period, seven, or 27 percent, were in public lockers; eight, or 31 percent were at various other airport locations; and 11, or 42 percent, involved aircraft. The current official threat estimate indicated that due to the increase in terrorist activities and the increasing use of explosives worldwide, the danger to lives and property is greater than ever."

Like the Southern hijacking, the disaster at LaGuardia Airport, New York City, on December 29, 1975, which left 11 dead and 54 injured, also has been a catalyst galvanizing the FAA and other Federal agencies to ever greater efforts in the battle against those who would use the vulnerability of the air transport system as a weapon of political terror.

The LaGuardia incident resulted in the immediate establishment of a joint government-industry task force. This group, comprised of government and aviation industry officials, was directed to review current security procedures and to recommend measures to prevent this type of crime against civil aviation. Specific actions designed to prevent the introduction of explosives into the airport/aircraft environment were immediately adopted by some air carriers and airport managers. These actions included increased security awareness, the closing or relocation of public storage lockers, and tighter control of checked baggage. The FAA initiated a comprehensive program of aviation explosives security surveys and seminars at the nation's air carrier airports.

The joint government-industry task force identified three areas of necessary concentration: public locker security, explosive detection research and development and strengthened security for checked baggage and cargo.

Explosives security surveys at the nation's airports have been initiated by FAA to identify explosives security needs and to develop appropriate and effective corrective measures.

Also the FAA is expanding the current explosives security training program to include the conduct of seminars at all airports and to maximize utilization of the explosives safety training now available.

In the area of explosives detection, the "detection dog team" program (dogs and handlers), initiated in 1972, has continued to expand due not only to the increasing threat but also because of the high degree of explosives detection surety these teams can provide. And in explosives detection research and development, the FAA continues to examine the possibilities of improving existing X-ray, vapor detection and other concepts as well as evaluating new locker design/modification concepts to minimize loss of life or airport damage resulting from a detonation.

With checked baggage and cargo, the FAA is working closely with the airlines to examine the problems and ramifications associated with passenger checked baggage operations, and is exploring the need for and feasibility of implementing increased security measures. Measures range from examining each piece of baggage to the development of less time-consuming but effective methods to determine quickly baggage and cargo that require special security attention.

The complexity of the whole problem is evident in a letter from FAA Administrator John L. McLucas to Transportation Secretary William T. Coleman, Jr., written shortly after the LaGuardia bombing:

"We do not now know whether the LaGuardia explosion was targeted against aviation or merely happened to occur in one of the lockers which are common to transportation terminals and other facilities serving the public.

"Whatever the connection, any strengthened security alternatives must be considered within the context of the U.S. air transportation system. There are 32 scheduled airlines operating a jet fleet of some 2,500 aircraft enplaning 500,000 passengers and more than 1,000,000 pieces of baggage on some 15,-000 flights each day. The airlines serve almost 500 United States airports each of which is different in many respects.

"Accordingly, security alternatives must weigh carefully the impact on efficient movement of passengers, baggage and cargo, especially whether passengers can or should be expected to arrive at airports hours in advance of flight departures, and whether U.S. airports can or should be converted into fortress-like transportation facilities."

"Ultimately," McLucas warned, "better methods and machines are not the entire answer, particularly if they induce a sense of complacency or relaxation of vigilance. When the FAA released its latest report on the number of hijackings and other criminal acts against aviation, some felt that the strict procedures introduced a few years back were no longer needed. But, the fact is that the threat is with us and our major concern is that people will not recognize this because of the program's success. So, too, with bombings, we must develop the best equipment and measures. But we all must realize that continued vigilance is equally vital."

Plans and programs are one thing. Action is another. To implement those plans and programs devised by the Washington task force, it takes men and women—professionals in security matters—in the field to make them produce results. It takes people like Jay Adsen and Mark Ludlow in the Western Region; Milt Ferris in Los Angeles; Jack Robitaille and Hideo Kiyomura in San Francisco; Bobby Tucker in Las Vegas, Nev.; Don Kelly in San Diego; and Bob Watmore in Phoenix, Ariz. It takes men and women like Lovilda Hayes, Principal Security Inspector (PSI) assigned to Continental Air Lines, and Harry Wisniewski, PSI assigned to Western.

Some of these folks and their counterparts across the nation were with the program from the very beginning. Others are newcomers recruited from the ranks of professional security specialists in industry or working for other government agencies. All of them know their jobs and all of them are all too aware of the odds against which they must prevail.

Adsen, for instance, was assigned to FAA security when the hijackings and bombings began in earnest. He had been a security specialist with the Atomic Energy Commission (AEC) engaged in traditional industrial security work—screening new employees for security clearances, conducting security education and managing physical security programs. His initial assignment with the FAA entailed the same general duties since the FAA, in its role working with the U.S. military services in time of emergency does require the handling and safekeeping of classified information. The acts of air piracy which began in 1961 were, however, building up to a crescendo and suddenly Adsen found himself involved in a different type of security effort—one where failure paid off in death, possibly for untold hundreds of men and women.

In Washington at the time, Adsen worked with the original task force (at a "low level," he modestly observes) studying this new challenge and devising programs to combat it.

"We already had security people, of course," he says, "like me, they were engaged in traditional industrial security work. But they were familiar with the FAA and with aviation so they became the nucleus of our new force. There also was an early program in being within Flight Standards wherein certain inspectors had been qualified in the use of firearms. These inspectors were placed aboard flights when it was expected that something might occur. This operation subsequently was expanded into the 'flying marshal' program."

Shortly, Adsen was sent to the Western Region—then comprising nine western states and subsequently broken up into three regions, the Western, the Northwest and the Rocky Mountain. Immediately he plunged into the task of implementing the programs developed by the Washington task force to combat air piracy. Fortunately, the FAA had a handful of security specialists like Adsen to get off the ground.

"The first program to be implemented in the Fall of 1970 was a volunteer one," Adsen recalls. "The air carriers did not have to accept it. We had a hell of an education job to do. Some carriers immediately undertook the program

SECURITY SERVICE

conscientiously. A number would not take it, or the threat, seriously. Some rejected it outright. Our hands were tied since it was completely voluntary."

"All of us were learning, however," Adsen adds. "This was a wild animal we were facing and we didn't know whether to grab it around the neck or attack from behind."

It remained for the Southern incident to arouse public sentiment to the point where Congress, the Executive Branch, the FAA and the airlines were forced to resolve their differences and adopt a mandatory program.

"That's when it really got interesting," Adsen says, "early in 1973 when they gave us some authority. Now we had to have many more professional security people. We recruited from other agencies, from industry, from wherever qualified men and women were available. Most of them, however, had little or no experience with airplanes or aviation. They were qualified in security measures but we had to train them in aviation."

For Adsen, another setback was to emerge. He had just established and staffed field offices up and down the west coast and extending east to the Rockies when the decision came to break up the area into three separate regions. From the standpoint of organization and resources, Adsen now had to fall back, regroup and play with the new hand he had been dealt. Ultimately, things settled down. In the new Western Region, now consisting of only the far southwestern states, Adsen got his field offices firmly established and staffed. There as in the other regions, the security teams got down to the business of checkmating the air pirate.

Air Transportation Security Field Offices (ATSFO) established early in this decade are not unlike those currently in being except that they had more resources. The FAA, in its planning, took into consideration the relatively large number of security personnel it would take to implement the new mandatory program. This was judged to be a "temporary" situation, however, and the plan included a programmed reduction of manpower after the preliminary work had all been accomplished.

"What the planners did not plan for," Adsen says, "is the fact that after the work load of establishing the program was completed, we would then have to monitor it. That takes manpower too, more than we have today. Certainly, three years later, we seem to have a handle on the hijacking problem, at least with the air carriers, but the threat hasn't disappeared. We still have a huge job to do and not enough manpower to accomplish it."

Initially, ATSFO's were staffed with a variety of specialists, specialists representing differing types of expertise—physical security, communications security, document control, electronics (experts in the sophisticated new detection gear used by airports to preclude carrying guns, bombs, incendiary devices, etc., aboard the aircraft). But in many areas today, the field office is a one-man or one-woman operation.

In all fairness to the agency, it must be recognized that much of the program now is in the hands of the air carriers, airport managements and local enforcement. Theoretically, this should reduce the work load significantly. However, like all the other aspects of FAA's regulatory responsibility, the security program must be constantly monitored and from a practical point of view the more cooperating organizations, the greater the task of monitoring the effort.

Also, there is another concern. It appears that as the incidence of successful air carrier hijacking decreased during the past three years, the number of successful attempts involving general aviation aircraft has increased. General aviation, as it is used here, includes air taxi operations, charter operations and private aircraft. All three are becoming the target for hijackers. A voluntary anti-hijacking security program is in being for air taxi operators but, according to statistics, few operators are cooperating. And in the case of charter operators and pilot/owners, the security responsibility rests squarely on their shoulders.

Here is a case in point taken from the May 1975 issue of the FAA Aviation News under the heading, "Skyjacking in General Aviation," with a sub-head, "With the success of airline anti-piracy measure, general aviation is becoming more of a target."

Out of Tampa the pilot of the Seneca headed south in the darkening Florida sky and gave the man in the right seat some unorthodox instructions.

"You're going to have to help me fly this thing," he said. "Since I don't have a copilot, you will have to assume his duties. First let's get the pressurization going. See that knob on the far side of the panel? To keep the pressure up so we can breathe you will have to keep pushing that knob in and out. If the pressure drops, we die."

Since the Seneca is not a pressurized airplane, and the knob the passenger was working so diligently was actually the cabin heater control, the orders given by the pilot were unusual to say the least. But then, this was an unusual flight; the reasons behind the instruction were sound. The pilot was trying to keep the other man's mind occupied—and away from the gun he held in his hand. Frank Haigney, a young charter pilot and amateur psychologist, was being hijacked to Cuba and he sensed that his life depended on how well he could handle the hijacker, keep him cool and keep his itchy finger off the trigger.

During the flight from Tampa to Cuba, which took just under three hours, Haigney invented a variety of make-believe chores to keep his ersatz copilot busy. He also made up touching stories about his personal life, designed to appeal to the hijacker's sympathy. His imaginative mind may have saved his life.

What was certainly the most memorable flight in the career of the 30-year-old pilot had begun in a routine manner. A man identifying himself as Robin Harrison of the Harrison Construction Company called the Tampa Flying Service at Peter O. Knight Airport at 4 p.m. on Saturday, December 14, to request a charter flight to Naples, Fla., in a twin. He wanted to leave about 7:30 that evening, remain overnight at Naples, then go on to Miami. The Seneca was marked off for the trip, and Frank Haigney was assigned as pilot.

At the appointed time the passenger appeared on the flight ramp—a clean-cut man in his mid-fifties—and the plane and pilot were ready. Only one detail remained. Since the customer was unknown at the flying service he would be expected to pay a cash deposit before the flight began. Haigney explained this to Harrison, who reached understandingly into his pocket. But instead of pulling out his wallet 'Harrison' pulled out a gun and pointed it at Haigney.

"This should take care of it. Let's go."

Haigney did not argue; he headed for the airplane, acutely aware of the gun at his back. As soon as the pilot and passenger were out of sight the line man who had observed the incident called the police.

Inside the airplane Haigney ran deliberately through his preflight check. He tried a stalling maneuver, ostensibly waiting for a second pilot whom, he insisted, he had to have before taking off. The hijacker was unconvinced and demanded that the pilot "get going, or I am going to shoot you in the leg." Haigney started the engines and taxied out to the runway at the uncontrolled airport. He dialed a number into the transponder and plugged his headphones into the radio jack.

"Where are we going?" he asked. "I have to file a flight plan."

"Head south," said 'Harrison,' "and move it."

The pilot concluded that it was unsafe to delay on the ground any longer, and when a last look around the field failed to disclose a police car racing to his rescue he took off. Now that he knew what he was up against his mind was racing almost as fast as the propellers. He sensed that if his gun-toting passenger had any suspicion he was making their situation known to Air Traffic Control, he might well pump a bullet into him. The only thing he could think of was to keep the man busy, so he put his imagination to work.

Once he had his passenger busy "pressurizing" the airplane (with the heater knob) Haigney tuned in to Miami Center, and requested a clearance to "Miami . . . possibly farther south." About halfway to Miami, 'Harrison' confirmed that he did indeed intend to go to Cuba, and Haigney asked the Center if they could give him radar vectors since he had no charts for the route. The Center complied, and also notified the Havana airport authorities of the hijacking in progress. Later, when Haigney advised that he was running short of fuel the Center requested, and received, permission for the landing to be expedited.

Meanwhile, Haigney continued to assign the other man "copilot" jobs to perform. Citing the importance of careful record-keeping, he fed 'Harrison' a constant stream of checkpoints and times to enter in a flight log. He would point out a light on the ground ahead, and ask the other man to tell him exactly when it passed under the wing. And through it all, he kept the hijacker pumping the heater knob.

He also kept him talking, making certain not to antagonize him. Haigney asked the man why he wanted to go to Cuba. Because he was "tired of living in the states," was the simple answer. Haigney, who was actually a bachelor, fabricated stories of a wife at home and a cluster of adoring children who, he said, would be destitute if anything happened to him.

The landing in Cuba at 10:20 p.m. was uneventful. Two uniformed immigration officers took the hijacker in tow, and the pilot was isolated in a hotel room.

Frank Haigney was lucky. On Monday, after less than two days in Havana, he was allowed to fly his airplane back to Tampa. (Swiss intermediaries had arranged to pay the approximately $500 in charges that the Cubans asked for release of the plane.

Other general aviation pilots and aircraft owners have been less fortunate. They have been shot, sequestered in foreign jails, had their aircraft impounded or damaged, etc.

The vulnerability of general aviation to air piracy; to being used by dissident groups as a medium of political blackmail; to criminal extortion plots; and as a means of personal retribution on the part of individuals psychologically or emotionally unbalanced is of growing concern to Adsen and his fellow aviation security specialists.

"This is happening all too frequently," he warns, "and could increase even more. We could be forced to extend our security program to include general aviation and that would be a really impossible task!"

What advice does the FAA have for general aviation and charter pilots? In general terms it goes like this.

Besides assuring passenger identification some of the other measures that can be taken to safeguard general aviation aircraft against the dangers of skyjacking are:

"Familiarize yourself with the recommended procedures for such 'special' emergencies (Part 4, Airman's Information Manual).

"Urging airport management to maintain an adequate guard in the general aviation area and to restrict unauthorized persons from access to the airport.

"Preparing yourself mentally to deal coolly with a pistol-packing paranoiac, if that situation should arise. *Offer no active resistance!* If, in your judgment, you can delay a skyjack departure by real, imaginary or exaggerated requirements, such as fueling, crew assistance, air traffic clearance, etc., you may do so, in hopes that police authorities may be alerted and arrive on the scene in time to foil the skyjacker. If you are forced to take off with him in the airplane, do what you can to avoid arousing his anger or suspicions, perhaps in the manner of the charter pilot described earlier. What non-pilot could ever resist the chance to play airplane driver?"

According to Adsen, the air carrier security program as it is implemented at those airports coming under Part 107 of the Federal Aviation Regulations (the part that provides for air carrier security) has had a beneficial side effect with respect to another mounting general aviation problem. In recent years, the theft of expensive avionics, other flight equipment and aircraft has increased alarmingly.

"At the majority of airports where air carrier security measures are in effect," Adsen says, "there has been a substantial decrease in aircraft and equipment theft. In fact, at some airports the decrease has been phenomenal."

The significant reduction in the number of successful hijackings through 1975 is somewhat misleading, misleading in the sense that it tends to give the impression that the threat also decreased along a similar curve. This, however, was not the case.

During the final six months of 1975, there was nearly a 20 percent increase in the number of persons—741—taken into custody because they had attempted to carry concealed weapons or explosives aboard an air carrier aircraft. During the same period there was a 16 percent increase in the total number of weapons and dangerous articles detected at the screening points. This on top of a 100 percent increase reflected in the previous semi-annual report to Congress.

The major increases occurred in the number of knives and other potential weapons like clubs, mace and tear gas canisters. While the latter in most cases, were not in the hands of potential hijackers, they did constitute a real danger to safe aircraft operation. There is some thought that in this respect the increased effectiveness of electronic detection systems and physical search has turned up what hitherto was an unknown safety threat. Another theory has it that the huge increase in these types of weapons is due entirely to public awareness and fear of the increasing crime rate.

During the same period some 2,440 guns were detected, nearly three quarters of them detected by X-ray machines. It is interesting to note that only one percent of the passengers declared that such a weapon was in their possession or in their hand baggage when faced with the pre-embarkation screening.

With the passenger screening program well underway, the FAA in 1975 turned its attention to the growing problem of bomb threats and terror bombings. A special school was established (with the aid of the U.S. Army) at the Huntsville Arsenal in Alabama. Selected FAA security specialists were exposed to intensive training in explosives. Two of those were Tim Horan and Pete Arcana assigned, respectively, to Los Angeles and San Francisco. They and their counterparts graduated with new titles—Civil Aviation Explosives Technicians—and new responsibilities. They had been back at their duty stations only a few days when the LaGuardia disaster spelled out in blood the critical importance of those new responsibilities.

"If we had been graduated just a few weeks earlier, perhaps the New York boys might have prevented the LaGuardia explosion," says Horan, a former Internal Revenue Service investigator with six years FAA experience, "we certainly knew we had our hands full when we left Huntsville, but I guess we didn't know just how full."

It's fortunate Horan is a bachelor because he has had little time to spend at home since December 1975. He is responsible for 21 airports in Arizona, Nevada and the southern half of California, conducting training programs for air carriers, airport managements and local law enforcement agencies at those airports and surveying the premises and facilities with a view to recommending methods and procedures, and in many instances, physical modifications to structures, that will reduce the vulnerability to bombings.

"To a large degree," he says, "it is a case of making the men and women who work at the airport aware—giving them security awareness. And, I don't mean just the management level. If this program is to work, everyone—the skycaps (porters), custodial personnel, clerks, mechanics, maintenance people, all of them, must be alert to notice anything out of the ordinary."

What kind of cooperation is Horan and his counterparts getting?

"Excellent, from the very outset," he says, "and now we are getting good feedback too. Those folks out there are really thinking and they are coming back with a lot of good ideas for improving the program."

One of the measures, that both Horan at his level and Adsen at the Region are involved with, is the "bomb" dog project.

"That was a tough one to sell," Adsen recalls. "At the beginning only a few airport managers and local law enforcement officials accepted it. Now it not only is widely accepted but the results are fantastic. What those dogs can do is simply unbelievable."

Under the project, monitored by the FAA, a local government can get a grant from the Federal Law Enforcement Assistance Agency (LEAA). Under the grant, it sends personnel to Lackland AFB, Texas (the Air Force's famous war dog training facility) where each handler is introduced to an animal and they are trained as a team. In most cases the dog also becomes the family pet spending 24 hours a day with his handler.

Looked upon with considerable doubt when it was first suggested, the "bomb dog" program has proved to be one of the most successful methods to control this type of problem. Unlike the narcotics dog who will tear into the material where he scents narcotics, the bomb dog is trained to first sniff out the explosive and then immediately come to a sitting position. In this manner inadvertent detonation of the bomb is avoided. This dog has just found the small, metal container of inert explosive used for training. He will now sit and as a reward the handler will let him play with a hard rubber ball. This handler—a member of the Los Angeles Police Department—also is a trained bomb expert. In many jurisdictions, dog handlers must call the bomb squad to complete the mission.

As opposed to the dogs trained to sniff out narcotics, the bomb dogs are taught not to disturb the scene but just to alert the handler to the presence of explosives. They are trained to immediately sit and receive a reward—the chance to play with a hard rubber ball. Experience so far with the animals has proven their noses to be virtually infallible.

Man/dog explosives detection teams (as they are formally called) now are in place or are available conveniently to almost every major air carrier airport in the nation and they are getting a workout. In addition to the real threats there are hundreds of false alarms resulting from threats made by pranksters and by cranks and as well as those resulting from passengers trying to be humorous. Many of these are patently unbelievable, but none can be totally disregarded until they have been investigated.

SECURITY SERVICE

On a monthly basis, bomb threats against aircraft averaged 162 during the final six months of 1975 and threats against airports average 52 a month. Some 22 of the threats were accompanied by extortion demands made to the airlines or airports. Since LaGuardia, many threats which might at one time have been considered a hoax, now are taken seriously creating a huge work load for security personnel, explosives detection teams and bomb disposal squads from local law enforcement agencies.

An analysis of the bomb threats to aircraft between July and December 1975 indicates that 377 were considered serious threats, nearly 40 percent of all those received.

This brings those responsible for civil aviation security to the conclusion that more funds and manpower must be forthcoming. While portions of the problem appear to be coming under control, other aspects continue to increase both with respect to their degree of seriousness and in their complexity.

"What the people holding the purse strings fail to recognize," Horan emphasizes, "is the plain fact that with every other phase of the FAA's regulatory responsibility, just let up in your efforts, reduce the number and frequency of inspections (and here it is important to avoid inspections on a scheduled basis) and remove surveillance and the result is predictable—the system goes to pot."

This isn't the first time in the 50-year history of U.S. aviation regulatory bodies that manpower has been thin nor will it be the last.

Traditionally, the gears of the bureaucracy mesh exceedingly slow.

Just as beacon keepers, radio operators, controllers, operations inspectors and other men and women in the field have filled the breech with dedication, perseverance and that priceless commodity called "voluntary overtime" for half a century, so will today's aviation security specialists manage to meet this new challenge.

For the men and women of the FAA (and in earlier years the CAA, the Bureau of Air Commerce) that too is part of their tradition.

GLOSSARY OF INITIALS AND ACRONYMS

ACDO	Air Carrier District Office
ACI	Air Carrier Certificate Inspector
ACM	Additional Crew Member
ADF	Automatic Direction Finder
ADIS	Automatic Data Interchange System
AEC	Atomic Energy Commission
AEDO	Aircraft Engineering District Office
AFRS	Armed Forces Radio Service
AID	Agency for International Development
AOPA	Aircraft Owners and Pilots Association
APIS	Approved Inspection System
ARSR	Air Route Surveillance Radar
ARTCC	Air Route Traffic Control Center
ARTS	Automated Radar Terminal System
ARVN	Army of the Republic of Vietnam
ASR	Airport Surveillance Radar
ATC	Approved Type Certificate
ATSFO	Air Transportation Security Field Office
BFR	Biennial Flight Review
CAA	Civil Aeronautics Administration
CAAG	Civil Aviation Assistance Group
CAB	Civil Aeronautics Board
CAMI	Civil AeroMedical Institute
CFI	Certified Flight Instructor
CIA	Central Intelligence Agency
CIC	Combat Information Center
CINCPAC	Commander-In-Chief, Pacific
CPT	Civilian Pilot Training (Program)
CRAF	Civil Reserve Air Fleet
DF	Direction Finding
DH	Decision Height
DME	Distance Measuring Equipment
DOD	Department of Defense
EMDO	Engineering and Manufacturing District Office
FAA	Federal Aviation Administration
FAF	Final Approach Fix
FAI	Federation Aeronautique Internationale
FAR	Federal Aviation Regulation
FINFO	Flight Inspection National Field Office
FSDO	Flight Standards District Office
FSS	Flight Service Station
GADO	General Aviation District Office
GCA	Ground Controlled Approach
HSI	Horizontal Situation Indicator
ICAO	International Civil Aviation Organization
IFO	International Field Office
IFR	Instrument Flight Rules
IIC	Inspector-In-Charge
ILS	Instrument Landing System
INSACS	Interstate Airways Communications Stations
LEAA	Law Enforcement Assistance Administration
MAC	Military Airlift Command
MDA	Minimum Descent Altitude
MEA	Minimum Enroute Altitude
NACA	National Advisory Committee on Aeronautics
NDB	Nondirectional Radio Beacon
NOTAM	Notice to Airmen
NTSB	National Transportation Safety Board
OMNI	Omnidirectional Radio Range Station (see VOR)
PA	Production Authority
PAR	Precision Approach Radar
PIC	Pilot-In-Command
PMA	Parts Manufacturing Approval
QASAR	Quality Assurance Systems Analysis Review

RAPCON	Radar Approach Control
RDF	Radio Direction Finder
RDP	Radar Data Processing
RTCA	Radio Technical Commission on Aviation
SAFI	Semi-Automated Flight Inspection
SCOMO	Saigon Commissioned Officers Mess
SIC	Second-In-Command
SID	Standard Instrument Departure
STC	Supplemental Type Certificate
TAC	Tactical Air Control
TACAN	Tactical Air Navigation (military system)
TCA	Terminal Control Area
TRACON	Terminal Radar Approach Control
TSO	Technical Standards Order
UHF	Ultra High Frequency
VFR	Visual Flight Rules
VHF	Very High Frequency
VHF/DF	Very High Frequency/Direction Finding
VOR	Very High Frequency Omnidirectional Radio Range
VORTAC	VOR/TACAN

Index